A Note on the Authors

Zuzana Růžičková was a celebrated Czech harpsichordist and a survivor of three Nazi concentration and slave labour camps. She recorded over one hundred albums, performed across the world o great acclaim, and became an influential teacher at the Prague ademy. Zuzana died in Prague in 2017 aged ninety.

dy Holden is the author of more than thirty published titles, y of them about the lives of remarkable women. A journalist rmer war correspondent, she wrote *Born Survivors*, about others and their babies who survived the Holocaust. She ffolk, England.

ONE HUNDRED MIRACLES

Music, Auschwitz, Survival and Love

ZUZANA RŮŽIČKOVÁ
WITH
WENDY HOLDEN

BLOOMSBURY PUBLISHING
LONDON • OXFORD • NEW YORK • NEW DELHI • SYDNEY

BLOOMSBURY PUBLISHING
Bloomsbury Publishing Plc
50 Bedford Square, London, WC1B 3DP, UK

BLOOMSBURY, BLOOMSBURY PUBLISHING and the Diana logo are trademarks
of Bloomsbury Publishing Plc

First published in Great Britain 2019
This edition published 2020

A catalogue record for this book is available from the British Library

ISBN: HB: 978-1-4088-9683-9; TPB: 978-1-4088-9680-8;
PB: 978-1-4088-9684-6; EBOOK: 978-1-4088-9681-5

2 4 6 8 10 9 7 5 3 1

Typeset by Newgen KnowledgeWorks Pvt. Ltd., Chennai, India
Printed and bound in Great Britain by CPI Group (UK) Ltd, Croydon CR0 4YY

FSC www.fsc.org MIX Paper from responsible sources FSC® C020471

To find out more about our authors and books visit www.bloomsbury.com
and sign up for our newsletters

Dedicated by Zuzana to Johann Sebastian Bach, whose music reminds us that there is still beauty in this world

Contents

Author's Note

The process of writing this memoir was an unusual and often challenging one. In the years since the Second World War, Zuzana had almost never refused a request for an interview. She gave them in person, on the telephone, via video, in documentaries, on television and radio programmes, all in several different languages – chiefly Czech, German, French, and English.

When I was invited to bring all these transcripts together and write her memoirs, I travelled to Prague in September 2017 for my own interviews, which were conducted at her home two weeks before she died. Zuzana was tiny, like a bird, with smoky grey eyes and a warm, open face. When she smiled, her eyes twinkled with mischief and joy. A heavy smoker, she lit one cigarette after the other as we sat for hours in her old-fashioned apartment or in a local restaurant, where she always ate a surprisingly generous quantity of food. Although – at ninety years old – she was tired, she was determined to answer my pages and pages of questions based on the existing material and my own extensive research. If she couldn't remember precise details such as dates and names, she would pour us a drink and ask me to fill them in for her. As we came to the end of our time together, she clasped my hand and asked me if I had everything I needed. I told her that I did, for now, but would see her again in a few months. She smiled and kissed me goodbye. Sadly that was the last time we were to meet.

After her unexpected death a week later everyone involved wanted to know if I had enough to proceed. My agent and our various international publishers were understandably concerned and her family and friends hopeful that the project could still go ahead. After reviewing all the material, I was delighted to tell them that it could. Zuzana's English was almost flawless and her remarkable story as set out in this book is told in her own words, transcribed from the answers she gave me and from those she gave to others who came before me, spanning many decades. These accounts were often almost identical, word for word, after years of telling the same stories over and over. Sometimes, however, they were conflicted, as can happen with memories of events long past. Occasionally, as she grew older, she was a little more forgetful. In a few of her interviews she claimed that she couldn't remember an event, whereas in others she was able to describe it with remarkable clarity. In the few instances where there was a discrepancy, I have drawn on her most coherent interviews and further corroborated the precise sequence of events using her personal letters, essays, and speeches as well as articles, archive material, a brief diary of her time in Auschwitz, and other historical documents. I have also relied on the testimonies of several people who shared her experiences during the war and afterwards, who were able to clarify certain points I could not otherwise accurately describe.

It was a considerable undertaking to weave all the material together, much of which had to be translated from the original. I have been enormously helped by the generosity of her previous interviewers and the patience of historians, archivists, documentarians, friends, family, translators, and musicians around the world. The recollections in this book are just as Zuzana remembered them. To the best of my ability, I have pieced them together in a way that I hope she would approve of.

My overriding impression was that Zuzana was determined to bear witness to history. Not just of the war years, but of the decades afterwards, which were often extremely challenging. I will be forever humbled by her courage and resilience in the face of so much suffering, prejudice, and adversity.

In spite of all that she endured, she remained a life-enhancing spirit who wished the world to know that she'd been healed by music and the love of her mother and husband. It has been one of the greatest privileges of my life to fulfil that wish.

Wendy Holden
London, 2018

1

Sibiu, Transylvania, 1960

'Welcome, Comrade!' The cultural director greeted me as warmly as ever in the remote Transylvanian city of Sibiu. 'A million thanks for coming back. We can't wait to hear you play for us again.'

It was the winter of 1960, and it had taken me the best part of a day to travel there from Kiev. When I eventually arrived alone, via a flight to Bucharest and then an ancient steam train that seemed to take forever to snake across the country, I was tired and extremely hungry.

My latest three-week recital tour of factories, shipyards, schools, colleges, and state buildings – the tenth that year – had been especially gruelling in the bitter cold of Ukraine, the Soviet Union, and Poland. Kiev had been particularly challenging, with an odd director who'd threatened not to pay me. I was desperate to go home to my family in Prague after this, my penultimate concert for the authorities that year.

I knew from previous visits to medieval Sibiu that my accommodation and my long-awaited supper would be basic. Fortunately, I had a little salami and a spare tin of sardines left in my suitcase, as well as a supply of Russian cigarettes.

Of all the other Eastern bloc countries I was obliged to perform in under the socialists, Romania was one of the hardest hit by dreadful poverty and a pervading sense of despair. The people of this former Hungarian province had suffered terribly at the hands of President

Gheorghiu-Dej and his senior minister Nicolae Ceauşescu, and were even more starved of contact with the outside world than we Czechs. I remember one trip to Timişoara where the hotel was so terrible, with such an insanely dirty bathtub, that I was afraid there would be bedbugs. I unpacked my little suitcase that my dear mum had packed so carefully for me and I started crying over it. I said to myself: if only my mum could see what kind of environment I was unpacking that little case in.

In Sibiu conditions were much the same, yet the musical director – who was thrilled by the arrival of any artist under the state cultural programme – somehow managed to lift my spirits every time, so grateful was he that I'd once again agreed to include his city in my itinerary.

'Everything is ready for you in your quarters,' he assured me, words that had gladdened my heart on my first visit there a few years earlier – until I saw my unheated room. With a blizzard predicted that bitter November night, I'd probably be sleeping in my coat.

My recital of early music the following evening would be in the hall of a building that doubled as a cinema. Accompanied by Sibiu's enthusiastic musicians, I didn't expect it to be my most memorable performance, but I knew that the appreciation would be genuine and heartfelt.

Long before I pulled on the green velvet ball gown that my mother had had her seamstress make for me, however, I was paraded around town as usual, having my photograph taken with Communist Party officials at the administrative headquarters before visiting workplaces and schools. The pupils were always most receptive, especially if they had musical ambitions, and seemed to regard me as a kind of celebrity.

In one classroom that day I spoke to a group who were the same age I had been when Hitler finally invaded Czechoslovakia – twelve years old. As always, I shared with them my passion for music and my deep connection with Johann Sebastian Bach. 'Bach was love at first hearing, when I was only eight years old,' I told them. In answer to their many questions, I explained why I'd not only dedicated my life to music, but switched from the piano to the harpsichord. 'Some people think of the harpsichord as a feudal instrument, a sixteenth-century wooden artefact that belongs in a museum, but to me it's still very much alive,' I told them. 'Bach composed his early keyboard music on organ and harpsichord and entrusted a third of his enormous legacy to the harpsichord, often specifying which instrument each piece should be played on. To be authentic and true to Bach's intent, I play the harpsichord.'

A hand shot up and a curious teenager asked, 'But what's so special about Bach? Why not Beethoven, for example?'

I smiled. 'Beethoven shakes his fist at the heavens,' I gestured with a clenched hand. 'In the music of Bach, there is the utmost joy of life and also the most desperate sadness. One always feels the deep sense of being human.'

Returning to my room to prepare for my evening performance, I'd just lit another cigarette when I was surprised to hear a knock at my door. The female concierge of the building, whose job it was to spy on me and report anything subversive, informed me that I had a telephone call.

Alarmed, I hurried to her room and cradled the receiver in my hands. I almost dropped it when I heard the sound of my husband's voice. Why was Viktor calling and from where? We didn't even possess a telephone. Few people in Prague did. Had something happened to my mother?

'Everything is well, Zuzana,' he reassured me, knowing I'd panic. 'I'm calling because your mother and I want you to change your travel plans. The weather forecast is very bad and we don't want you to fly home in the middle of a snowstorm. Can you come by train instead?'

I peered out of the window at the snowflakes swirling crazily by the light of a street lamp. It didn't seem any worse than when I'd arrived, and I was about to reason with him. Then I heard my mother urging Viktor to persuade me and I knew the lengths they must have gone to in order to make the call.

'Very well,' I replied a little reluctantly, for the journey would take twice as long and I was expected to start on a new recording almost as soon as I returned. 'I'll ask the concert agency what they can do.'

With the director's help, an employee at the agency agreed to alter my travel schedule. I had one more concert to give in the city of Arad, on the border with Hungary, and hoped I could travel home from there. The authorities said I could. 'There's no need for you to go all the way back to Bucharest first,' the employee told me. 'You can take the midnight train to the Hungarian border and then catch another train to Prague, via Vienna and Ostrava.' He scribbled something onto my existing ticket, stamped it and sent me on my way.

When I took my place at the harpsichord later that night and paused for my usual moment of reflection, I saw in the front row some of the children I'd spoken to earlier, their faces tilted expectantly towards me. As I began to play Bach's Italian Concerto, I could see them listening attentively to each note I teased out of the instrument, which was gratifyingly well tuned.

Quickly losing myself in the music, I went into the semi-meditative state that I always did once my fingers touched the keys. Whenever I played Bach, it was the same. There is such beauty in his structure. I have a tectonic rather than a visual memory and as the melodies begin to build, in my mind I imagine a building. I know where the highs and lows are. Bach's modulation moves me forward like corridors. I absolutely know where and when to turn the corner. I instinctively know how it is built. I understand the architecture and where it is heading – the corridors leading to rooms; stairs leading to upper levels, and ultimately to a final melody that completes the structure perfectly.

Long after I have played the final note, it always takes me a while to come back to myself – and the applause.

As usual I was presented with a bouquet and – offstage – the director handed me an envelope containing my fee in Romanian leu. I couldn't open it as I was on strict instructions to hand it over to the state within twenty-four hours of arriving back in Prague, along with my passport and the other payments from the tour.

I'm sure the Sibiu director suspected that I only received a small portion from those who controlled my bookings, because he embraced me warmly once again. 'We cannot offer you much, Comrade Růžičková,' he said, 'but please don't say no if we ask for you again. It means so much to have someone like you here.'

Someone like you.

Looking into his eyes, I pondered his choice of words. I doubted that he knew my history. I supposed he was referring to the fact that his district was so rarely visited by one of the few musicians from behind the Iron Curtain who was allowed to record albums and – occasionally – even travel to the West.

Assuring him that I'd be back, I accepted his offer to escort me to the station later that night in the thickening snow. Sibiu's medieval heart was extremely picturesque, but on the outskirts it was clear that, for most of its citizens, winter was just another unwelcome hardship. Walking to the platform, we had to sidestep people so poor they had strips of cloths wrapped around their feet instead of shoes.

Exactly on time, the train pulled in a few minutes before midnight in billowing clouds of steam. I was eager to get on board, but the senior conductor had other ideas. Having examined my paperwork, he informed me that it wasn't valid.

'Your reservation is from Bucharest,' he told me flatly. 'There's no place for you on this train.'

I could have wept. I longed for the city I'd made my home after the war and was horribly homesick for Viktor and my mother. I wanted nothing more than to get back to our two-room apartment where Mummy had the only bed and my husband and I slept on a mattress under the piano.

'But I have to get back to Prague,' I protested, 'and this is my only way out.'

The director tried to intervene and addressed the conductor directly. 'Comrade, this is Zuzana Růžičková, the harpsichord virtuoso. She is an honoured guest of the party. You must do all you can to help her.'

The official seemed unimpressed. I wondered if he'd refused to join the Communist Party, just as Viktor and I had.

'Surely you can find me somewhere on this train?' I pleaded finally.

'Very well,' he conceded with a sigh. 'You can take an empty berth in the Czech sleeping car, but be prepared for someone with a valid ticket to board in Ostrava and kick you out.'

Thanking him, I hurried to the sleeping carriage before he changed his mind.

It took all my strength to lift my suitcase onto the upper bunk, laden as it was with books and ball gowns, my music, and a few items of food. At less than a metre and a half tall and weighing less than fifty kilos I'd never had an athletic physique – much to the disappointment of my father, who'd always hoped for a sporty child.

Settling onto the lower bunk with a book by my favourite author, Thomas Mann, I waved farewell to the avuncular director who stood on the platform wreathed in steam and snow. As the train lurched forwards and he slipped from view, I was reminded of my last station farewell from the director of the Kiev Philharmonic, who'd been something of an enigma.

Just as in Sibiu, I'd arrived in the Ukrainian Socialist Soviet Republic late and tired. Eager to get to my room and eat something – for I was always hungry – I first had to locate the director, who I found sitting in a small office heated with a little stove.

It was like a scene directly from a film. The director was a bear of a man who sat behind a large table with black cloth oversleeves to protect the arms of his white shirt. His secretary sat in one corner. The room was terribly hot and stuffy.

'Hello, Director. I am Zuzana Růžičková and I am pleased to be here,' I told him politely. I then presented him with the necessary forms so that the authorities could work out what taxes to deduct before I received my fee.

The director went red in the face. 'What's this?' he barked, stabbing at my documents with his finger.

'My engagement contract, Comrade,' I explained. 'It requires your signature – as usual.'

Without a word he grabbed my papers and threw them into the air. Jumping to his feet, he bellowed, 'I shan't sign them. I refuse to sign another thing. I'm tired of all this paperwork, stuck in this airless office!' Marching towards the door, he turned only to yell, 'I'm going out. Leave me alone.'

I began to protest, but caught the eye of his mousy secretary who shook her head and pressed a finger to her lips. The door slammed and we heard the director thump off down the corridor as she helped me gather up my papers.

'Don't worry,' she assured me, as if his behaviour was nothing out of the ordinary. 'I'll deal with those for you.'

'You will? Oh, thank you.'

She arranged the bundle on her desk, but just as she was about to give them an official stamp, the door burst open and the director stalked back in, eyes blazing. 'What are you doing? We won't sign those! I forbid it. I don't care if I lose my job. I'm on strike!'

'But Director,' I cried, 'without these papers I'll be in terrible trouble and I shan't be paid.' Unmoved, he marched out, leaving me speechless. Thankfully, his aide ignored him and within minutes I was hurrying from his office with my completed contract.

The following evening, just as I was climbing the grand staircase of the concert hall where I was to perform, the same woman stepped out of the shadows to tell me the director had invited me to dinner after my recital.

'What? After the way he treated me?'

'He *has* to take you to dinner,' she replied. Lowering her voice, she added, 'It is expected.'

I had no choice but to agree.

The concert went well, but later in the hotel restaurant the director and I sat in virtual silence. Finally, he said, 'I know that I didn't behave well to you, Comrade, but you have to understand that life is so very difficult for me here – because I am a Jew.'

Taking a deep breath, I looked him in the eye and said, 'So am I.'

Squinting for a moment he examined my expression with suspicion before exclaiming, 'Prove it.'

I looked around the half-empty restaurant, unsure quite what to do. His face betrayed nothing, so I rolled up my left sleeve and showed him the tattoo neatly inked into my forearm in Auschwitz by an expressionless functionary in a striped uniform.

The director waved his hand dismissively. 'Oh, lots of people have those!' Before I could protest, he leaned forward and hissed, 'Show me your passport.'

I reached into my bag and handed him what he wanted, but he was dismayed to discover that my Czech papers gave no indication of anything other than my citizenship. Tossing it back at me across the table, he commanded, 'Say something in Yiddish.'

I almost laughed. I was thirty-three years old and, although I knew a little Hebrew, I had hardly ever spoken Yiddish in my life. My wealthy and largely non-observant parents had only ever taken me to the synagogue in Plzeň for special occasions and on high holidays. We were an assimilated family who celebrated Hanukkah but also Christmas each year, complete with a glittering tree. I knew a little Hebrew from my grandfather singing at family feasts, but my only contact with those who spoke Yiddish had been in the concentration and slave labour camps of Terezín, Auschwitz, Hamburg, and Bergen-Belsen.

Wracking my brain, I closed my eyes as my brain filtered words from a time I tried hard to forget. '*Meshuggeneh*!' I came up with suddenly.

'Ah, but what does it mean?' the director asked, testing me on a language he clearly knew well.

'Crazy?'

'What else?'

'*Kvetch*?' I tried. 'I believe that means to complain.'

He nodded.

'Oh, and *mensch*, which means a good man.'

Apparently satisfied, the director flashed me his first smile, completely transforming his face. 'Welcome to Kiev, Comrade,' he cried, extending a paw of a hand. 'I can't wait to introduce you to my Jewish family.'

I thought he was joking until I left Kiev for Sibiu the following morning. He was there, waiting for me at the station, with a huge crowd of people he proudly introduced as his parents, grandparents, aunts, cousins, and children, all of whom pressed around me as if I were a movie star.

'I brought them all to say goodbye!' he boomed over their heads. 'Please come back soon.'

I did return to Kiev a few years later, but the director was nowhere to be seen. I could only assume that he'd been fired.

After crossing the Romanian border from Arad into Hungary my train trundled slowly towards Vienna, where we were shunted into a siding and hooked up to a modern diesel locomotive.

When we reached Ostrava I fully expected to be evicted from my solitary berth but, blissfully, no one arrived to claim my bunk. I read a little, ate a little, and smoked a little, but I was fast asleep when I was suddenly thrown from my bed.

The first thing I knew, I hit the floor with a thud. Then my suitcase crashed down on me from the upper bunk. I tried to get up, but realised that my carriage was at an oblique angle and I was too weak to lift the weight of the case from my back. I have no idea how long I lay trapped, but when I finally managed to wriggle free, I could hear shouting and the sound of metal grating against metal.

The next few hours were spent in a painful daze. Someone helped me off the train and I stubbornly insisted that my suitcase be taken off with me. When I finally emerged from the wreckage, all I could see was thick fog. All I could smell was fire. There was debris everywhere. I had to pick my way across broken glass and the remnants of carriages splintered like matchwood. Bodies were strewn around in the snow. I'd lost all track of time and had no idea if it was day or night, but it felt like night and I could see flames licking at the scene of devastation behind me.

Those of us who survived were shepherded away by public security guards and taken to an unheated building in the nearby village that we later learned was Stéblová in eastern Bohemia. Local citizens brought us some water, bread, and a little cherry brandy to warm us up before hurrying to the crash site. We were left shivering in various stages of shock and injury.

At some point, a man came to tend to the wounded and told us what had happened. A passenger steam train had collided with us head on at speed and there were many dead and injured. To prevent the boiler from exploding someone had thrown the coals onto the embankment, but they'd accidentally ignited spilled diesel from our train and caused a fire. Further down the track, he said, people were swarming around the wreckage to free the injured who were being ferried to hospitals in nearby Hradec Králové and Pardubice.

In spite of my sore back, I refused medical treatment and asked for arrangements to be made to get me back to Prague as soon as possible. 'I have an important appointment,' I repeated. 'I need to get home.'

It took two days in treacherous conditions, but, eventually, via a bus to Hradec Králové, a train and a tram, I finally made it. The scene of the crash was approximately 120 kilometres from Prague, so I didn't arrive until the early hours of the morning. When Viktor opened the door to our apartment building, fully dressed despite the hour, he looked like he'd seen a ghost.

'You're alive!' he cried, enfolding me in his arms. My brilliant composer husband, who'd married a young Jew fresh from the camps despite all my warnings, couldn't believe his eyes. Standing back and checking again, he declared, 'It's a revenant! You've come back from the dead, Zuzana – again!'

I nodded, too tired and cold to speak.

Climbing the six flights of stairs to our apartment took all my strength, not least because my back was causing me a great deal of pain. As we made slow progress, Viktor told me that he and my mother had heard a brief news item on the wireless about the train crash, but the authorities had issued no further details.

It was a long time before we learned that senior party officials had decided to keep the worst train disaster in Czech history largely secret to prevent the news from being 'abused by enemies of socialism'. The media didn't immediately report that 118 people had died and more than a hundred had been injured. They didn't even cover the subsequent trial in which the surviving driver, conductor, and train chief were jailed for misreading the signals in the fog.

Desperate for news the night after the crash, Viktor had to call in a great many favours to discover more. Fortunately, one influential friend had connections with Prague railway station, so he rang there and asked if the sleeping berths from Romania had been involved in the crash.

'Yes,' came the reply. 'The last three international passenger wagons were completely crushed. There were no survivors.'

He and my mother then rang the local hospitals to see if I was listed among the injured, but could find no record. Believing then that my change of travel plans had inadvertently caused my death they were distraught.

When I reached the top of the stairs my mother, also fully clothed, stood waiting for me, her arms open. 'Zuzanka,' she whispered, wide-eyed, unable to say more.

By the time Viktor and I lay down on our mattress under the grand piano it was already dawn but I still asked him to set the alarm. He looked shocked. 'But why?'

'I have to be at the Domovina Hall first thing,' I reminded him. 'The building has been booked for the recording and everyone will be waiting.'

He began to protest but then he looked into my eyes. Ever since I was a little girl, my eyes couldn't lie. It was a trait I'd inherited from my father. Viktor knew what I was thinking. I didn't even have to say it: *What would Bach do?* He rolled over and set the alarm.

The one concession I made to his concerns was to rise even earlier and have myself checked over at the hospital first. 'I might have lumbago or I may have bruised my back,' I informed the doctor who examined me, adding only: 'A suitcase fell on me.' He ordered an X-ray, promising to contact me later with the results.

I can't now recall what piece of music I recorded in the hall that day for Supraphon, the Czech record label that had become such a champion of mine. I thought afterwards that it might have been something by Domenico Scarlatti, an Italian contemporary of Bach's and a prolific composer for the harpsichord.

The sleeve notes from that time tell me, however, that it was the Goldberg Variations, one of Bach's most challenging pieces and a work I had aspired to record ever since I was a little girl. Reportedly commissioned by a Russian count who had insomnia and wanted his harpsichordist Johann Gottlieb Goldberg to play these pieces at night to entertain him, the variations are mathematically perfect, with a dazzling number of numerological patterns which Bach described as 'prepared for the soul's delight of lovers of music'.

I can't recall feeling much delight that day. I only know that I fulfilled all my obligations, pushing on through the pain to spend four or five hours at the keyboard. As always, my fellow musicians and diligent recording staff assisted me. When the producer decided they had enough material and asked if I wanted to stay and listen to what they'd taped so far, I shook my head.

Feeling feverish, I told him, 'Thank you, but I'm rather tired after all my travelling and think I may be developing a cold. I'd like to go home now.'

I must have delivered my foreign currency and my passport to the authorities as required. I would then have caught the tram back to our apartment near the four-storey nineteenth-century Hotel Flora in Vinohrady district, where Viktor and I often went for lunch (until it was demolished to make way for a shopping mall and Metro station). But I don't remember doing anything before turning the corner on our street and seeing an ambulance outside our block, its rear doors open. Quickening my pace as best I could, I reached the front door to come face to face with the doctor I'd seen hours earlier.

'Where have you been, Mrs Růžičková?' he cried, clearly agitated. 'We've been waiting for you.'

'Why? What's wrong?' I asked, fearing something might be amiss with my mother.

'It's your X-ray results,' the doctor explained. 'You must be admitted to hospital immediately.'

Confused, I asked, 'What? Why?'

'My dear Comrade, you have broken a cervical vertebra in your back.' He went on to tell me I was lucky not to have been paralysed. Under strict instructions not to move, I spent the next three weeks lying flat on my back in hospital and several weeks afterwards laced into a spinal brace. The recording company sent me a bouquet of flowers with a note saying that the record turned out very well, in spite of my pain.

My greatest luck was that my injury didn't affect my playing and – just as I'd fought my way back to health in 1945 – I did so once again. Bruised but unbowed, I couldn't wait to return home to Viktor and my mother, grateful once more for yet another miracle that allowed me to spend that Christmas with the two people who meant more to me than life itself.

2

Plzeň, 1927

'*Nursemaid required for female infant, six months old. Must be able to sing.*' The advertisement my mother placed in the Plzeň newspaper in 1927 must have puzzled many. Several of those who applied suggested that the singing requirement was an unnecessary indulgence for such a small child, but my mother insisted: 'Her previous nurse always sang to her and she loved it.'

To prove the point that I had an unusually developed musical ear, she held me on her lap during each interview and asked every potential nursemaid to sing to me. Whenever they were off-key I howled so loudly that, through a process of elimination, my mother found the perfect nurse. Mummy said that my reaction to poor singing was the first intimation she had that I might one day become a musician.

That my parents were very indulgent of me is without doubt. I was their only child and I didn't know poverty. When somebody asks me how I would have ended up if I hadn't gone to concentration camps, I tell them that I would probably have been an unbearably spoiled child. My mother Leopoldina, known as 'Poldi', was thirty when I was born and my father Jaroslav Růžička was thirty-four. A Jewish *shadchen* or matchmaker had arranged their marriage, as was the tradition, but that didn't mean they were unhappy. Far from it. They were devoted to each other and had one of the most beautiful marriages that I have ever known.

Mummy longed to study medicine, but instead she ran a porcelain shop in the town of Dobříš in eastern Bohemia and then worked in accounts for a company that made paints and lacquers, before taking a position as a senior secretary in the Auto-Štádler vehicle export plant in Plzeň. Cultured and elegant, she attended boarding school where she learned German, and then spent quite a lot of time in Vienna with her sister, Elsa, going to theatres, concerts, and museums. My mother was strikingly beautiful, but considered herself ugly in spite of having several men in love with her, including one who was married. As a younger woman, she'd fallen for the brother of one of her brother-in-laws, an older man who was lame. He adored her too, but was later rejected as unsuitable by her parents, who hired the matchmaker instead.

My father, who'd been a first lieutenant in the 35th Plzeň Infantry Regiment during the First World War and been shot in the lung, looked almost Prussian in posture and not at all Jewish. He never spoke about the war, but his wound affected him for the rest of his life, particularly in his sporting activities. He studied at an academy of commerce before going to work in his father's toy store Hračky Růžička (*hračky* means toys) at Solní 2, Plzeň. By the time he and Mummy were formally introduced he'd just returned from four years in Chicago in the United States, where he'd been apprenticed at the Leader department store on Paulina and 18th streets, co-owned by relatives named Ginsburg. My great-aunt Malvina had emigrated to the United States in 1912 and married one of the Ginsburg sons. They settled in the largely Czech district of Chicago they'd named Pilsen after our town. Zdeněk Ginsburg and his three younger brothers quickly established themselves in the dry goods business with other relatives, members of the Oplatka family. By selling everything from school uniforms to feather duvets, and specifically targeting immigrant Czechs, the store continued to serve its loyal customers right up until the 1970s.

They had other talents too. One of the Ginsburg sons, Roderick, founded the Czechoslovak Society of Arts and Sciences and became famous for translating Czech works including Karel Hynek Mácha's poem 'May', Karel Havlíček's Tyrolean Elegies and the poetry of

Ján Kollár. Another son married into a family that was prominent politically. All were so friendly and welcoming to their Czech cousin that my father thoroughly enjoyed his time in Chicago, even though he had to work his way up from the warehouse and learn how a department store was run.

My father loved his time in America. He would probably have stayed there, but his father Heinrich, known as Jindřich, got sick and wrote to his eldest son and heir, asking him to run the Plzeň store with his younger brother Karel. After four years he returned, somewhat reluctantly, fluent in English and well versed in the principles of American commerce. That's when he was matched with my mother, whom he married in 1923. Their wedding gift from my maternal grandmother was a cook called Emily who took care of us all. Four years later I was born on 14 January 1927, whereupon my grandmother also trained a maid for Mummy and, later, I had a governess. I was given the name Zuzana Eva Miriam. Zuzana is the Czech word for Susanna, which means lily in Hebrew, and my parents chose it from a movie they saw together when my mother was pregnant with me. Eva was the name of a favourite cousin, and Miriam was my Jewish name. Zuzana was not a popular choice, however, and it created quite a scandal in my mother's family. My grandmother was appalled and wrote to Mummy and told her, 'Zuzi is a name you give a dog!'

Although my father was deeply patriotic, I think he might never have come home from America but for a sense of familial duty. In time, though, he took over the running of the toyshop with his younger brother Karel, to whom he was very close. Karel had deserted from the Austro-Hungarian Army during the First World War to join the Foreign Legion in Italy. The two brothers inherited their father's skill in salesmanship, if not his rather flamboyant style. My paternal grandfather had white hair down to his shoulders, wore a cape, and became famous for dressing the shop windows with themes for different occasions. One year for the holiday of St Nicholas, the theme was Hell, with devils and fire. Another time he filled the window with model trains. Whatever theme he chose, it would always attract a lot of children. To this day, I meet people who say that they would stand with their noses against the window at the Růžička toy store.

Inside was sold every kind of toy, including skates, puppets, balls, spinning tops, and scooters. When my father took over he drew on his experience in Chicago and opened a new 'bargain' section, accessed by its own entrance, that sold gloves, umbrellas, shoes, lingerie, bedding, jewellery, and lighting, so that customers could buy everything they needed in one place. I have an old photograph in which the shop windows are crammed from floor to ceiling with all manner of goods.

My father also dreamed up American-style advertising slogans such as 'Don't Forget Růžička!' that he placed in the local newspapers and had erected on huge billboards around town. Business was soon thriving and salesmen flocked to my father, eager to sell their wares. From as far back as I can recall I had a nursery full of toys. I was never keen on the dolls but I loved anything shiny and especially paste jewellery.

Mummy helped in the store and kept the accounts. With the blessing of their husbands and my grandfather, she and Karel's wife, Kamila, did something unusual for women of the time and opened a shop of their own called 'Filiálka' (which means branch) on Klatovská třída in a different district. They ran that independently and it was successful. The wives tried to outdo their men so there was some healthy competition between the two, and my father was supportive and kind.

We were very happy, the three of us, and used to cuddle each other a lot, long before it became fashionable. My mother, especially, was a 'cuddle bear', even though she was also a great worrier and always looked rather sad. Both my parents often worked late into the evening but when they came home I was their only focus as they asked me about my day and spoiled me. With German and English governesses, I grew up surrounded by three languages – Czech, German, and English – and we switched from one to the other effortlessly. Perhaps because my parents were out at work all day I became something of a neurotic child, though, and developed terrible anxieties that something might happen to them. My mother was, in turn, over-protective of me and would have liked another child to keep me company, but my father was extremely pessimistic about the state of the world in the 1930s and said that he didn't want to bring another child into it.

His decision saved our lives because with a younger sibling in tow we might well have gone straight to the gas chambers later on, as some of my close relatives did.

I didn't miss having a brother or sister because I had my cousin Dášenka, known as Dagmar. We were inseparable. Only one month younger than me, she was the eldest child of my Uncle Karel and Aunt Kamila. Dagmar and I dressed the same, we went to the same elementary school, and were known as Zuzi and Dagmar – 'the Růžička girls' – by all our teachers. We also spent holidays together, skiing in the winter with our parents, or hiking in the Krkonoše Mountains in the summer.

Dagmar lived with her parents and younger brother Miloš, known as Milošek, in a second-floor apartment adjacent to ours at Plachého 4 in central Plzeň. From my bedroom window I could look straight across a courtyard into Dagmar's bedroom. Every morning we'd open our windows and cheerily call to each other, 'Good morning cousin! Are you coming?'

From my other window I could see Mummy's shop from where she'd wave at me in the doorway when she closed up at six. We would then walk together through the public gardens around the synagogue to pick up my father at his store. He would often meet us halfway on his bicycle and I would be so happy that we were a family again. I would receive my pocket money of five crowns and we would go together to buy my favourite magazine *Malý hlasatel* ('Small Announcer') and some flowers for my mother.

I was an inquisitive child, fascinated by everything, especially aircraft, and at the age of six announced that I'd be a pilot when I grew up. Then I fell in love with books, so declared my intention to become a writer. Dagmar was obsessed with nature and animals and decided early on that she would become a veterinary doctor. She had a kitten called Evinka and I had tropical fish in an aquarium in my bedroom, including one with a fan for a tail, which I called 'Lady Windermere's Fan' after a Wilde play that I liked. I also had a pet canary called Jerry, named after my father Jaroslav, but I'm sure Dagmar took far more interest in him than I ever did.

My father (who we called Tata) encouraged our English from an early age by reading us children's stories such as *Peter Pan*, *Winnie-the-Pooh* and *Alice in Wonderland*. Dagmar especially loved Winnie-the-Pooh and dreamed of owning her own donkey called Eeyore. She was slower at languages than I was though, so dear 'Tata' lost his patience and she eventually dropped out of his lessons. After that, my father taught me English on my own and in the most wonderful way. He had me write down each new word in the chapter we were reading and tell him their meanings when he came home. If I wasn't good enough we wouldn't read on, so the incentive was enormous.

Mummy was immensely elegant and that made a great impression on me. I loved the way she always used to be beautifully dressed. She had lovely garments specially stitched for us by a local seamstress, and Dagmar and I were often dressed alike, although Mummy also had matching mother and daughter outfits created just for us. We especially loved to dress up in costumes. Once I dressed as Cio-Cio-San from *Madame Butterfly* in my mother's bathrobe complete with turban and chrysanthemums. Another time I was Mata Hari, and for a school play I was a simple postwoman in uniform.

My father was a keen amateur photographer, with his own darkroom set up in a small room within our apartment, so he took dozens of photos of us all that were fortunately saved by friends during the war and I still treasure to this day. There's a favourite one of Dagmar and I posing as wild flowers for our school production of *The Mother Earth*, in which I was a forget-me-not and she was a daisy. Oh, how we loved to dress up!

When I was a little girl our house was filled with music. Emily the cook sang me old folk songs about wolves and babies, and my father was a fine baritone who played the violin. We didn't have our own piano but my mother played other people's whenever she could and I loved to watch her hands flying across the keys. We sang together as a family from the morning when my father was shaving until the evenings when we sang bedtime songs. Everything I heard I memorised and then sang. My father had a wonderful ear and could always tell if I was out of tune.

Tata taught me songs in every language, especially Czech and English, even Russian. I remember learning 'London's Burning', 'My Bonnie Lies Over the Ocean', and a funny poem called 'My Mother is Full of Kisses'. It had the lines: *'A kiss when I wake up in the morning, a kiss when I go to bed, a kiss when I burn my fingers, and a kiss when I bump my head.'*

My favourite song, though, was an old American song called 'Silver Threads', which had the lyrics, '*Darling, I am growing old, silver threads among the gold… Life is fading fast away. But, my darling, you will be, always young and fair to me.*'

If I heard it again now, I think I'd weep.

My father's purchase of a radio was a big event in our home. Unfortunately, I was terrified of it and used to run away screaming whenever it was turned on. Complaining that it was far too loud, I even refused to enter the room where it sat.

Mummy took me to see a paediatrician who examined me, pronounced my hearing perfectly normal, and told her, 'Your home is too silent. Perhaps you and your husband should quarrel more?'

To help me overcome my fear of the radio, Tata made up a story featuring two characters called Antenna and Amplion who had exciting adventures inside its polished mahogany case. He invented another funny one about a nightingale that tried to teach a cow and a goose to sing. My father was very well educated and not entirely happy working as a merchant. I think he would have preferred to have furthered his education and played the violin. A naturally introverted man, he had studied philosophy and was politically aware. As the eldest son of a storekeeper, however, the life of a thinker was not possible, so he had little choice but to run the store and do all he could to make it a success. Secretly, he planned to make enough money so that he could sell or leave the store to his brother, retire at fifty and build his dream house, a villa complete with a tennis court. We had all this planned and spoke of it often, and of how he would collect a fine dowry for me.

Each night he would read to my mother and me. It might be articles from the English or American newspapers he had sent to him from relatives. These were, of course, greatly delayed but nevertheless much anticipated. I would always dive for the comics, while he read stories from the news.

He also liked to read us fantastical stories by Rudyard Kipling, or something from H. G. Wells's gripping *War of the Worlds*. He had access to all kinds of books that he drew from the shelves of his extensive library. I particularly liked it when he read Homer to me, the *Odyssey* and the *Iliad*, both books that influenced me greatly – especially the rhythm of them. I think my good sense of rhythm and metre in music came from that kind Jewish shopkeeper reading those classical stories to me as a child.

His parents had been ill-suited emotionally, although the marriage was surprisingly harmonious. His father Jindřich was a staunch Czech patriot who was born in Plzeň but lived in Vienna for many years, where he established a branch of Sokol, the gymnastics movement based on the principle of 'a strong mind in a sound body'. The word '*sokol*' means 'falcon' and they wore wonderful uniforms and carried colourful flags to inspire Czech patriotism. In the early 1900s, he was banished from Vienna for his association with the organisation, which played an important role in the development of Czech nationalism in the interwar years. This would lead to its brutal suppression by the Nazis later and give them yet another reason to persecute us.

Ever since my grandfather's banishment there was a strong feeling on that side of the family against Vienna and an ingrained hatred of the Austro-Hungarian Empire. They also vehemently objected to the rise of the National Socialist German Worker's Party, or Nazi Party, that began in 1920 with the slogan 'One People, One Nation, One Leader' and had vicious anti-Semitic themes.

Moving back to Plzeň after his bruising experiences in Vienna, my grandfather married my grandmother Paula, who came from a wealthy merchant's family in Prague, and they had five children in quick succession – each of them given patriotic Czech names. There was Vlasta, then my father, Jaroslav, followed by his sisters Jiřina and Zdena, and then finally their brother Karel. None of the sisters married Jews, which gave them a different status and later affected how quickly they were sent to the camps in the Second World War.

When my grandfather first moved to Czechoslovakia from Vienna, he set up a business that imported and exported iron, before starting to sell toys from the shop whose windows he loved to decorate like the grand Viennese stores. He never lost his passion for health and fitness, though, and – as a great nature lover – spent all his spare time either in the natural history museum or out in the forest watching birds, identifying wild flowers, or chasing butterflies. He would cycle with Dagmar and me to a village called Švihov where he liked to live a simple life each summer. We would visit its beautiful Gothic castle and moat, and walk every day in the woods to learn about the plants and animals. It was he who first gave Dagmar the idea of becoming a vet.

My grandmother Paula, by contrast, was a lively socialite from the city who loved to travel and enjoyed music and culture. Theirs was the most amiable relationship because they resolved their many differences in the most reasonable way. In spite of having five children at home, my grandmother would drive to Nice to spend her summer holidays with friends. She would send us the first violets from there and return fully refreshed, bearing exotic, edible gifts. She also loved music of every kind and encouraged it in her children and grandchildren. Her daughter Vlasta was a wonderful alto who had ambitions to be a professional musician. She sang the role of Háta in the first performance of Smetana's comic opera *The Bartered Bride* in Paris, but, as the daughter of a well-known family, a career in the theatre was impossible, so she was married off to a wealthy man named Arnošt Karas and remained bitter and unhappy about it for the rest of her short life.

I called my grandmother Paula '*Babička*' and, although she was not musical herself, she loved the arts and took me to the theatre often. First to the matinees of children's shows from the age of six, then to operettas and ballets, and later to operas, including my first opera – *Carmen* – which I adored for both its music and its high emotion. Dagmar came too and my cousin Eva Šenková. We loved everything, completely.

My grandmother was involved in several charities including the Society of Czech Ladies and Misses and a fund in support of poor Jewish students. She also arranged a season of string quartets by the Chamber Music Association, and a performance of the Beethoven Quartet Cycle by the Kolisch Quartet. There was a Spring Festival of Opera each year for which we always took a family box in the theatre. Watching those musicians coax such beautiful sounds from their instruments enthralled me and led to my final and enduring ambition to become a musician.

I would get myself so wound up about hearing a new concert that I almost made myself ill from the excitement and, sitting in that box, I sometimes even forgot to breathe.

Although my mother came from a religious but not orthodox Jewish family, we were not observant. Her father always led the Hebrew singing at Passover and the Seder feast but no one kept kosher or spoke Yiddish. On the contrary, the family was bilingual in Czech and German and completely assimilated.

My father had never lived in Vienna with his parents, so he didn't speak German well and didn't even like Czech Jews speaking German in coffee houses, as he feared that this might antagonise other Czechs. He was also an avowed atheist who never even closed the shop on the Sabbath, but nor did he ever dispute my mother's quiet faith.

When my mother went to the synagogue on Yom Kippur, it would have been customary for my father to take her flowers. It took our housekeeper Rézi, known as Emily, who was Czech and an ardent Catholic, to tell him, 'You have to take flowers to Mrs Růžičková.' And when he left for the synagogue with his bouquet, she ran after him, crying, 'But Mr Růžička you don't have a hat!' So he was not at all familiar with Jewish customs, but he went because he loved my mother so.

Growing up I had little sense of being Jewish or different from others in any way, although I did go to the synagogue with my mother on the high holidays. Dagmar was the same. Our parents raised us with total freedom, including religious freedom, and didn't try to influence us in any way. As I loved any kind of ceremony, I enjoyed visiting the synagogue for Rosh Hashanah and Yom Kippur, but that was the only place I came into contact with Jewishness. I'd always loved anything with music, but my interest wasn't based on faith and I was equally interested in the ancient Greeks and Romans with all their mythical gods.

I even took part in the Catholic procession for Corpus Christi and received a blessing from the bishop after bearing a cup of peonies to the altar. He gave me a holy picture, which I have kept to this day. The feast of taking the wafer representing 'the body of Christ' was the greatest joy for me. The curious thing to me now is that nobody back then in President Masaryk's republic said, 'You don't belong here. You're Jewish', especially as it was well known in town that the Růžičkas were Jewish, even though it was traditionally a gypsy name. Nor did my parents tell me not to attend those ceremonies. We were part of a community that was considered to be a bastion of social democracy and I was allowed to go anywhere. It was all so tolerant and democratic.

Dagmar and I started at the local school, Cvičná škola in Koperníkova Street, on the same day. Even though we were in the same classes there was never any rivalry between us. The school was highly regarded as a place where teachers were trained, so we were taught everything from languages to the arts, classics to mathematics. With my natural hypersensitivity to noise – first discovered when I hid from the family radio – I often had to sit in the silence of the staff room because my head throbbed from hearing things so acutely.

As well as our regular studies all the pupils had weekly religious classes, which meant that Dagmar and I went to see a wonderful old rabbi at the beautiful Great Synagogue in Plzeň, the second largest in Europe. Similarly, the Catholic and the Protestant students went to their churches to meet with their priests. My parents left it up to me whether I wished to attend these Jewish classes or not, but I enjoyed them very much because the rabbi explained everything so nicely and taught the parables as if they were fairy tales. Best of all for my over-sensitive hearing, the religious studies were much quieter, with just five or six pupils, unlike the regular classes with twenty or more.

As far as I was concerned, I was a Czech child having a Jewish education and that was that. I took no pride in being Jewish and I certainly didn't consider myself 'chosen'. I never once had the fear that someone might persecute me for it. I experienced no anti-Semitism, not a single incident, and I'd never witnessed any to anyone else either. After our religious studies, Dagmar and I would meet up with the other children to go to the park together or to swim in the lake, none of us giving faith or race a second thought.

All of my childhood memories are happy ones. I think if you have a sweet childhood like I did then you can survive almost anything in later life. Nothing can really spoil it for you.

My mother used to say that to make lemonade you have to put the sugar in before the lemon. If you do it the other way around it will always taste sour. That is really a metaphor for life, because the sweetness stays with you forever if you taste it before the bitterness.

Fortunately, my parents were very much in love with each other and I was part of their love. Some of my best and most vivid memories are of our two or three weeks together each summer in Dobříš in eastern Bohemia, where the majority of my mother's family lived as part of a large and influential Jewish community. Mummy was the youngest of four, although her younger brother Josef, known as 'Pepa', committed suicide after the First World War. He had studied chemistry in Prague with his friends and classmates Maksymilian Faktorowicz (the Polish beautician Max Factor) and the conductor Walter Susskind. When he returned home from the war he never adjusted and could no longer cope with ordinary life after the trauma of the trenches. When a love affair ended, he couldn't cope and killed himself. His suicide was rarely talked about.

My grandfather Leopold co-owned a company called Schwartz & Lederer that employed the wives of miners and metal workers, working from home making gloves from imported leathers, which he sold in his shop. In Dobříš, he was almost considered part of the gentry and my grandmother Zdenka Fleischmannová was also greatly respected. She and her numerous younger siblings had reportedly been orphaned following an epidemic, probably of the Spanish flu, and Zdenka cared for them like a mother. They were only saved from destitution by their uncles who'd formed a famous synagogue trio that sang all over the world. The three brothers were blond and blue-eyed, popular and wealthy, and they sent money home for their nieces and nephews, a kindness my grandmother never forgot. Even after she was grown up with children of her own, she would send a doctor to a sick child in the village or hand out baskets of food to the poor, regardless of who they were.

As a fourteen-year-old surrogate mother, Zdenka was a beautiful girl who would go shopping at the local grocery store. My grandfather was a young apprentice there who became mesmerised by her, not only for her looks, but also for how she took care of the whole family. Allegedly, he told her that he would wait for her, which he did and when his 'Zdenička' turned eighteen, they got married.

My grandparents celebrated all the Jewish holidays and my grandmother always had a wonderful Sabbath table decked with polished silver candles and white linen. She made delicious challah bread and the smell of warm yeast, beet soup, and roast chicken takes me straight back to those early days. What I loved most in their house, however, was my grandfather's book-lined study. It was like an Aladdin's cave in which he used to sit and smoke the pipe he'd allow me to light for him as a special treat.

Dobříš felt like a second home to me because I had so many relatives there. An aunt Růzena owned a large house in the town and was known for hosting spirited soirées for local intellectuals. Another aunt, Hermine, and her husband Emil, lived locally with their two boys named Hanuš and Jiří. Hanuš was four years older than me and became my first love, even though he generally preferred to play with his tin soldiers than spend time with me. I was bitterly disappointed when my mother explained that I couldn't marry a first cousin.

The town of Dobříš boasted a rococo castle owned by an Austrian count who was a member of the Colloredo-Mansfeld dynasty. Thanks to a family connection with the estate manager, our little group of cousins and friends were given the key to the back gate of the castle grounds and allowed to step inside. I was the only girl – the rest were all boys – and we had so much fun playing in that magical kingdom. The countess was a former model from Paris who'd commissioned a park like a mini Versailles, laid out with a parterre and roses. She also had a beautiful potager and tried to encourage the locals to eat more fresh vegetables. We children were only allowed in the English park with its woodland and fields of wild flowers, but roaming those meadows and picking fruit from the trees was like some sort of childhood dream for a girl who'd grown up in a city.

I felt very lucky and was perfectly happy there.

Summers spent in the fresh air were magical for me but also increasingly necessary because, from the age of six, I developed serious chest problems and became a virtual invalid. That was the greatest cloud of my youth as from then until the age of twelve I was ill with bronchitis or flu most of the time. Then I had my tonsils taken out and that just made me worse, so I was extremely weak.

As my parents still worked full-time they hired a nanny called Karla, a village girl who was perfectly suited to me as she was very musical. We sang folk songs and arias together, which only made me long to study music more. Then Karla developed tuberculosis and was sent to a sanatorium to recover. I started coughing then and so did Dagmar. I was also unfashionably thin at a time when plump girls were in vogue. People used to comment on it and wonder out loud if I had TB, which was a disease that terrified people then because it so often led to their deaths.

My mother – the woman who always wanted to be a doctor – also feared the worst and she took me to Prague immediately. The whole family said she was crazy and that we girls were coughing on purpose. They pointed out that Dagmar was healthy, plump, and pink and couldn't possibly have been ill. In Prague, I was X-rayed as a precaution, and the doctors confirmed that I had TB too. Dagmar was never checked.

After a particularly bad episode in 1935, my mother was advised to take me to a sanatorium at Breitenstein in the Austrian Alps near the Semmering Pass for six months. Painfully thin, I was wrapped in blankets and ordered to have plenty of bed rest in between steam treatments that reddened my face and wrinkled my skin. At each meal my plate was loaded with leafy green vegetables, which I hated, but my time there saved my life.

My father came to the mountains every weekend and for three weeks in the summer. It was not long after the Austrian Chancellor, Engelbert Dollfuss, had been assassinated for banning the Nazi Party in Austria, and there was a great deal of discussion about that. I remember sitting with Tata in the grounds of the sanatorium one day as he sang me some of his favourite patriotic Czech songs.

After a while a man approached and told him to stop. 'You shouldn't sing those here,' he warned. 'Chancellor Hitler wouldn't like it.'

It was the first time I'd ever heard that name.

I was still too thin by the time we eventually returned home to Plzeň so I was encouraged to gain more weight. One of my favourite dishes was *svíčková* and *knedliky* – beef with dumplings – but even that lost its appeal after a while and I often pushed the plate away.

It was rare for my father to punish me for anything but one day I refused to eat a plate of buttered noodles at a time when my mother was especially worried about me being too skinny. Tata made me stand in the corner throughout lunch but I didn't mind. I'd rather stand in the corner than eat noodles, but the memory of my stubborn refusal that day was to mock me cruelly in later years.

Because of my poor health I didn't attend school for much of my childhood but had governesses and private tutors instead who improved my languages and other skills. I was a diligent little girl who completed all my studies but I was very lonely too, as my teachers were not good company and I was hardly ever allowed to play with other children for fear of infection. The only other child I saw was Dagmar, who was a normal healthy girl until she developed a cough, which her mother Kamila dismissed as nothing and refused to have treated.

Left alone for hours on end, I longed for a piano and music lessons but was frequently told that I shouldn't exert myself. Instead, I spent much of my time reading in my room after my kind nurse Anča had made up the fire in the stove to keep me warm. I had my own library, commissioned from the local bookshop and catalogued for me personally by the owner. There was a wall of books opposite my bed, each of which was numbered and colour-coded. Blue was for history, yellow for fairy tales, green for the classics and so on. I had a little leather catalogue that listed them all so that I could sit in bed and ask my governess to fetch me down book 34B or 72A.

At the age of nine, I developed pneumonia and became gravely ill. I remember my parents standing around my bed as our family doctor fretted over my fever, and Anča mopped my brow. It was March 1936. Mother wrung her hands repeatedly and was on the brink of tears.

'Zuzi, if you will only get better you can have anything you desire,' she pleaded. 'Anything at all!'

My eyes flicked open. 'Piano lessons,' I told her hoarsely, with a fresh determination to get well.

Mummy kept her promise once I'd recovered, but first she had to find me a suitable teacher. Being a shopkeeper, she knew almost everyone in the town, so she asked the advice of one of her customers, a woman without children who frequently bought toys for her nephews and nieces. Madame Marie Provazníková-Šašková was a 53-year-old pianist and organist who'd graduated from the Prague Conservatory and was a member of a chamber trio that performed locally and accompanied visiting soloists. She came from a musical family in eastern Bohemia where her father, Alois Provazník, had been a cantor and choirmaster, her sister Luisa was a famous singer, and her brother Anatol a composer.

'Madame', as we all called her, never had much success as a soloist because of her rather manly features. She taught piano instead but took on a few students and never beginners, so my mother hoped only that she might be able to recommend a teacher for me.

'I shall have to test her first,' she announced before coming to the apartment to hear me sing.

I chose a complicated Czech song, which I slightly regretted once I stood before this imposing woman in a blue silk dress. I must have been all right, though, because she turned to Mummy afterwards and said, 'I'll keep her.'

'Excuse me?' my mother enquired.

'I will teach this child myself.'

Her decision to take me on as her student turned out to be one of the first miracles of my life.

To begin with I went to Madame's apartment to study and play her piano. Before too long, she announced that I needed my own instrument before recommending a store. The shopkeeper was a giant of a man who listened attentively as my mother told him, 'My daughter appears to be gifted so we would like to buy her a nice piano.'

His face screwed up into a scowl and he shook his head. 'Don't let her become a pianist,' he bellowed. 'My son is one and he doesn't earn any money at all!' Striding towards me so that I took a few steps back, he cried, 'I would chop her hands off before I'd let her become a professional musician!'

Terrified, I quickly hid my hands behind my back.

Mummy seemed unfazed and insisted he show us his range of pianos. As I peeped out from behind her skirts, she examined several and sat me at a few until she eventually chose a German-made upright called a Förster. She asked him to arrange delivery and a few days later it was carried up the stairs with much huffing and puffing and placed within sight of my sickbed in my bedroom.

From then on, Madame came to see me once a week for a formal lesson and then every Sunday we played and played mostly for amusement. Ignoring my weak chest, she smoked cigarettes and drank coffee while she listened and taught me everything I needed to know about music. I worked my way through the complete scores of Carl Czerny's *Art of Finger Dexterity* and was taught how to sit with the correct posture, as well as theory and positioning.

One thing that became apparent to everyone was that I needed glasses. Reading a book at close quarters was fine but following the complicated patterns of clefs and quavers from a distance was too demanding for my eyes. As soon as I was fitted with my first pair of steel-rimmed spectacles my playing improved and I have worn glasses ever since.

Madame had a rather unusual teaching technique in that whenever she saw that a piece of music wasn't going so well or that I was tiring of it, she switched me to something else. My mother was concerned about this and feared that I'd never learn anything, but Madame told her firmly, 'The most important thing is that she doesn't get bored.' Mummy was also worried that I would never be a concert pianist because I couldn't memorise the music at all and always had to play from notes. Once again, Madame reassured her, saying quietly, 'This will develop.' She was right because in later life I became quite famous for playing and recording without reading the score.

On Sundays we played everything together – she playing the upper part and I playing the lower part. Madame really loved me and often came not to teach me but just to play four hands for fun. She was a wonderful teacher who taught me expression and intonation and passed on her own great passion for music, which has remained with me my whole life.

Together we played through the whole repertoire – everything from Brahms and Haydn's symphonies to Smetana's *Má Vlast*, to Beethoven, Purcell, Tchaikovsky and Dvořák. I played Chopin, Mendelssohn, and Saint-Saëns – the Rondo Capriccioso. I kept a little notebook in which I recorded all that I played and it is incredible to me that we sight-read almost everything. We used musical scores, of course, but she rarely gave me any notes in advance, so I learned early to play by sight-reading a piece for the first time, known as *prima vista*, which was the most wonderful training of all. Still now, if I play a piece of music once, I can more or less remember it forever.

Even more remarkably, from the earliest stages I felt the music in a way I can't really describe. It felt as if it was a part of me somehow, as if I was reconnecting with something inside. Little did I know then just how important that connection would become.

The first time I was formally introduced to Johann Sebastian Bach it really was love at first playing. Madame had me play the Prelude in C from *The Well-Tempered Clavier*, a piece that I'd never heard before but which instantly felt so familiar.

Bach later wrote of these twenty-four pairs of preludes and fugues that they were 'for the profit and use of musical youth desirous of learning, and especially for the pastime of those already skilled in this study'. Playing them for the first time, it was almost as if I didn't need the score, and in feeling the music, really feeling it, I was transported to a place I'd never been to before.

Seeing how much I loved studying music my parents took me to a concert at the Peklo Culture House in Plzeň in 1936, featuring the famous Czech violinist Jan Kubelík and his conductor son Rafael. The son was at the piano and the father played well, but you could see that he was worn out. He died a few years later. I never forgot it, though, and how I had to dress up for the occasion on a rare evening out with my parents that year.

My first public performance was at Christmas, which my parents and I celebrated with a huge tree that we decorated together, not long after Mummy and I had marked Hanukkah that year. It was 1936 and I'd only been having piano lessons for seven months, but I already knew how to read music. I somehow knew. That day in our apartment I played a children's tune Madame had taught me called 'Merry Christmas' and I performed it perfectly for my parents. They seemed impressed.

Madame's Christmas gift to me was Bach's 48 Preludes and Fugues, each one written in a different key, beautifully bound. She handed them to me with great reverence and said, 'One day soon, Zuzanka, you will play these. You may even be able to accomplish something as challenging as Bach's Goldberg Variations.' Smiling, she added, 'That would fulfil all that I ever dreamed of for myself.'

She made me feel so special from the start and inspired me so much that I decided then that I would love to master the Variations for her one day.

Once she discovered how much I was in love with Bach, she suggested that I consider switching from the piano to the organ so as to become a better interpreter of his early music. 'Bach didn't write for the piano,' she told my parents simply.

They consulted my doctor about her suggestion but he immediately objected. 'Impossible!' he declared. 'Organs are only in cold, damp churches. They would be a disaster for Zuzana's weak chest.'

Madame relented and continued with my piano lessons but suggested that I might one day study the harpsichord, a little-known baroque string instrument on which Bach – switching from the organ – composed many of his earliest pieces and twenty-four of his preludes and fugues. It was no longer popular as an instrument and the few still in use were extremely old. There wasn't a single harpsichord in Plzeň that I was aware of, but Madame was still eager that I should consider it.

'The harpsichord plucks at the strings with a small quill rather than beats them with hammers, which gives it a sharper tone and a wider register,' she enthused. 'Playing it is a very different discipline to that of the piano. There's a second keyboard above the first so it's really like two instruments in one that you can play together or independently.' She went on to explain that, because the strings are plucked not beaten, the player has to create the illusion of light and shade by using the 'space' between the notes, via the use of articulation and overholding notes to produce a singing sound. 'Playing the harpsichord involves not only interpretation but a full understanding of the theory and mechanics of the instrument itself.'

Excited to share her private passion, she played me recordings by a world-famous harpsichordist named Wanda Landowska, mostly compositions by the French composer Francis Poulenc and the Spanish composer Manuel de Falla. I was fascinated to hear them and to learn how the tone or colour was changed by a clutch and a series of levers similar to the organ, but I was still utterly devoted to my piano.

For the next year I did nothing but play, spending all my free time with music. I devoured it in the same way as I devoured books, especially once my father opened up his library to me, telling Mummy, 'Let her read anything she likes. If she doesn't understand something, she can ask.' Whenever I was ill with my chest again, I'd remain in my room, diligently studying or losing myself in the works of the world's greatest writers until it was time for me to practise my piano for two sessions of three hours each.

The more Madame heard me play the more convinced she was that I should take up music as a profession and start studying the piano exclusively with immediate effect. My mother was horrified by the idea and they had several heated debates about it. Although she was a little scared of my teacher – whom she referred to as *Milostpaní,* which means 'Gracious Madam' – this was something she hadn't expected and she strongly resisted. Mummy knew how many sacrifices musicians have to make and how devoted they have to be, often to the exclusion of everything else. Citing the piano-shop owner and his penniless son, she argued, 'But Zuzana will never earn anything. She must at least complete her formal education.'

'No, no, that would be too late!' Madame insisted. 'The teenage years are absolutely crucial for the development of a musician.'

There were also arguments between my parents about it behind closed doors, from where I often heard their voices rising in dramatic debate. I could see both sides actually because I already knew that going into music as a career was a big risk. Either you are successful or you are nothing. You can be an average doctor or an average lawyer, but you can't be an average musician.

My father was far more fatalistic about my future and, being a spiritual person, he knew how much music resonated with me. In the end, he summoned me into the room they called the salon and asked, 'What would you like to do, Zuzka?'

I looked from Mummy to him and replied softly, 'I dearly wish to study music, Tata.'

My mother glanced at my father, nodded and let out a sigh. 'Very well ... Let her do it.'

Her one stipulation was that I continue my studies until the age of fourteen before concentrating wholly on music.

Madame didn't waste any time and immediately wrote to Wanda Landowska in Paris to ask if she'd accept me as a fourteen-year-old student at her Ecole de Musique Ancienne, which she had established in the Parisian suburb of Saint-Leu-la-Forêt. On reading Madame's glowing accounts of my ability, Ms Landowska agreed and sent all the requirements for admission to her classes. They included the finer points of theory, harmony, and counterpoint, so Madame arranged for me to take lessons in these with the composer Josef Bartovský, professor of music at the teacher's seminary in Plzeň.

Madame's next instruction was that I needed to take better care of my hands, as my growing fingers were fragile and needed to be protected for playing only. A pianist's fingers can't be knocked for fear of any break in the bone and they had to be kept from getting too cold or developing chilblains. It was a decree that had the inadvertent effect of upsetting my father. As a devotee of the Sokol school of thought so revered by his father, he'd always dreamed that I'd be an athlete. In spite of my mother's neuroses about me catching a cold or getting overtired, he was convinced that fresh air and vigorous exercise was exactly what I needed. After Madame spoke to them, though, I had to abandon all games and was allowed only to swim in (warm) lakes or play table tennis. Giving up activities such as eurhythmics, skiing, tennis and skating was no great disappointment as I had inherited my mother's fear that outdoor activities might adversely affect my health – but it was a huge disappointment to Tata.

Because of my lungs, my mother and I continued to visit the mountains a great deal and my father would join us whenever he could. We went often to Karlsbad in the Black Forest and to Mariánské Lázně in the Krkonoše range, but in the summer of 1937 we stayed at a Czech resort called Špindlerův Mlýn, a place we returned to for a couple of years. Jindřich Matiegka, the rector of the Charles University in Prague, went there as well and he got along with my father well. Whenever he was going on a hike, he would always wait to see if Mr Růžička was coming along as well.

Wherever we went we always took lots of luggage, my sweet nanny-nurse Ança, and sometimes Emily the cook, although sometimes Mummy cooked. I hated going away if it meant missing my piano lessons, but to my delight I discovered a piano in the dining room at our hotel in Špindlerův Mlýn and immediately settled down to play some Bach.

As I lost myself in the music once more, a grey-haired gentleman wandered into the room to listen. I didn't know him and I didn't care. Afterwards, he sought out my parents and introduced himself as Karl Straube, the cantor at Leipzig, a position Johann Sebastian Bach had once occupied.

'I was astonished!' he told them. 'I heard the music and thought it must be a colleague playing. I couldn't believe it when I found a small child at the piano. You must do everything you can to further her musical education.'

The last thing my parents wanted was a child prodigy but they assured him I was receiving suitable tuition and sent him on his way. To my surprise, my mother was disgusted with me.

'You are not to show off, Zuzana!' she scolded. Her words really stung. At another spa resort later that year, I sang for an old lady who asked me to but then I ran to my mother crying. 'Forgive me Mummy!' I wailed. 'I've been showing off again.'

It was only later that I learned that my mother had always hoped I'd become a medical doctor, which was a profession that was impossible for the daughter of a good family to take up in her youth. She didn't lack the courage to pursue her dream but there were other difficulties, too, as my grandparents had just lost their youngest son to suicide after the First World War and she didn't feel she could leave them for university. In any event, I had absolutely no talent for the natural sciences and only desired music. Tata was not only completely behind me, but already excited by the thought of accompanying me to Paris and on world recital tours where he could show me the America he'd fallen in love with as a young man.

I have often questioned why my father didn't arrange for the three of us to leave Czechoslovakia while we still could. After all, we had his relatives in Chicago we could have gone to without any problem at that time. He was so deeply interested in politics that he knew enough of what was happening in Germany, with the rise of Hitler and his Nazi Party, to fear fathering a second child. Our 'President Liberator' Tomáš Garrigue Masaryk was one of the first to voice his concerns about Hitler and even though he died in 1937, his successor Edvard Beneš continued to warn of the threat of Nazism.

My father's patriotism was too deep, I think. Tata had been born in Plzeň in 1893, when it was still in the Austro-Hungarian Empire. He was twenty-five years old when our democracy was formed, a change that had a profound affect on him. Like many of his countrymen, he was so proud that his people had gained their independence at the end of the First World War. He was Czech before he was Jewish and his national identity was as fundamental to him as music was to me. He had fought for his country in the last war. With a bullet in his chest, he'd almost died for it. If Czechoslovakia was going to be in any trouble, then he felt it was his patriotic and moral duty to stay.

Besides, what would he go to and how? Even if we did escape to Chicago, he would never be his own boss, whereas in Plzeň he had two successful toyshops with employees dependent on him for their livelihood. We had friends and relatives from both families close by. Furthermore, his only child looked destined to become a gifted musician thanks to a devoted local teacher who was determined to help me reach the top of my profession. How could he give all that up?

Like so many Jews and Gentiles before the war, my father believed that the educated German population would see sense and put a stop to Hitler and his anti-Semitic ravings. Germany was, after all, a country with the greatest literature and culture, music, art, and science. It had an intellectual and artistic stature that the rest of Europe had long aspired to and its influence on us all was immense. Nor could my father bring himself to believe that another world war would follow so closely on the heels of the previous 'war to end all wars'.

As far as he was concerned, all we had to do was sit it out, safe in the knowledge that if anything terrible happened our allies in the West would surely come to our aid.

3

Prague, 1949

The first time I ever played the harpsichord was at the Academy of Performing Arts in Prague two years after I'd been accepted to study piano there in September 1947. I was twenty years old and had spent the intervening period since the war working tirelessly to catch up on my musical education.

While continuing with my piano lessons for a year under the tutelage of one of the academy's finest professors, Albín Ším, I also learned to play the organ and then began to study how to master the harpsichord thanks to the expert tuition of his colleague Dr Oldřich Kredba. Only after closely examining the history of the harpsichord, including the theory and mechanics of it, and appreciating the differences between it and the piano as well as the best means of manipulation, did I finally come to the instrument, place my hands on the keys and begin to play.

Just as when I'd first heard the preludes on the piano as a child, I fell immediately in love. The music of Bach truly came alive.

I'd never forgotten what Madame had told me about the harpsichord when I was little, or how she'd arranged for me to train with Wanda Landowska in France. Sadly, that was never to be.

Miss Landowska, a Polish-French Jew, was recording the Scarlatti keyboard sonatas in Paris at the moment the Nazis invaded. In spite of bombs falling all around her (some of which can be heard on the recording), she kept her nerve and continued playing until the end.

Her home and all her possessions including her prized instrument were stolen so she fled with virtually only the clothes on her back and arrived in New York on the day Pearl Harbor was bombed. She remained in America until her death aged eighty in 1959.

Because Czechoslovakia was liberated by the Soviets and the Americans in 1945 and then the communists took over, I ended up living behind what became known as the Iron Curtain. This meant that I was not allowed to travel to such a capitalist country as America for a long time and never had the chance to meet the great harpsichordist. I wasn't even allowed to write to her, because we were forbidden from having any contact with the West.

Miss Landowska's recordings were familiar to me, though, or at least those my beloved teacher used to play. Later in life I was able to talk at length to one of her final students before she died, a Colombian harpsichordist named Rafael Puyana. He was the sweetest man and he told me, 'If Wanda would have known you, she would have carried you in her arms and just loved you.' I was so touched by his words.

I also never forgot how Madame campaigned unsuccessfully for me to learn the pipe organ – the world's first ever keyboard instrument – a huge beast designed principally for churches. After the organ came the sensitive clavichord, designed for intimate musical recitals at home. The versatile harpsichord, designed later, was perfect for public performances in court, but the piano – or 'pianoforte' – that I played wasn't invented until the 1700s in Italy by a man named Bartolomeo Cristofori.

When Bach was first shown a German prototype of the new-fangled piano in 1736 he declared it too heavy to play and didn't approve of the higher notes, which he claimed were too soft to allow a full range. It wasn't until almost twenty years later and only in his final years that he agreed to endorse an updated design. Even then he wrote nothing for piano, and his last ever composition, the *Musical Offering*, a suite of sixteen movements written in response to a challenge by Frederick the Great after he'd shown off his collection of pianofortes, was written on a harpsichord.

The moment I began to play Bach's keyboard instrument of choice, I understood his reasoning exactly. Once I heard how entirely differently the works sounded – especially his fugues – I felt a sense of déjà vu. It was as if I had come home. There was such an affinity, as if I'd once lived in the court of Elizabeth I and played harpsichord for kings and queens, dukes and earls.

From then on, I resolved to play the harpsichord whenever I could, in between honing my piano skills to impress my most difficult professor at the academy, František Rauch, who never failed to assure me daily how much I had yet to learn.

Eager to make up for time lost in the camps and absorb everything I could, I took a composition class and had musicology lessons with a professor who encouraged me to speak up in class and not sit in silence because I didn't feel as well educated as the other students. I became friendly with two cellists who'd served in the British RAF during the war, and another group of musicians who had formed the Smetana Quartet just after. Their violist was Václav Neumann who would go on to become principal conductor of the Philharmonic and a champion of Czech music.

I also applied for a chamber music class under the supervision of the cellist Professor Karel Pravoslav Sádlo, in which I was expected to accompany fellow musicians. For my audition, Sádlo – whom we all referred to affectionately as 'KPS' – asked me to tell him if I thought a violoncello was correctly tuned and then he had me accompany the cellist on the piano playing Beethoven's Cello Sonata in G Minor. Luckily, I passed.

Sádlo was an authoritative and respected figure in his fifties who earned another student nickname, 'the Old Man'. He acted like a father figure to young musicians such as me and took special care of those of us who had suffered during the war. In the 1920s he had taken in a teenage cellist from a broken home who went on to become the world famous Miloš Sádlo – who was so grateful to his benefactor that he took his surname.

One day KPS asked me to distribute some leaflets for a student of his who was about to give her first public piano recital as part of her final exam. 'Please give your friends these tickets and she'll do the same for you when it's your turn,' he explained.

I hung my head and began to weep, which surprised him, so he asked me what was wrong.

'My professor won't let me give such a recital,' I explained. 'He doesn't think I'm good enough.'

The 'Old Man' went to see Professor Rauch and challenged his decision, but he was unrepentant. 'It will be a fiasco,' Rauch insisted. 'Her hands and her nerves are ruined.'

It was true that my once-lovely young girl's fingers had become fossilised by frostbite in the bitter winter of 1944–45. The fingerprints had been virtually worn away by blisters that never healed, and my knuckles were deformed and gnarled from months of slave labour. My joints had become stiff and inflexible and didn't move in the right way. It was only through sheer diligence in practising the piano for up to twelve hours every day that I finally made it into the academy after two intensive years of studying in order to finish my education.

KPS, who knew my story, quietly told Rauch, 'Hands are not everything. It's the heart that matters.'

Professor Sádlo was so kind to me and helped me through so much, especially my terrible stage fright. I often found it difficult to play in front of fellow students or accompany others. Even after the war, I was to learn a great deal about what the human mind can endure through my concert life.

'I can't go on! I've forgotten the programme,' I'd protest, getting myself horribly worked up. 'I just can't do it.'

KPS used to sigh and say, 'But dear Zuzana, everyone will be so disappointed, and the cellists especially, so you simply must go on. You know you want to play and you know you will play well.'

I'd nod, take a deep breath, and go on, and afterwards he would tease me terribly and tell people grandly, 'And – after all the drama – suddenly a radiant Zuzana walked onto the podium!'

In February 1948 the Communist Party – with Soviet backing – assumed control and placed Czechoslovakia in a communist state.

This coup d'état – or as we referred to it, a putsch – led to the murder of the Foreign Minister, former President Tomáš Garrigue Masaryk's son, and the resignation of President Beneš, leaving many of us terribly afraid of where this would lead.

After feeling so betrayed by the West in abandoning us to Hitler in 1939 and afterwards, the majority of Czechs were grateful to the Soviets for our liberty and so turned their hopes to them. Many began embracing socialism and rejecting the once-popular Western values. Even Jews felt that way at the time because communism promised that all men would be equal and all beliefs recognised. It would solve everything, they promised.

What we got instead was Stalinism, and that was quite different.

My mother showed incredible courage in the face of this new political upheaval. She was busy working back at the smaller of our two stores in Plzeň and gradually rebuilding her life. Running the store had given her a reason to live again and she relished being back among people and making some money. Trying to allay my fears she'd say, 'Maybe society will change for the better and workers' lives will be improved.' She spoke to many people about the situation and really tried to understand the whole thing. Having lived through Nazi occupation she was determined to be better informed this time.

Secretly though, she feared for the consequences as much as I did and was worried her store might be taken away from her once more. She was right to be concerned. There was no warning. It all happened so suddenly. A former employee of my parents, a really good shop assistant whom we'd thought of as a friend, walked in with her husband out of the blue and told my mother, 'You are a capitalist and you are no longer allowed to have this place. The shop belongs to the party and the party has given it to me. We are taking over.' They'd applied to the communists and were set up as 'national caretakers' – good party members who were rewarded with the homes, businesses and possessions of those who'd fallen out of favour with the state. Their announcement was shocking and frightening and Mummy was really shattered by it. She was, once again, a second-class citizen.

The woman was especially arrogant and later came to discuss business with my mother in their brand-new car, a Tatra sedan, gloating at their newfound wealth. Mummy was upset and angry at first, but then she accepted it, saying, 'When I compare this to what happened before, it isn't the worst.' The communists also confiscated her apartment and offered her a much smaller one. They then allocated her a job as a supervisor and quality controller in a state-run toyshop, with a much smaller income and the promise of a minimal pension. Fortunately, she had made quite a lot of money in the shop in the three years since the war and she put most of it in a bank account for me so that I wouldn't have to teach piano for the rest of my life.

Ironically, the young daughter of the couple who seized her store became seriously ill not long afterwards and the only thing that could help her was some medicine that was only available in America. The 'caretakers' wrote to Mummy, far less arrogant this time, and begged for her help. My mother's response illustrates her character well. She didn't hesitate for a moment, even though they'd stolen her store. She immediately contacted her sister Elsa in New York and had the medicine sent over, to be paid for in instalments, which helped the child greatly. The family was enormously grateful and the daughter wrote to my mother until Mummy's death. My mother was like that all her life. Even though the communists had robbed her, she always tried to find some good in a situation and even claimed that people were better off under the regime, although I'm sure she didn't really believe that.

I, meanwhile, was still so wrapped up in my music and focused on my studies that I didn't really know and didn't really care what was happening in politics. Like many of my fellow students I never joined the Communist Party, but after being pressed to join its Youth Union I was sent for schooling in Marxism–Leninism for two weeks. It was almost military in its rigour. We had military exercises during the night and were subjected to very thorough brainwashing. At the end of it we had an interview with a schooling officer, and when asked what I was reading, I made the mistake of being honest and saying Freud, which of course was banned. As a consequence,

I received a bad political report and was called before a committee to be questioned about my attitude to Marxism and Freudism.

I was lucky I wasn't expelled from the academy, but I was given a lot of books on Marxism–Leninism to read and had to take special examinations. At the academy we were obliged to see the whole of music history from the perspective of socialist realism. I had to read the history of the Communist Party, all the Stalin books, and those of Lenin. The examinations were strict and quite a lot of students were expelled because they didn't pass. Eventually I dropped out of my academic classes and never took Russian as others had to, claiming that with all my classes as well as practising three to five hours every day, I simply didn't have enough time.

I was always too busy for communism.

Even then, at twenty-one years old, I didn't fully realise that we'd swapped one dictatorship for another and that our hard-won democracy would be lost to us again for another forty years. I couldn't allow myself to believe that the same situation in history would repeat itself and thought that talk of it was some kind of joke. I was so deeply involved with my music and still fighting for my life. Getting through each day required all my concentration and diligence. I was closed up with my music and nothing else was important to me. This lack of political interest was my great mistake.

The same year as the communist takeover, I came into contact with another great musician who had suffered at their hands. The celebrated conductor Václav Talich heard me play the Bach Triple Piano Concerto with another student and invited me to work with him as part of the Czech Chamber Orchestra he had founded after the war. 'Come to my family villa in the country,' he told me. 'I'd like to prepare you for the Mozart Coronation Mass in C Major.'

It was the greatest honour from someone who had been concertmaster of the Berlin Philharmonic, the chief conductor of the Czech Philharmonic, and the administrator of opera at the National Theatre in Prague. Talich had once said: 'In art there is no such thing as a goal definitively achieved. Artistic growth is a series of errors and a search that lasts as long as an artist's life.' I couldn't agree more.

Even though he had been a hero of our nation during the German occupation, bravely defending Czech musical culture, in 1945 he was accused of collaborating with the Nazis, for which he was imprisoned and banned from conducting. He set up his chamber orchestra on his release and took only a handful of young soloists into his programme, so I considered it another miracle that he had chosen me.

I travelled to his lovely villa in Beroun, central Bohemia, on a hot sunny day and his daughter welcomed me warmly. He then gave me a lesson, which was unforgettable. Even though he was in his mid-sixties and not in good health after his imprisonment, we worked all the phrases and we even danced a little and sang together. During a break, his daughter suggested we go into the garden where she would bring us coffee.

As it was so hot I took off the cardigan I was wearing over a sleeveless blouse. Talich took one look at my arm, noticed my number for the first time, and he began to cry.

'Can you believe they accused me of collaborating with the people who did this?' he sobbed.

I told him it was all right and that I didn't believe any of the stories, but he couldn't be consoled. His daughter eventually accompanied me to the door and said, 'Please don't come back to see my father anymore, Ms Růžičková. It is too much for him to face you every day.'

In response to the rise of the communists, Talich and his players decided to dissolve the chamber orchestra before they were forced to. His suspicions were confirmed and he was forbidden from conducting again until 1954, when he performed at his last public concert. He stayed in touch, however, and remained a fan of my music until his dying day, coming to almost all of my concerts. After his death in 1961, his daughter came in his place.

I feel very fortunate to have worked with him, if only for that one golden afternoon.

*

One fateful day in 1951, as I walked down a corridor at the famous Rudolfinum concert hall on the banks of the river Vltava, I heard the voice of a female alto accompanied by piano coming from the Small Hall.

The beauty of the music stopped me in my tracks, so I waited and listened right to the end. When it was over and some fellow students emerged, I asked them, 'Who was that? Who wrote that music?' They told me it was a work called 'Birds' Weddings' written by Viktor Kalabis, a composition student I knew, but I fell in love with his music long before I fell in love with him.

Viktor was a rather serious 27-year-old from eastern Bohemia, studying composition and conducting. Three years older than me, he had studied under composer Emil Hlobil at the Prague Conservatory, as well as musicology at the philosophical faculty of Charles University – until Hitler interrupted his studies. A bespectacled Gentile with poor vision, Viktor was forced by the Nazis to work in factories during the war. I knew who he was as he sometimes joined a group of us for lunch. We were all so poor that we'd choose the cheapest items on the menu and share them between us.

Viktor might have sat at our table and shared our food but he didn't join in. He was never someone who laughed or joked like the rest of us. In fact, he always looked rather worried. I asked him once why he was so serious and he made his first joke – 'Of course I'm serious. I'm married with two children!' – something I momentarily believed. The truth was that he'd read a great deal about what was happening in the Soviet Union and was already worried about our future.

My MA graduation piano recital took place on 23 April 1951. Each student not only had to give a feature-length recital but could also compete for a chance to perform with an orchestra. The first prize was to play with the Czech Philharmonic and there were runner-up prizes that enabled winners to play with a regional or municipal orchestra. I was terribly nervous and uncertain which piece of music I should play.

It was a year since I had been one of three young pianists chosen to perform the works of Bach at the academy in honour of the bicentenary of his death, a concerto in C major for three pianos and a string orchestra. That was a wonderful experience, if nerve-wracking, but this was my chance to shine as a solo artist and I knew that my choice of music would be pivotal. In the end, my programme featured the composers Beethoven, Debussy, Chopin, Mozart, and Prokofiev. Despite my crippling nerves, it was well received and I even won the competition to play with the Czech Philharmonic. Mummy was as pleased and relieved as I was.

My next decision was what to play with the Philharmonic, so I agonised once more. Then I remembered that my beloved Madame had especially liked the charming pieces for piano by the Czech librettist Bohuslav Martinů, a man who went on to be a great composer of modern classical music. As a lifelong devotee of baroque music, I'd only come to Martinů's contemporary compositions after the war when I was asked to accompany his violin sonata, and became enchanted. It was like tasting a delicious new dish and wanting to eat even more of it. Excited by this new discovery, I decided to play his 1940 Sinfonietta Giocosa for piano and orchestra.

Once I announced my decision, the dean – who was an ardent communist – summoned me to his office. 'I hear you want to play the Martinů?'

'Yes,' I replied. 'I have only recently discovered him, but I'm already a fan.'

'Do you know he is a renegade and a traitor to our nation?' the dean asked, his eyes narrowing.

'No.' I couldn't hide my disappointment.

'If you play Martinů you will not graduate.'

It was only afterwards that I learned the full story of Martinů's history. The young composer had lived in Paris for much of his adult life and from there he wrote a Field Mass in honour of the Czech resistance during the war. The Nazis blacklisted him for it, so he fled to America in 1941 as the German army approached Paris. For the so-called 'crime' of deserting his country, he was decreed a traitor to his homeland by the post-war Czech government and his music was banned for a number of years.

I left the dean's office knowing that my mother would be desperate if I didn't graduate after all the money it had cost her and all the worry I had put her through, so I had no choice but to think of something else. Eventually, I chose Mozart's Piano Concerto in D Major No. 26, known as the Coronation Concerto.

Martinů wasn't the only composer who was banned. During my composition classes I'd heard several pieces by others who were blacklisted, including Stravinsky and Bartók, both of whom had either done something to offend the communists or been labelled traitors. Just to play a note of Stravinsky was dangerous, but the students loved him and followed his way of composing, which was considered decadent and formalistic at a time when they were supposed to compose music based on social realism.

Regardless of their political or personal affiliations, the work of these forbidden composers was still studied and admired at the seminars and presentations of contemporary music at the Prague Music Theatre. Jaroslav Šeda, who at the time worked for the recording company Gramofonové Závody but who would later become the director of Supraphon, organised many of these events. Listening to this new music was a huge departure from the early music I knew and loved, but I found it exciting and stimulating in a way that I'm sure Madame never would have.

Later that year I was invited to perform the piano part in Brahms' Violin Sonata in F Major, as well as Bach's Italian Concerto and his Fantasia and Fugue on harpsichord, all of which were well received. I was also given the chance to play both instruments to showcase works by Bach and Scarlatti. One of my unkinder critics said afterwards that it was like using a horse and carriage when I could have had a car.

I would say that my second great love after Bach was Domenico Scarlatti, whose father, Alessandro, was the number-one composer in Italy and the founder of the Neapolitan school of opera. Domenico became the organist at St Peter's in Rome. Then one day he gave harpsichord lessons to a Portuguese princess, who later became the queen of Spain. When she returned to Portugal and married into the Spanish royal house, Scarlatti took his wife to live there and remained in the services of the Portuguese and then the Spanish courts for the rest of his life, occasionally going to live with shepherds in the hills. He didn't write anything but harpsichord sonatas after his move to Spain, and he wrote more than five hundred of them. Unusually, he didn't care to have them published. The printer had to beg him on his knees to publish the first thirty, and the majority weren't published until after his death.

I played a lot of Scarlatti, who always reminded me of Goya. He had these Spanish accents – sometimes drama, sometimes dancing. There was no polyphony. His was a volcano of ideas and of different moods. When I am born again as a harpsichordist, I will record all the Scarlatti.

Having graduated and started to make a name for myself, I was offered the chance to teach compulsory piano to a group of composers at the department of composition in the academy, which I did for fifteen years. They were short of piano teachers and several of its students, including Viktor Kalabis, needed to complete the education that had been interrupted by war.

I was years younger, and several inches shorter, than most of the composers I had to teach, many of whom were already famous or making names for themselves. The pay was minimal but I needed every *koruna* I could make and it was far more rewarding working with proper musicians than teaching children finger dexterity in their homes.

Viktor arrived for my class with his best friend, the composer František Kovaříček, and three others. Having already heard Viktor play I told him that I was sure there was nothing I could teach him. I suggested he skip my class and just take the exam, for he would surely pass. Smiling, he told me, 'I don't want to do that. I'd prefer to have lessons with you.'

It was clear to me from the start that there was one leader in this group and that was Viktor. The others were all much taller than he was, full of talent and enthusiasm, but they still looked to him for advice and guidance. Politically, they were absolutely on the wrong side and not for the communists at all, and Viktor was the epitome of that philosophy.

Before too long, he and I ended up sitting side by side at a piano playing four hands, just as I had once done with dear Madame. We played Stravinsky's *Le Sacre du Printemps*, and some Bartók. From the outset, I was impressed by his expertise and his quiet, thoughtful manner, but I was far too busy focusing on furthering my own musical education to consider embarking on a relationship.

My biggest priority was preparing for my first harpsichord recital at the Rudolfinum. Even though it would be in the Small Hall playing to a maximum of 190 people (as opposed to the Dvořák Hall that seats more than 1,100) my stage fright took over and I panicked, convinced that I'd never be brave enough to perform in such a historic venue.

The neo-classical Rudolfinum was designed in 1885 as a 'monumental house of arts' and became Prague's chief musical venue. It is home to one of Europe's oldest concert halls – a place where Dvořák himself conducted his own compositions. In 1919 it was adapted to house the newly minted Czech government. When the Nazis came in 1939 they restored the building as a concert hall for the German Philharmonic and then after the war it became the home of the Czech Philharmonic.

I had been to many recitals and concerts there but I'd never been on stage before so I was keen to prepare as much as I could. Where better than in the building itself? Getting up early one morning, I discovered a cleaning lady entering via a back door at 6 a.m. With a smile and a pleading look, I persuaded her to let me in so that I could practise secretly on the very instrument I'd be playing in a few weeks' time. It sat alone in a cold corridor beyond the main hall and each morning from 6 a.m. to just before 9 a.m. when the staff began to arrive, I played to my heart's content – wearing my coat and hat.

What I was doing was not only forbidden by the authorities, but would have met with the disapproval of everyone from my professors to my mother. My luck ran out when the director of the Rudolfinum caught me and made it quite clear that I had no business being there. A few days later, though, he heard me playing piano in a recital at the academy and found me afterwards to tell me that I could carry on with my secret sessions after all. I was so grateful.

Even more frightening than the director, though, was the Polish tuner Xavier Skolek, who took care of the instruments for the Czech Philharmonic. Like many professional tuners, Mr Skolek felt a sense of ownership as custodian of the instruments he cared for. Harpsichords are especially sensitive to temperature, humidity and heavy-handedness, and always need to be tuned directly before a concert. If there is an unexpected problem such as a broken quill or a crack in the resonance plate the concert can be delayed or even cancelled. Understandably, when the tuner discovered me playing 'illicitly' in the corridor early one morning he was angry and asked me what I was doing there.

After I explained that I had the director's permission he reluctantly let me continue as he stood listening, his head tilted critically. When I had finished, his manner changed completely and we started talking. He told me that he had once been the harpsichord tuner for Wanda Landowska, a connection that moved me deeply. After that, he and I were to work together for many years.

By the time I finally took to the stage at the Rudolfinum a few weeks later, I was shaking all over with nerves. Standing in the wings, I did not believe that I would be able to go on. I nearly didn't, as my mother had brought my gown for the recital from Plzeň, but forgot the petticoat it needed because my dress was see-through. Fortunately, she was able to rent me a substitute from a costume shop just in time.

The hall that night was packed with fellow students and some celebrated musicians, including Karel Hoffmeister, a pianist and professor of the Prague Conservatory's Masters School. All were curious as to how my recital would go. They were especially interested to hear the harpsichord being played, because hardly anybody played it any more. The last soloist who'd played in the Rudolfinum had been a Czech named Frank Pelleg who had emigrated to Palestine before the war. His real name was Pollak, but he changed it to Pelleg – as a nod to Bach, whose name translates to 'creek' in German, while 'Peleg' is the Hebrew name for channel or canal.

I was not completely unknown, but I was not Pelleg, and I was so afraid that I would let myself and everyone else down, including my dear mother, sitting in the audience. I was just so sorry that Madame was too old and frail to attend.

As always though, once I stepped onto the stage and sat at the instrument my fears faded away. Whenever I perform I am completely inside the music. Everything else melts away. I don't even remember the recital or concert afterwards and often have to ask people how I played.

Apparently, that night I performed well and everyone seemed satisfied. I played music by Purcell, Bach's French Suite in G Major, and some Scarlatti sonatas.

Afterwards Professor Kredba kindly told me, 'I have nothing more to teach you.'

There was one other person sitting in the audience that night who I wanted to impress – Viktor, to whom I was becoming increasingly close.

One night, a group of us went to a bar to drink wine and commiserate after being forced to learn the new socialist songs we'd be expected to sing en masse for the 1 May International Workers' Day celebrated by the communists. Viktor was sitting behind me while we learned these songs and, as usual, I'd been at the heart of the group, being merry, making fun of the silly words, and telling jokes.

Anything to fit in.

Later at the pub Viktor cornered me as I was leaving and asked, 'Do you ever talk seriously, or do you always make fun of everything?' He went on to tell me that my 'fake smiles' didn't impress him. 'I don't believe them for they're not real. I think you have a problem that you are trying to hide. Would you like to tell me about it?'

He did not know I was Jewish as he had met several other people with the name Růžička who were either of gypsy blood or pure Aryan. Nor did he know my full story. Few did. It wasn't that I hid my past but nobody ever asked, and only a handful knew that I'd been in the camps after Sádlo told them. Even then most people knew little of what really happened. They were told nothing during the war and afterwards the communists never wanted it discussed. That directive came straight from Moscow. If anyone spoke of Terezín, they usually just said that Czechs were imprisoned there. There was no mention of the Jews.

Even though he knew so little, Viktor had somehow sensed that my forced laughter was a masquerade and an attempt to appear normal. His frank questioning opened the floodgates and I burst into tears. Nobody had ever asked me anything as probing as that. Later that night, as he walked me the five kilometres back to where I lived, I told him everything and we made a real connection. He was an excellent listener and a good amateur psychiatrist. When he took leave of me he kissed me. From then on, we were inseparable and it was Viktor, above all, who was to save my life.

He was my latest miracle.

Viktor graduated that year, but was denied his doctorate because his thesis on Bartók and Stravinsky was declared too 'formalistic and decadent'. It was clearly not in line with communist thinking. The weekend of his graduation concert, in which Miloš Sádlo was to play his cello concerto, I remained in Prague to hear it. My mother knew then that I had more than a passing admiration for this young composer. After the concert I presented Viktor with a posy of flowers, which he sweetly pressed in a book and kept for years.

His best friend, František, needed to be convinced that we were right for each other, so he asked to meet me in a bar the next time I returned to Prague from visiting my mother. 'I need to have a serious talk with you,' he told me ominously.

Once we'd ordered our wine and sat at a table in the corner, František – his expression grave – told me that Viktor had only ever had two girlfriends, neither of whom had been right for him. Before he met me, he'd decided to not complicate his life with women but dedicate himself to his music instead. Then I came along.

He added, 'When Viktor commits to a relationship in the way he has with you, then that is serious and I don't want him to get hurt.'

Sipping my wine, I said, 'I have no intention of hurting Viktor.'

František continued. 'He wants to marry you, but this won't be an easy thing. In Viktor's life music is number one, his parents are number two, and you will be number three.'

I was shocked then. I had never really thought about marriage, and the idea that Viktor wanted to marry me secretly upset me. I wasn't going to let František know, though, so I forced a laugh. 'I don't think that's a difficulty at all,' I told him. 'The first thing in my life is my music, and the second is my mother, so if Viktor and I are in third place with each other then I would say we are perfectly matched.'

František frowned. I leaned forward and touched his arm. 'It's fine, František. I'm happy that he loves his music and I'm happy that he loves his parents. The important thing is that we love each other.'

After our meeting I rushed back to Plzeň and burst into tears in my mother's arms as I told her what had happened. 'I don't want to get married,' I cried, 'but I don't want to lose Viktor either because he is such a rare man. I doubt I will ever find such a person again.'

In the end, and after much thought, I decided that if this was how I had to keep him then, yes, I would marry him after all.

I assumed that Viktor had sent his friend to speak to me and let me know he was planning to marry me, so the next time I saw him I blurted, 'When do you want to get married?'

He seemed rather shocked by my proposal and all he could stammer was, 'I think you should meet my parents first.' It was only later that I found out that he had no idea about the private discussion with František, and my unexpected suggestion of marriage scared him as much as it had scared me. He acted courageously, however, and even presented himself to my mother formally to ask for my hand. However, he always joked afterwards that he only married me to get out of his piano lessons.

Viktor's parents Karel and Viktorie were welcoming and I liked them very much. They had a flat in a beautiful part of south Bohemia, and Viktor went back there all the time to compose on their piano. His mother was a gifted painter and an amateur actress who spoke French and also played the piano. Her grandfather had been a graduate of the Prague Conservatory. She died two years after Viktor and I married, so I was sad that I never got to know her better. His father was a senior postmaster and I don't suppose he thought I was the ideal daughter-in-law at all, but we bonded eventually. The couple had both worked at the post office in the east Bohemian town of Solnice, where Viktor had gone to school and developed an early fascination with the town's brass band. As a small child, he used to stand in front of the bandstand and pretend to conduct the musicians.

One of the pieces they played, and which he liked very much as he and his family promenaded through the park, was a Czech marching song by Julius Fučík known as the 'Marinarella'. It always brought him happy memories, although it was later to have very different associations for me.

The conductor was so enchanted with Viktor's enthusiasm that he offered to teach him how to play the piano, so Viktor gave his first concert in the local town hall aged sixteen.

Like me he, too, had suffered from a bad chest in his youth and was sent to stay with relatives in the Bohemian town of Jindřichův Hradec for a year. Eventually, his parents joined him. During the economic crisis of the 1930s, married couples who were state employees were no longer permitted to work together so his mother had to give up her job and his father was able to relocate.

When the war started, Viktor's father was allowed to remain in his position at the post office but Viktor, aged nineteen, managed to carry on with his studies while teaching singing and German in a girls' school in Mělník, thirty kilometres north of Prague. After two years he was sent to a factory that made aircraft parts, working as a riveter in a place that was so noisy he almost lost his hearing.

In spite of the war, Viktor was as eager as I was not to miss out on his musical education, so he travelled to Prague when he could to take composition lessons from the composer Jaroslav Řídký and the conductor Pavel Dědeček. The Allies bombed the city during one of his visits, so he had to hide in the shelters where he tapped out the beat for his next work on his knee.

Just as with me, the music came first.

Viktor and I were very much in love, but we almost didn't get married when new and frightening political developments in our country began to threaten our happiness. It wasn't that I didn't care for him desperately. I did, and had been ready to marry him ever since František told me of his intentions. But things had changed in Czechoslovakia and 1952 was a year of great turmoil. Lots of people were arrested as traitors for allegedly being in touch with Western powers, some of them high-ranking party officials and politicians, but most were Jews. There was a growing feeling of incredible oppression and I was increasingly worried about the consequences for Viktor of marrying me.

The problem was that there had been an enormous rise in anti-Semitism in our country after the war, caused in part by the high number of Jewish intellectuals among the communists. After the putsch when the party assumed control under Secretary General Rudolf Slánský, a Jew, anti-Semitic attacks across the country only increased.

The communist leadership was split over how much it should emulate hard-line Soviet policies and went on a witch-hunt for 'disloyal' elements at the same time as starting a purge on Jews from the higher echelons. In 1950 the Czech politician Milada Horáková was the first 'traitor' to be tried, accused with twelve others of leading an alleged plot to overthrow the communist regime. A Gentile, Milada was a staunch patriot and feminist who had joined the Czech resistance during the war, been arrested by the Gestapo, and sent to Terezín and prisons in Germany. Following her latest incarceration, in 1949, she was subjected to intensive physical and psychological torture by the Czech secret police, the feared StB.

All the factory workers were forced to sign a proclamation against this 'traitor', demanding her execution. At her trial she and three of her co-defendants were duly sentenced to death, in spite of appeals by her family and protests by eminent people around the world including Albert Einstein, the British prime minister Winston Churchill, and former American First Lady, Eleanor Roosevelt. Milada, who kept her dignity to the end, was hanged for fabricated charges of crimes of conspiracy and treason that she did not commit. It was the cruellest thing.

That was just the start of the show trials. When the anti-Jewish line became official Soviet policy thanks to Stalin, the authorities began to prosecute as many prominent Jews as they could, starting with the high-up party officials like Secretary General Slánský and ten other party members in what became known as 'The Jewish Processes'. Each was accused of participating in a Trotskyite-Titoite-Zionist conspiracy and convicted.

Every day the state radio announcer blared out damning criticism of the 'Jewish traitors' in a threatening voice. Everybody was afraid and we all had to sign petitions for the 'traitors' to be executed for crimes against our 'happy and developing country'. The prisoners were confessing and then retracting, claiming they'd been drugged and made to memorise their confessions, but one after another was condemned to death. The secretary general was convicted and hanged and three others were sentenced to life imprisonment. Many more were sent to uranium mines and labour camps. In total, more than 200,000 people were arrested and imprisoned.

It was so very frightening because it felt like the horror of the war was happening again in some kind of dreadful symmetry. My only hope was that with Viktor and me fresh out of college and my mother a mere quality controller none of us were important enough to be prosecuted, but we also knew that was no guarantee.

Anyone who allied themselves with a Jew became known as a 'White Jew', and their name was put on a list that would affect their lives for as long as the communists were in power. I knew that Viktor had a great career ahead of him and I was so afraid for him. Marrying me would be such a courageous and yet foolish thing to do because he already had a reputation for not being politically correct. To wed a Jewess in the middle of this politically difficult time would seal his fate and could be extremely dangerous.

Thinking it would be best if we split up, I told Viktor that he couldn't marry me after all. 'I won't permit it,' I declared, a few months into our engagement. 'If you do, it will ruin everything for you and could be double the damage for us both.'

Viktor just smiled. 'Never mind,' he replied. 'I love you.'

Refusing to take no for an answer, Viktor persuaded me that we should continue our engagement and make plans for our wedding regardless of the world around us. We'd originally planned to marry in May 1953, because Viktor was still a student in my piano class until then, and it was against academy rules for us to be in a personal relationship. Politically, he was still under suspicion, and there was a really big question about how he would make his livelihood as a non-party member. He was earning a bit of money composing music for radio and I had some concerts and my teaching salary, but we were still terribly poor. Both of us lived in dismal sub-lets in Prague, in between going home to our parents, and were trying to save enough to afford our first flat together. We also wanted to get enough money to pay for all the marriage formalities, a ring and my wedding dress.

The Czech government had passed a law after the war that made it possible for newlyweds to be given an apartment and some money for essentials, which we hoped to benefit from, but in September 1952 it announced that this law would be scrapped from 1 January 1953. Hurrying to the old town hall, I asked if we could rearrange the wedding date to before the New Year in the hope that we'd still qualify.

The end of that year was a disastrous time to get married. Viktor was staying with his parents in Jindřichův Hradec, trying to meet a deadline for a new piece of music – the Strážnice Suite, commissioned by Czechoslovak Radio – and I had two big concerts coming up, including the demanding Goldberg Variations.

I also had a joint concert planned for the evening of 7 December with Dr Jiří Reinberger, a professor at the academy and a classical organist. It was a huge honour to play with him and Viktor was determined to travel from the country to hear me play, a trip that would use up the last of our funds. Rather than come to Prague twice in the same month, he suggested we kill two birds with one stone and get married the morning after my recital.

The concert went marvellously well and the chain-smoking Dr Reinberger became another friend. To a packed house, we introduced and then played Bach's Chorale Cantatas, written when he was cantor in Leipzig and forming part of a set of Protestant chorales based on Luther's *Catechism* – the large ones for the organ and the smaller ones for harpsichord.

I felt so privileged to play Bach with such a renowned and talented organist and on the eve of my marriage to someone who completely understood me.

The day Viktor and I quietly married was Tuesday 8 December, 1952. We'd been seeing each other for over a year by then and had faced so many obstacles that the last-minute hitches surrounding our big day were just fresh hurdles to overcome.

Our wedding day dawned frosty and dull, but we didn't mind. Wrapped up warm, I wore a brown coat and hat over a regular dress. The only flowers available for sale at that time were red carnations for the communists, so that's what Viktor bought for my bouquet.

Laughing, we hurried to the Old Town Hall in the shadow of the Astronomical Clock and went through all the formalities, witnessed by my mother, Viktor's parents and two of his friends. Mummy liked her future son-in-law but she wasn't so happy about the speed with which we had got engaged, which at the time she thought unseemly.

It had taken Viktor so long to persuade me to finally go ahead and marry him that he raced through his vows in case I changed my mind. After our marriage certificate had been signed and stamped at the town hall we all went to lunch in a local restaurant where Viktor informed me that his wedding gift was the piano concerto he'd been working on, his first ever, to be known as Piano Concerto No. 1, Op. 12. This was a pretty, light-hearted piece, inspired by Mozart's *Exsultate, jubilate* motet, which he said summed up how he felt about me.

Then my mother presented us with her wedding gift – bed and breakfast in a suite in the beautiful Palace Hotel right in the centre of Prague, not far from Wenceslas Square.

This was such a luxury we could hardly believe it. We were really so very poor and were thrilled to be spending our wedding night in such a grand hotel. We were especially looking forward to a luxurious lie-in with a proper double bed and a hearty breakfast.

Unfortunately, there was yet another last-minute hitch. On the afternoon of our wedding we heard from Viktor's best friend František that he and my other composer students had been called up for military service. We knew that Viktor would be excluded because of his poor vision but were appalled to think these four talented young men would be forced into the military at a critical time for their studies. The best they could hope for was to join the army orchestra, but František said they'd already been told that privilege would be denied them because they were considered 'politically suspect'.

Viktor had a professor he admired and who liked him in return, so he contacted him the afternoon of our wedding to ask for his help. 'Come and see me before class tomorrow morning and I'll see what I can do,' the professor said. 'Be in my office in the philosophical faculty by 7.30.'

I could have let Viktor go alone while I languished in our comfortable bed, but I so loved him for being unselfish and faithful to his friends on such a morning that I got up with him at 6 a.m. We drank a quick coffee in his dressing room and then left our warm suite to wait in the freezing cold faculty building for the professor to arrive. He eventually did and Viktor spoke to him at length, but in the end he could do nothing and we knew that our friends, my students, would be leaving us soon. Disappointed, we hurried back to our hotel to eat our breakfast and enjoy the last few hours of our honeymoon.

Viktor helped me so much during the first years of our marriage. He gave me the spiritual strength to keep surviving even through all these new and frightening challenges. He held me when I cried out in my sleep, and he soothed me after every nightmare. I was often crippled by my memories, but Viktor constantly reminded me that I had survived and could now devote myself to my music. He also assured me how good I was as a musician and I trusted him because I respected his opinion. With Viktor there were no platitudes and I knew he couldn't lie about something as important as that.

In time I came to realise that I only wanted three things from life: to be alive and not hungry; to make music, and to have my mother and Viktor.

Most importantly of all, he made me talk and talk about my experiences. He was the first person to make me rest because I was a terrible workaholic, and he would make me stop practising after three hours and tell me, 'You need to clear your head.' We would cycle to the Divoká Šárka nature reserve on the outskirts of the city and walk in the woods. I soon found that the walk did me a lot of good, but when I came home I would practise for three more hours. I am no expert in Jewish culture, but I always liked the concept of the Sabbath Soul – a day of rest when the soul is obliged to celebrate creation. Keeping one day a week free gives you a chance to reflect on life's lessons and regain focus. And I loved that the tradition is not only for the people but also for the beasts of burden, so that they can rest too.

Viktor continually promised me that we were living in unusual times, and that what happened with the war was rare. He claimed that nothing like the Nazis would ever happen again. I knew he didn't really believe that and neither did I, but it was good to hear him say it anyway.

The truth was that he was extremely pessimistic about political developments. He knew a lot about what was happening in the Soviet Union. He read all these memoirs of Russian émigrés and he knew that the next developments in Czechoslovakia would not be good. But he tried to hope for the best and he tried to help me lead a normal life again. I discovered in Viktor a person who was gentle and very truthful, and whom I could absolutely rely on. And that was a far better medicine for me than trying to be optimistic about our situation.

Throughout our long and happy marriage, whenever he came home from work, depressed about the latest situation, he would tell me, 'I need to clear my head.' Without another word, the two of us would sit at the piano and play four hands together night after night. He used to say that he needed to make himself clean. I always played the bass and Viktor the upper voices. He was a better pianist and we played Brahms, Beethoven, everything. We both adored Stravinsky and I was always happy to play Bach, of course, but we also played a great deal of Haydn and Mahler. Viktor loved Hindemith's piano sonatas as well as those by Bartók and Honegger. We would play and play until my mother told us that our evening meal was ready.

Dear Viktor always said that next to his music he had one wish for his life – to rid me of the trauma of war, to heal me, and make me feel like a normal person again. He said that the greatest tragedy of those who had suffered my fate was that they somehow felt excluded from the human race.

It took his love to cure me and, just like my parents, we two were very much in love – until the end of our days.

4

Prague, 1938

'Zuzana, wait!' my cousin Dagmar called after me as I hurtled headlong through the school gates and down the street, crying. My satchel flying, I ignored her and hurried straight to the hairdresser's where I knew my mother was being coiffured. It was spring 1938 and I thought my world was about to end.

'Mummy, Mummy!' I cried as I threw myself onto her lap in the hair salon. Face down in her skirt I wept.

'What is it, darling?' she asked, horrified, removing my glasses and lifting my face. 'What on earth is the matter?'

'There will be a war!' I cried. 'Tata will be sent away to fight! He could be killed and never come home again!'

My mother looked up at her stylist and silently gestured for her to slip away. Cradling me in her arms, she stroked my head and tried to soothe me. 'Now what brought this on?' she asked.

Hiccupping, I told her that my teachers at school that afternoon had held a mock air raid and handed each of us gas masks before training us in how to use them. 'They said that if we didn't put them on in time, we could choke to death!'

To me, those horrible rubber masks were tangible proof of something unthinkable and I was deeply shocked.

'Darling, please don't worry,' my mother said, wiping away my tears. 'Wars are all in the past. They will never happen again. This is just an exercise, like a drill.'

I thought back to all those stony-faced conferences my mother and father had been having recently when my aunts and uncles and even relatives from Vienna came to call. I'd naively assumed they'd been talking about the state of the business or taxation matters, but I now realised that we'd all been living in the shadow of war and that they'd been keeping things from me. No matter what my mother said or how much she tried to comfort me, I could not be consoled.

At eleven years old, I had never once heard my father speak of his experiences in the First World War, but I'd been raised in the belief that his was the last war. The notion of another conflict being possible changed my life and more or less ended my idyllic childhood, there and then.

The events of the following months only served to frighten me more. After Hitler annexed Austria in the Anschluss in March 1938, he set his sights on Czechoslovakia, seizing the Sudetenland in our western province later that year. My father was so outraged by this move that he immediately volunteered for the Czech army, which he didn't have to do because of his war wound, but he was determined to fight once more for his country. The Czech army was efficient and well prepared and we had treaties with England and France to help us if we were ever invaded. He implored my mother to take me to Dobříš in Bohemia to stay with her family until he returned and then, to my abject horror, he bade us farewell and left for the front.

Not long afterwards, the unthinkable happened. England and France, the major powers of Europe, broke their treaties with us and, along with Italy, signed the Munich Agreement, giving Germany our Sudetenland as an appeasement. The thinking was that if they did that, Hitler would be satisfied. British Prime Minister Neville Chamberlain and French premier Edouard Daladier were greeted on their return to London and Paris with cheering and flowers. They were thought of as peacemakers, but really it was the beginning of the end.

The Munich Agreement was such a terrible blow for Tata. He felt so betrayed. The whole country did. With no foreign support and the nation in turmoil, he had no choice but to give up his hopes of fighting for his country and return home where we were reunited in Plzeň to wait for the next disaster.

Being so young, I had no idea what was about to happen. I'd recently started at the classical gymnasium, or school, and was happy to be going as I'd been so sickly as a child that I had missed a great deal. I took classes in mathematics, chemistry, physics, history, geography and German. My first form teacher was a woman named Milada Tománková, whom I loved, and she me, even though she frequently complained of my 'appalling' handwriting, for which I always received below average marks. Later, I found out from tests that I was naturally more left-handed, which helped me tremendously when I was playing. In most cases, people find their left hand technically weaker than their right hand, but I didn't have any difficulties. I think that it even helped me with Bach's polyphony. I could feel the voices and was able to interpret each hand separately.

My happiness at being at school was, however, overshadowed by the aftermath of events in Munich and then in November 1938 the news of Kristallnacht – the Night of the Broken Glass – when hundreds of Jewish homes, schools and synagogues across Germany were attacked and innocent people murdered or sent away to concentration camps.

I remember my parents listening solemnly to the BBC news on the radio, but I still didn't really understand what was going on nor yet appreciate that it had anything to do with us. That was until the *Wehrmacht* arrived in Prague in March 1939, sending shock waves reverberating through every home in the land.

I don't know which shook me more – the thought of armed German soldiers patrolling our capital in tanks or the fact that my parents were still keeping things from me. From then on, I insisted that I be kept fully informed. I bombarded them with daily questions about the political situation and started to read everything I could on the subject in the hope that I wouldn't be caught unawares again.

They did their best to distract me and I remember Mummy taking me to the cinema to see my first film, the Disney cartoon

Snow White, which enchanted and mesmerised me. I loved it so much I planned on seeing every new film that came out after that, but the Nazis had other ideas. It would be six long years before I was permitted to set foot inside a cinema again.

As their Nuremberg laws began to take effect in our country, delineating what Jews across occupied lands could or could not do, there were suddenly posters put up on street corners for everyone to read. They announced that the schools were closed to Jews, the cinemas were closed to Jews, and we were only allowed to shop at certain stores and within certain hours, usually when all the best things had been sold. All Jews had to wear a Star of David on their outer clothing and so immediately a lot of people avoided us on the street because it was dangerous to even talk to a Jew. We were barred from public and the trams, and had to stop our usual employment. Jewish shopfronts were painted with the yellow star or the word 'Žid' or 'Jude', for Jew.

The bad feelings against us developed gradually. Some of my classmates and even some of my friends were either pro-German or avoided me because of the six-pointed star. Or maybe they were just afraid. Many more were nice, but it was the nasty ones I remember. One was Hans Ledeč, a German boy who lived downstairs whom we used to talk and play with, even though he was a bit older. When the Nazis came he joined the Hitlerjugend (Hitler Youth) and was immediately different to us – cold and hostile. He pestered me and started to be nasty, telling me that I was not welcome and didn't belong in Plzeň.

'If I don't belong in this country then where do I belong?' I asked my father, confused and upset. 'Why didn't you ever tell me that I didn't belong here or was from a different race? What will happen to us?'

I went to the library and started reading every book I could find on the Jewish race, faith, and history. I wanted to find out what the source of anti-Semitism was, whether it was religious, social, or racial. Up until that point I hadn't even been aware of its existence. I was so appalled by what I read – the centuries of persecution and pogroms Jews had faced – that, at twelve years old, I became an ardent Zionist. It seemed to me that the only way to get out of the Devil's circle was to create your own. My natural conclusion was that I belonged somewhere else – maybe Palestine or one of the other countries that were being considered for an independent Jewish state – so we should all move there.

Mummy was worried that my new reasoning would devastate my deeply patriotic father. She feared it might bring him into ridicule for having a Zionist daughter when he had always boasted to his Sokol friends about being so assimilated. She begged me not to read any Zionist books in front of him. Instead I read them when I was alone in the bathroom, but he found out anyway and, when he did, his reaction surprised us both.

'If you feel that strongly about it then I think it is best that you be fully informed,' he told me in a tired voice. 'Maybe I am wrong and you are right, Zuzka. You need to come to your own conclusions.' He always accepted my opinions, which was a wonderful thing for a father to do.

After that I became almost proud of being Jewish, once I knew the history of Judaism. I realised that this was part of my history too and even debated the point with my father and his friends, telling them, 'Now you must see that assimilation doesn't work! Jews have always been persecuted and the only answer is for us to form our own state.' I don't think he ever changed his mind and was devoted to his country to the end, but I believe he at least understood my line of thinking.

I joined a Zionist youth movement called Maccabi Hatzair that seemed to offer a path out of the chaos. Set up in Czechoslovakia in 1929, it had similar principles to Sokol in terms of promoting physical education and sporting activities, but with the added element of learning Hebrew. We called our group Kadima (which means 'Forward' in Hebrew) and were prepared for life on a kibbutz in 'the Promised Land', once a Jewish state had been established.

Dagmar refused to join our band of ten girls and five boys and her decision really shocked me, as I'd always thought of us almost as twins. We didn't quarrel, we just discussed it, but she asserted her independence and chose to stay in the opposite camp of the assimilated Czech Jews. She believed simply that she was Czech and that the suppression by the Nazis was happening to all the Czechs, just a little bit more to the Jews. Zionism was not for her. It was the beginning of our inevitable separation after years of closeness, a transition that had begun in school when she chose to study natural sciences instead of Greek and Latin with me.

I was disappointed that she didn't share my enthusiasm, but it did not stop me allying myself ever more closely to my new friends and especially to the golden young couple who led the group: Tylda (known as 'Tilla') Fischlová and Karel Schleissner, both of whom I respected and loved. Tilla was a pretty blonde from Plzeň, chubby with blue eyes, eight years older than me. Karel was from Sudetenland, very Jewish-looking with black hair combed into a side parting, brown eyes and a little moustache. He was extremely handsome and a good man. They were deeply in love and I was convinced they would marry and have a wonderful family together, probably in Palestine.

They gave us lessons that first summer after Czechoslovakia was occupied, which, ironically, was when I finally recovered my health and became a normal child. Almost every day we went swimming together in the 'Jewish lake' in the České údolí valley. This was the only place we were allowed to use as we were no longer allowed to swim with Aryan children, and so it became a place to meet our parents, friends, and fellow Maccabis. At the lake we were all Jews together and being part of a group of young people who sustained each other and had a common goal helped a lot. It made me appreciate the strength of the Jewish faith.

Once it was decreed that we were banned from public transport and had to comply with an 8 p.m. curfew, we had to allow plenty of time to get home or face arrest, but we sometimes lost track of the hours by the lake. That was when we first encountered members of the fascist youth movement called Vlajka, which means 'the Flag'. They were what we referred to as Czech Nazis – older boys aged eighteen to twenty who were on the lookout for Jewish children. I don't think they were especially anti-Semitic; they were just fascist bullies. They used to lie in wait for us on the road back from the lake and beat everyone up for being out after curfew. That was my first ever experience of violence. We always tried to run away, but sometimes they caught us. I got really hurt only once, taking a physical beating with hands and fists, but thankfully they didn't break my glasses. The boys in our group were hurt far more often.

My father still felt deeply betrayed by the West and was terribly depressed. A few fellow Sokol members had been rounded up, and each day brought news of more trouble. Jews were banned from keeping radios, but we managed to hang onto ours somehow and glumly listened to the BBC from London every night. Tata tried not to show his true feelings to me, but I sensed that he was tormented and expected us all to be arrested any day.

One evening as he and I were coming home from the lake, long before curfew, our cook Emily was waiting for us on a corner and stepped into our path. 'The Gestapo are looking for you and other members of Sokol,' she warned my father. 'It's too dangerous for you to go home.'

Tata thanked her and told me that he'd hide in the woods. 'Go home and make sure Mummy is safe and then come to me tomorrow,' he told me. 'We'll meet in our special place.'

I ran home, my heart in my mouth, to find two members of the Gestapo waiting in our apartment. They had clearly been there for some time from the look of the overflowing ashtray. My mother was surprisingly calm and kept telling them, 'I really don't know where my husband is. I never know. I just trust that he will come home when he can. You could wait here forever.' They finally believed her and went away.

The next morning I ran to the woods with food and clothing and found my father just where he'd said. He had to remain in hiding for a week because the Gestapo came looking for him every day. His brother Karel also had to hide, as the authorities wanted him for deserting from the Austrian army during the First World War.

When the Gestapo realised that they were unlikely to find my father at home and decided that he'd be rounded up eventually for being a Jew, they came to our home only to steal. They arrived on a weekly basis, usually two men in uniform with a Sudeten

Czech named Haas who helped them search for food, chocolate, and jewellery. A lot of Sudetens helped the Germans against the Jews, which had consequences later.

It was terrifying to hear them hammering on the door and demanding entry. They'd burst in, shouting and kicking things around, opening drawers and cupboards, threatening us all the time as they searched every room. I had never heard shouting like that and would have to cover my ears. They'd stay for around an hour, taking anything they liked and telling us, 'We'll get rid of all you Jews soon. None of you will survive and you won't need any of these things where you're going.'

Their threats were terrible and we didn't know what was going to happen to us every time they came. I was so terribly afraid.

My mother was very courageous and often stood up to them. During one search they found a large salami she'd hidden in the chimney. When the Gestapo officer said: '*Das ist nicht für sie, das ist für deutsche Kinder*' (This is not for you, this is for German children), Mummy replied in perfect German: '*Aber wir haben auch ein Kind und das will auch essen*' (But we have a child, too, and she also wants to eat), and they somehow left it there. She was a really great personality in the way she stood up to them. Incredibly, they never mistreated her for her insolence. And once they had left, we put everything back where it belonged and went on living. What else could we do?

The Gestapo eventually stopped coming when they realised there was nothing left to steal. We had no income as my father's shop had been taken away from him and placed in the care of a *Treuhänder*, or trustee, a man who'd clearly believed the Nazi propaganda. Having seen the terrible anti-Semitic posters pinned up everywhere by the Germans, he imagined Jews to have beards and horns and was surprised that Tata was handsome, non-observant, and didn't look Jewish at all. To begin with my father was allowed to work in the shop alongside the trustee, but my father was an extremely proud man and he never accepted his new position.

The trustee grew to like him and he tried to be kind. He knew that they had stolen the business from him and eventually said,

'Herr Růžička, please, you can take whatever you want from the shop.'

My father was incensed. 'That is not for you to say!' he replied sharply. 'The shop is mine.'

Later the *Treuhänder* secretly offered to give him half the earnings from the store, but he wouldn't even accept so much as a cigarette from this man. He made him feel that he was the thief.

Shortly afterwards my father was sent to the town of Horní Bříza, fourteen kilometres away, to work in a kaolin factory. He wasn't able to come home from there, which worried us all, so one of his Sokol friends took him into his factory in Plzeň instead. Then we lost our beautiful flat and had to move into a much smaller apartment with a family of German Jews. We gave away most of our belongings or asked friends to keep special things for us and then we had to cross the city to our new home with only what we could carry. Although we thought we were being treated unfairly, we never considered ourselves inferior in any way. Our new flatmates were very kind and took care of us. We celebrated all the Jewish festivities with them and gave each other little presents.

Best of all, they had a gramophone and a large room in which they gave dance lessons. They even hired a proper tutor. We'd move the furniture to the four corners and play records and it is there that I first learned to dance, gliding around the floor to marvellous Glenn Miller tunes or one of my favourites – 'Smoke Gets in Your Eyes' by the singer Leslie Hutchinson, known by all as 'Hutch', and one of my early teenage crushes.

It may seem naive to look back on those days now, but although each new development was worse than the last, we still felt that the situation wouldn't endure. We may have lived in constant fear of dreadful things happening, but – to my surprise – I didn't collapse emotionally and neither did my mother. We grew stronger.

The hope that we clung to was a blessing and a curse, because we went on hoping even though our hopes were repeatedly crushed.

I was still so young and believed that somehow we'd survive and end up moving to a new Jewish state. My parents believed the

Western armies would step in to defeat the Nazis and save us so that we could remain in Czechoslovakia and carry on as before. We knew many Jews who had already fled and others who still planned to do so despite the growing risks. They had asked their Gentile friends to conceal their most precious belongings, just as our friends already had with our photographs, Persian rugs, porcelain, gold, and jewellery, but it was terribly dangerous for those caught hiding anything. The Nazis had frozen Jewish bank accounts and ordered that every household meticulously catalogue their possessions and assets before handing them over for 'safekeeping' to the Third Reich.

My father still had many friends in Sokol and almost every day some of the 'brothers' called by to see what they could do to help. They still wore their special uniforms and met in secret as 'hawks' or falcons. He was such an influential figure in the town they didn't want him to desert them either. 'Don't worry,' they assured him. 'It won't be as bad here for Jews as in Germany. We'll take care of you. You belong to us. Nothing can happen to you or your family, and this won't take long. France and England will help us and in half a year everything will be over.'

They made him an honorary Aryan, and then they offered to hide all three of us until after the war if necessary, but Tata declined. He was a realist and he told them solemnly, 'You can't make that kind of promise. None of us know how long that might be for.'

In the coming months, my parents did finally entertain the idea of us leaving the country. There was talk of opportunities in Latin America so, although I don't think my father ever had any intention of leaving, to appease my mother he started to take secret Spanish lessons, which I took with him. Tata and I also had English conversation classes with an Englishman in case we could move to London. Mummy's nerves often got the better of her but she nevertheless busied herself learning how to make ties because she thought that perhaps she could earn a living somewhere doing that.

Her sister Elsa had fled Vienna with her husband Leo in 1937, before the Anschluss, and emigrated to New York. Leo owned a silk umbrella business and had re-established it there. Their son Otto was in frequent contact with my parents and repeatedly urged them to flee as well. The Ginsburg family in Chicago had even sent a signed affidavit vouching for us all and giving us the authority to apply to the American embassy for a visa. My father had that document in his pocket but still he declined, saying, 'I would emigrate any other time but I cannot desert my nation when she is in danger.'

I never queried him and I took his decision as mine. I was always as patriotic and even though I had dreams of starting a new life in Palestine, I still believed in the future of Czechoslovakia. My mother felt quite differently and when the borders were closed in the autumn of 1941 and it was impossible for an entire family to escape anymore, I'm afraid that she made life even harder for my father. He was terribly despondent by then, but she berated him daily with recriminations about how he should have taken us to safety while he still could.

The psychological pressure of what he'd decided for us all weighed heavily on his shoulders. Eventually they decided to save me, at least, so after much secret discussion they brought up the possibility of me taking a place on one of the Kindertransports of Jewish children to England.

I was horrified and immediately and vehemently objected. 'I would die if I had to leave you!' I declared. 'I am absolutely not going.' As always, they treated me as an adult and respected my decision with, I think, some relief, as none of us wanted to be apart.

Before the Nazis came, Dagmar and I were supposed to attend a Jewish high school in Brno, but because the Nuremburg laws banned all Jewish children from going to school, we never went. Those same laws forbade Gentiles from teaching Jews, but my brave Madame allowed me to visit her secretly for piano lessons even though I had to half-conceal my star under my scarf. The punishment would have been severe for us both if we'd been caught and she only taught me when her husband was working (as an engineer at the Plzeň Škoda Works that had been commandeered by the Nazis to make tanks). I remember we played a lot of Dvořák and Mendelssohn at that time, often four hands. Madame was a courageous and beautiful human being.

Many others showed remarkable bravery too. Older children organised lessons for those who were missing out on school, volunteering to come to our homes in secret to help those of us for whom further education was now '*Verboten*'. The teachers in Brno sent all the books, materials and exam papers we needed and our former school director Mr Spala, another Gentile, taught us at his house. He was devastated by the political situation and kept saying that Masaryk, our nation's first president, should never have broken up the Austro-Hungarian Empire.

His comments seemed so odd to us at the time. We thought him such an old-fashioned man who spoke nonsense. We had no idea. And so we carried on, coping as best we could despite the almost daily threats to our existence.

The 'transports' started in October 1941. It was such an ordinary word for something that came to represent our worst fears. An estimated 6,000 Czech Jews were sent 'East' from Prague and Brno to work for the Third Reich in ghettos in Poland and Belorussia. None of their relatives knew where they had been sent and few ever returned, which led to rampant speculation and wild rumours that they had all been killed.

Two months later, a Czech ghetto was established in a once-sleepy garrison town called Terezín, about fifty kilometres north of Prague. The Nazis renamed it Theresienstadt and it was to be a model ghetto, a show-off concentration camp billed as 'a gift from Adolf Hitler to the Jews'. It was, they said, a place for Jews to live in safety and call their own. The whole concept was devised as a publicity stunt to show how 'the Jewish problem' was being solved, while at the same time masking its true purpose – as a transit camp for the extermination centres in the East.

All 75,000 remaining Czech Jews were to be sent to Terezín ultimately, especially those who were '*prominentní*' or being watched by the West – the artists and the scientists, professors, musicians, intelligentsia and playwrights. The ghetto would later be promoted as somewhere for war veterans and elderly Jews who might not easily stand 'the strain of resettlement'. It was then inundated with prominent and wealthy Jews from all the countries Hitler had invaded across Europe, most of whom had been promised luxury accommodation in what turned out to be one of the most terrible frauds in the history of mankind.

So-called 'invitation cards' began to be delivered to the homes of Jewish families in Plzeň informing them of their transport numbers and advising them that they had two days to prepare before presenting themselves at the Sokolovna, a huge local gymnastics centre. From there, they would board trains to their new 'home'.

There were rumours of transports taking all of Dobříš's Jews, too, and Mummy was very worried about my grandmother Zdenka. My dear grandfather Leopold, with his pipe and books, had already died aged eighty-one following heart surgery, and my grandmother wasn't coping well on her own. On the eve of Yom Kippur in September 1941 she had her maid prepare the Sabbath table as usual with the best silver and china, her prayer book and the candles. She marked the Day of Atonement in traditional fashion, went to bed, swallowed some pills, and never woke up. She knew what was coming.

On 7 December 1941, a month or so after the Plzeň transports began and in direct response to the Japanese bombing of Pearl Harbor, the Americans entered the war. There was suddenly hope again. Everyone believed that the hostilities had to end soon. We would never have believed that it would last another four years.

Instead of celebrating the news, scores of Jewish teenagers, including Dagmar and I, were summoned by the Gestapo to the headquarters of the Jewish Community. That was when the biggest shock of my childhood happened. The Gestapo informed us that we young people were to be sent onto the streets in pairs to distribute transport invitation cards to their recipients, most of whom believed that what we held in our hands amounted to a death sentence for them and their families.

Dagmar and I quickly paired up in the belief that we could support each other in our grim task but there was little comfort to be had. We were both so scared and stunned by what we'd been ordered to do. Each delivery round took all day from 8 a.m. until 8 p.m. as we walked hand in hand through the streets and made our way to the doors of the unfortunate ones. Word quickly got around so some of the scenes that greeted us were truly awful. People knew who we were and why we were there and some were expecting it and were already prepared. Other desperate families screamed and wept and pleaded and became hysterical and some went quite mad.

Several of those who knew our family tried to bribe us to claim that they weren't at home, or negotiate with us to somehow misplace their little white card, but we didn't dare risk it. We were under strict instructions to deliver all those we'd been allocated, ensuring that each recipient sign for them, before returning to the Gestapo headquarters by 6 p.m. with every name and address so that the administrators could add them to their lists and complete their paperwork.

The Germans were so very thorough.

I think we may have only delivered those wretched cards for a few weeks but it felt much longer. Dagmar and I clung to each other after every 'successful' delivery and wept. Many were angry with us for delivering the orders. It was terrible. There was weeping and lamentation everywhere. The sights we saw were too horrible and I still can't think about some of the things we witnessed. We didn't tell our parents the details, so as to spare them. Those few days truly marked the end of my childhood. Aged just fourteen, I had no idea that the world was like that. I'd been raised in an idyllic and loving home. I had never known unkindness or suffering and suddenly I came face to face with the worst that man can do.

Dagmar and I arrived at one apartment and found that the entire family had gassed themselves. They'd already been discovered and the door was swinging open. There were dead bodies everywhere, including small children. They must have known we were coming. I had never seen a body before and the sight that met us there that day haunts me still. Elsewhere there was water and blood coming out of the bathroom, after people had taken their own lives.

Late one evening, when we finally returned to the SS HQ, we were kept waiting for hours as the officials checked and double-checked our lists. We had to write down where we had been, who we had visited and to whom we had given the cards, dictating everything to a Gestapo officer. We were exhausted and traumatised and it was already long past curfew under martial law so we were also worried about getting home safely. Slumped onto chairs waiting to be released, we were shaken by the sudden arrival of my father standing in the doorway, wearing his Star of David like a badge of honour. It must have been about ten o'clock and it was almost suicidal for a Jewish man to have been seen out on the streets after curfew wearing that but he never accepted being a second-class citizen.

'What are you doing with these children?' he demanded. He was as white as a sheet and confronted them most fiercely. He always turned pale when he was furious. 'You know they mustn't be out this late. They are in danger and must leave immediately!'

The Gestapo looked up at this defiant Jew in amazement. When they didn't respond, he announced, 'I'm taking them home!' before grabbing us by the hand and leading us away. Nobody said anything and nobody stopped him. That night Tata was once more my hero.

A few weeks later, in late January 1942, not long after my fifteenth birthday, a teenager we knew appeared at our door with our 'invitation' to Terezín. Dagmar and I were out delivering at the time but we knew that someone had delivered the order to us. We had been expecting it as my Uncle Karel, Aunt Kamila, Dagmar and her seven-year-old brother Miloselk had received theirs the previous day.

Our order gave us two days' notice before we had to report to the authorities at the Sokolovna at 5 a.m. My father's parents were on the same transport along with many of our friends, so at least we would all be together. Dagmar and her family would go the day before.

My mother hid her anxiety by busying herself getting everything organised. It was a nightmare for her, and for any mother. Our former cook Emily came to help, as did our maid. We were only allowed a suitcase each – effectively two and a half for the family, with my small bag – and the total weight could not exceed fifty kilograms – fifty kilos for a lifetime. We could take no cash or jewellery, although friends suggested sewing money and gems into the linings of our coats. The orders were to leave everything else behind including all our valuables. Like everyone transported before us, we agonised over what to pack. Mummy had been advised to take pots and pans and to select our warmest clothes, which we decided to wear in order to reduce the weight.

We didn't know when we'd next eat or what it might be, so Emily helped Mummy pack dried peas, flour, some cans of fish, and tobacco. The curious thing is that even with these strict limitations most people who went to Terezín still took either books or violins – even cellos – determined to continue some sort of cultural life. Even if it meant they couldn't take as much warm clothing or food, they were prepared to sacrifice that for their instruments. This is why, once they arrived, people were immediately able to form a quartet or put on a play. We were no exception. I obviously couldn't take my piano and most of my books were too heavy so I selected a few cherished volumes. I was allowed to take some music and I pored over my scores for ages and eventually picked Bach's French and English suites, some of his earliest pieces.

I dreaded saying goodbye to Madame, my teacher and mentor from the age of nine. I took her a copy of the official photograph my father arranged to have taken in the days before we left. I still have a copy in which you can tell I'd been crying. Madame was very brave and didn't show any emotion in front of me. She gave me my lesson as usual and then asked, 'What would you like to play for our last piece together today?'

She made no suggestion that this might be the last piece we ever played together, but I knew what we were both thinking.

Without hesitating, I chose one of the pieces of music I was taking with me – Bach's English Suite No. 5 in E Minor with its poignant sarabande. It was such wonderfully simple music, and so moving. It showed a face which one doesn't usually associate with Bach. It showed tenderness.

Leaning against each other slightly, Madame and I sat side by side on the piano stool and played it, four hands.

5

Ostrava, 1954

Finding work after I graduated in 1951 was never going to be easy with so many unemployed in Czechoslovakia and the country still in post-war shock. So when friends at the Prague Academy told me that a new state-run agency called Pragokoncert was running a competition at the Rudolfinum for a pianist to travel with a singer, violinist and cellist and 'bring music to the people', I immediately put my name down.

The agency had been set up in 1948 to promote cultural, musical, and artistic events in the towns and villages, many of which had been largely abandoned and isolated during Nazi occupation and then deeply divided by the expulsion of every remaining German citizen after the war. Pragokoncert imitated a similar set-up in the Soviet Union and, as there, it hired an entire troupe of clowns and acrobats to perform along with popular singers and classical musicians like me.

Touring in an old bus to play in smoky pubs and half-bombed factories was never how I'd imagined my musical career would begin, but the chance of a paid job on a contract would at least mean a regular wage and a few more comforts as Viktor and I saved for our future together.

The auditions took place behind a screen. I was told that I needed one classical and one modern piece so I had something prepared – Prokofiev's Piano Sonata No. 3 and Beethoven's Piano Sonata No. 31.

With little notice, I sat at the piano hidden from the judges. It was the first time I had played behind a screen and I must say it was rather pleasant. I don't even know who they were. The screen wasn't there so much for us, but rather for them. They really didn't know who was playing.

To my surprise, they wrote to me and informed me that I had won the competition as piano soloist for Pragokoncert. I had no idea what that really meant. The job started almost immediately and I was to remain in it for four years. My fellow 'winners' were the soprano Ludmila Dvořáková, the cellist Josef 'Pepik' Chuchro, and the violinist Václav Snítil, all of us in desperate need of money. Together we became the so-called 'Prague Variety Show'. There were hundreds of times after winning when I pondered my decision to enter the competition. The schedule was punishing, the accommodation dreadful, and the work often thankless. All of us musicians often felt as if we had no future. Performing ahead of us might be a strongman lifting weights (who had to ask the cellist for help with the dumb-bells), a contortionist, a clown named Uncle Jedlička or a woman who trained puppies. There was a moderator who would oversee the entire event as workers or miners fresh from the bowels of the earth sat stony-faced in a fog of cigarette smoke, blankly watching our endeavours. Every day, we would think, 'Oh, God, what is he going to make us do today?'

Sometimes I might appear with the other musicians playing Dvořák or Bach, and sometimes on my own. I also had to accompany the soprano, who sang popular songs. Whenever I was playing solo, the moderator would summon me on to the stage – usually just a platform pulled off the bus for the occasion – and tell the impassive audience excitedly, 'Now Zuzanka is going to play something for you!'

There was rarely any applause as I took my seat before the moderator would ask, 'Do you know the scale, Zuzana? Can you play it for us? – c, d, e, f, g, a, B, c', and I would dutifully perform like one of the trained dogs.

'Now can you play the letter C?' he'd ask, with a knowing wink, as I did as I was bid.

'And now, Beethoven's *Appassionata*!' he'd declare triumphantly, as I launched into Beethoven's Piano Sonata No. 23 in F Minor. The upright piano on which I was supposed to play didn't have wheels and instead, for some reason, had the base of a rocking horse so, whenever I leaned on it, it moved away.

I can laugh about it today, but I must say that it was not at all laughable. It was such a crazy degradation and so humiliating. We would gather after the concert in one grim hotel room, wrapped in blankets as it was always cold, and we would ask ourselves what would happen to us next. We thought that this would be our future because this was how culture was promoted in the Soviet Union. We were really afraid of what would happen to us – and we were the privileged ones, those who had won the audition as the soloists of Pragokoncert, which soon earned the nickname the HAÚ (MCH), the Music and Circus Headquarters. People envied us because there was some money for it.

In the mornings they might send us to play to small children from kindergartens and first forms from elementary schools. When Chuchro no longer enjoyed it, he would put down his cello and say, 'Kids, I'll tell you a fairy tale.' And he told them fairy tales, which were far more successful than Dvořák in B minor.

The factories were better to perform in than the dingy pubs, and we were often instructed to play the folk piece 'Červená sukýnka' (Little Red Skirt) until we were blue in the face, to boost their working abilities. But there at least we would have some interesting discussions afterwards with the workers, many of whom were surprisingly knowledgeable and asked intelligent questions about technique and the history of each composition. I remember one packed factory at a mine in Ostrava in 1954 where all the workers were given an hour off to listen to our music before their next shift. They stood before us in a vast hall wearing their grubby overalls, arms folded, ready to be entertained. On that occasion the soprano Ludmila Dvořáková was performing with the violinist and the 'Old Man' Professor Sádlo – KPS – had come along to introduce us and open a discussion afterwards.

'Does anyone have any questions?' he asked, smiling at the crowd after our performance of Haydn's Symphony No. 104 in D Major.

A hand shot up. 'Yes. What does the violinist get paid for a concert?' a young man asked.

There was a general murmur of approval as people nodded and laughed.

KPS turned to the violinist. 'Well, Comrade, can you please tell us how much you are paid for playing for us today?'

The violinist stated the sum quietly – I think it was something like 600 Czech crowns (approximately £20 now) – and there was a huge uproar with men shouting and waving fists and crying out, 'What? We have to work an entire month for that and he just plays one afternoon!'

The professor smiled and waited for them to calm down. Looking around the hall, he asked, 'Do you have someone among you who is really strong?'

The workers started to goad one another and there was a general hubbub before they agreed on a giant of a worker whose name, we were told, was Franta.

'Would you please come up on stage?' KPS asked the man they pushed to the front.

'Yes! Yes!' the crowd cried, cheering and laughing.

KPS took the violin from my colleague and handed it to Franta, who held it gingerly in his enormous hands. 'Now, Comrade,' he explained, 'I want you to stand just as the violinist stood for the past hour, with the instrument on your shoulder and your hands held high as if you are playing Haydn for us too, okay?'

Everyone cheered and laughed as Franta adopted the required position – with a few minor adjustments from KPS and the violinist – and stared out at his fellow workers with a triumphant grin.

The professor smiled at them all and glanced down at his watch and said, 'Let's see how long Franta can hold this position, shall we?'

Meanwhile, we played some music as Ludmila sang 'Písničky na jednu stránku' (One Page Songs) and Franta began to wilt. Within minutes, I could see his arms began to tremble, and then his knees. His face went red and then blue and he grimaced at the strain the position was beginning to take on his shoulders. The hall erupted with noise as the men yelled their encouragement, stamped their feet, banged tin plates against the walls, calling Franta's name and urging him not to let them down.

'Franta! Franta! Franta!' the workers chanted, pressing forward to get a better look at their champion. I watched money exchanging hands and the noise rose to a deafening level as Franta's whole body began to vibrate with the strain.

He lasted just over fifteen minutes according to the professor's watch. Unable to stand it a moment longer, he dropped his arms and hung his head in shame as the men booed and shouted.

When they had finally stopped their din, KPS patted Franta consolingly on the back and asked everyone to give him a round of applause. 'Now maybe you can understand why the violinist earns his fee,' he said. 'He not only stands like that for an entire evening but he also has the talent and the knowledge to play the most beautiful music. Please now, let's give all our musicians a huge round of applause.'

The workers admitted defeat by deafening us with their newfound appreciation.

It was men just like those factory workers who risked so much to rebel against our communist masters the year after Viktor and I were married. Aside from the general sense of oppression under Stalinism, there was turmoil brewing in our troubled country.

Even though Stalin had died in March 1953, the government pushed ahead with a Soviet-inspired reform programme in which agriculture was collectivised and the focus shifted to heavy industry. Food became scarce, the cost of state-supplied goods rocketed, and inflation rose to twenty-eight per cent.

There were terrible rumours about our economy being on the brink of collapse and that money reform might be necessary. Then, at the end of May, the newly installed President Antonín Zápotocký gave a speech saying that these rumours were entirely false and only designed to destroy faith in the socialist state. The next morning all the banks were closed. It happened overnight. The value of our currency was less than fifty-to-one. We only had permission to go to the post office and take out a certain sum of money. Suddenly the whole nation became paupers.

The move was intended to hit speculators and hoarders and crush other 'bourgeois class enemies'. Banks were instructed to block any large cash withdrawals in what was widely considered to be state theft.

Viktor and I were living with my mother in a small modern apartment in Plzeň at the time. An industrial town in which workers dominated, it had a very different philosophy to other parts of Czechoslovakia because the Americans, not the Russians, had liberated it from the Nazis. On 1 June 1954, some five thousand workers, many of them from the huge Škoda engineering and armaments plant, broke out of their factories and took to the streets to protest at their already paltry wages being effectively slashed by eighty per cent. From our apartment just across the street from the district courthouse, the Palace of Justice, we witnessed everything. The workers were joined in the main square by students and other protestors, many of whom waved Czech flags and chanted, 'Down with the communists!' or 'We want free elections!' before marching on the government offices.

In a remarkable act of resistance that was to become the fulcrum of the rebellion, they tore down the Soviet flags and the huge pictures of Stalin and Lenin. Busts of communist leaders were hurled into the main square. They sang our national anthem and they stormed the Palace of Justice to free political prisoners. The police wouldn't intervene so the authorities had to call in the army. Many soldiers also refused to fight the workers, so they then summoned the people's militia, who were ardent communists.

Viktor was busy working at home on a new concerto and tried to remain focused. I couldn't work at all so I put on my coat and went to the square to see what was going on. I soon hurried away, but as I did so I noticed unmarked cars driven by the StB secret police cruising around taking photographs of everyone who was there. It was all looking increasingly dangerous and when I came home and Viktor turned on the radio for news, the events went unreported and instead they played nothing but Strauss waltzes, which sent shivers down my spine. 'This will end badly,' he predicted, and he was right.

When the militia arrived, fighting broke out, shots were fired, water cannons were used to drench the crowds and scores of rioters were injured. Martial law was imposed and hundreds of people were taken prisoner by the StB, whose officers swept through the crowds arresting anyone who even had wet clothing. In a series of show trials, the leaders of the rebellion were imprisoned for up to fourteen years and one was reportedly executed. At least two women prisoners died in captivity. From our apartment we saw it all: first the rebellion, then the release of prisoners, followed by the prosecution of all those who were being tried, including teenagers accompanied by their weeping parents, begging for mercy.

Once again there were dire and unexpected repercussions for us. The government could not publicly admit that communist workers had staged a counter-revolution, so they claimed that former capitalists had planned the entire rebellion.

The Communist Party unleashed a wave of vindictive measures on anyone it could blame. Property and homes were confiscated, hundreds lost their jobs or were demoted, and trade unionists expelled. The authorities seized their chance to remove 'enemy elements' from the city and announced almost immediate forced resettlement of entire families to barren areas in the Sudetenland near the German border, where abandoned and dilapidated buildings damaged by war were the only available properties.

Although my mother had already had her shop and her apartment taken away, she and her family were still considered 'subversive' as Jewish capitalists, so the authorities decreed that she should be among the other 'capitalists' evicted from Plzeň and resettled elsewhere. It was just like before. I hated Plzeň for that.

A policeman arrived with the proclamation that we had to sign, giving us twelve hours to leave our homes with all our belongings before being taken in trucks to these deserted villages.

The idea of trucks coming for us absolutely broke my mother. It was just like the camps. And even if we survived the resettlement, once we were evicted we would be deemed 'politically unreliable', and our identity cards stamped with the notation 'Action June 1, 1953' – a stigma that would have been disastrous for us all. If this had happened, as it very nearly did, Viktor and I would never have been able to continue our studies or work on our music. There would have been no composer Viktor Kalabis and no musician Zuzana Růžičková. We would not have been able to get anything other than the lowest menial jobs. I would have had to work in the fields, and Viktor probably in the mines.

There was no time to challenge it or think about escape before being banished to what we knew were virtually uninhabitable houses. We were in a desperate situation.

Then, another miracle happened. Anča, my former nanny-nurse, the one who had taken such great care of me when I had tuberculosis as a child and who'd holidayed with us in the mountains, had become a senior communist in Plzeň and was on the municipal committee. When she learned of our eviction order she immediately withdrew it, although we knew we still had to leave and could probably never return to our hometown to live.

Anča had been part of our family – as all our staff had been – and she did what she could at great risk to herself. We were warned that the order could only be postponed and would be reinstated imminently so we had approximately two days to find somewhere else to live.

Viktor had some dismal lodgings in Prague at the time so that he could continue to work in the city. His accommodation was a small room off a kitchen, a broom cupboard and just enough room for a bed. The landlady was kind, though, and she allowed him to play her upright piano. He had left his previous lodgings when he discovered his landlady was racist.

'Are you Jewish?" she had asked me one day, after she spotted the number on my arm. 'I don't like Jews.'

Viktor turned to her in fury. 'Why? How many do you know?'

'I never met one before,' she replied, sneering. 'But I know all about them.'

We had already applied for a flat of our own in Prague, but were still waiting for approval, which had to be granted by an official – a controller – who came to see where and how you were living before he allocated new accommodation. Viktor hurried to the city to speed the process along and was lucky because, at the eleventh hour, the controller arrived and, hearing of our dilemma, promised to help us. He had two children, one a harpist and the other a conductor, and he was sympathetic and understood about our passion for music. He promised to get us a flat the following day and advised Viktor to return to Plzeň with our decree, remind the authorities that we had recently got married, claim we had a flat in Prague, and that we were taking my mother with us.

Together we helped Mummy pack some essential belongings – once more – and summoned friends who took away our best furniture. We hired a truck and loaded up the grand piano and the rest of our belongings, and just as we were leaving, a policeman arrived with our new 'invitation'.

'Where are you going?' he asked, brusquely. 'You are supposed to go to the Sudeten.'

Viktor said quite calmly, 'We have just got married, we have a flat in Prague, and we are moving there with my wife's mother.'

The policeman could have arrested us on the spot, but the police in Plzeň were not so sympathetic to the party, especially after recent events and – incredibly – he let us go.

All the way to the city I expected to be apprehended at any moment. I knew we could be imprisoned for our insolence and our lives ruined. I had visions of us living together in some bleak hovel in the borderlands with no proper work, no money, and no music. By the time we finally opened the door to our rooms and stumbled inside in the dark, I promptly fainted.

Our new apartment on the top floor of a building in the Vinohrady district was small for three adults. It had belonged to an architect who lived in a villa outside Prague. The controller went to see him and told him, 'You won't need your apartment in Prague anymore. It's being given to students.'

We didn't manage to get all our furniture in, but we were determined to squeeze my grand piano into one of the rooms. Getting it up the six flights of stairs was an adventure in itself, with scraps of carpet laid on the stone steps and several men huffing and puffing their way to the top. One room was a kitchen and my mother slept in there with her head virtually in the icebox, so the other room was for us – and the piano. There was no choice but to slide a mattress under the piano and make up our bed there every night to sleep.

It was a major adjustment to live on top of each other all the time. My mother suddenly had no work and no friends and was left alone all day while we went out to teach or study, and only came home for meals and to sleep. It must have been hell for her.

For the next ten years or more we lived like that until an old lady who lived next door died and we applied for the rest of the flat. It was not at all convenient, but it was better than the Sudetenland – and at least we were safe.

The Plzeň uprising was one of many in our country in the summer of 1953, as workers in other cities took to the streets to protest at the government's crippling reforms. It was widely considered to have been the first anti-Stalinist rebellion in Eastern Europe and had broad significance for the future of Czechoslovakia.

The so-called 'strong hand' crackdowns that followed it were gradually relaxed and some concessions granted to those who had been persecuted. Retail prices were lowered and new houses built. In many ways it helped to force the government to adopt a softer stance and led to what became known as 'socialist consumerism' and a 'new course' designed to improve the lives of workers.

For the two of us, crammed into our tiny apartment with my mother, though, the standard of living only got worse. We had no telephone and no bathroom, just a basin with hot water. Food was expensive, so we lived on basics and saved our money for luxuries such as cigarettes and wine. I have to say, though, we made the most of it; we spent so many happy evenings and hours together there. We read and we listened to music, or we played it, and our tastes were varied. I had a secret fondness for adventure stories about the North Pole explorers, but I also loved crime stories and thrillers, especially Agatha Christie. Viktor loathed them and said he could always work out how they would end by the third page. He read a lot of classical Czech literature, especially Karel Čapek and Alois Jirásek. We both loved Mann, who wrote about our world so perfectly. I read all his works in German but there are some wonderful Czech translations, which I read to Viktor later on and which gave us new insight and appreciation. We thought we both knew the texts, but when I read them out loud it was different.

As for music, we didn't listen to popular music at all, although I argued that at least country music had a story. Viktor loved listening to anything by Bohuslav Martinů but he played a great deal of Stravinsky too. The professor of the gymnasium once asked Viktor what he listened to for relaxation, and he replied 'Stravinsky.'

The professor, said, 'Come on, nothing popular?'

Viktor smiled. 'Do you play chess?' he asked.

'Yes.'

'Then why would you play dominoes?'

The rooms next door to ours were rented out by the state to a man we hardly ever saw but whom we suspected of being in the secret police. We knew we were being watched and listened to all of the time. Everything we did was scrutinised. Every six months I faced a complex evaluation, which was in two parts – the professional and the political. I always had a good professional evaluation and an extremely bad political one. It was a dangerous position to be in, so to show that I was active in some small way I volunteered to collect the fees for the unions. That was the extent of my political work.

It was worse for Viktor, who was not only under suspicion because of his political inclinations but doubly condemned for marrying a Jew. He was writing some music for radio but the only work he could get after he graduated was reading student composers' scores or teaching students how to conduct. The authorities decreed that every university and every high school was required to have a certain percentage of students from the working classes, most of whom were labourers in factories who'd never had any formal education. They sent people into the factories to select the ones who could maybe play the guitar or the accordion and made them take examinations so that they could be given scholarships for composition and conducting.

Viktor was given the obligatory task of teaching these young men and women how to read scores and it was heartbreaking for him because they didn't even understand the essentials of reading music or know what a clef was. They were extremely poor and many from broken homes or without parents after the war. My dear Viktorek was very conscientious and he took it all seriously. He would come home and say, 'What will happen to these people? They will never be able to compose or conduct no matter how hard they are made to study. And if they are unable to stand before a great orchestra and do what's expected of them, they'll make hell for them.'

He painstakingly gave them some tasks to perform so that they could at least read something basic. When they came to the next lesson, however, they hadn't done the work and didn't know anything. Only one of his students showed any serious promise and he was hopeful that he might make a musician of him, but the boy also never studied hard enough or completed his homework. Exasperated, Viktor eventually asked him, 'Why aren't you working?' and the youth replied that he didn't have the time. Each of the students had been appointed head of this or that party youth movement and their entire week was taken up with working in the factory, followed by compulsory political activities and lessons on Marxism–Leninism.

'Who is your composition professor?' Viktor asked. When he learned it was a younger colleague, he said, 'Then please ask your professor to relieve you for at least half a year of your political functions so that you can complete this course.'

Unfortunately, the professor – an ardent communist – wrote a letter to the head of the faculty claiming that Viktor was trying to get his students to give up their political studies. That was the end. His casual suggestion was considered a 'treacherous act' against the state. He was immediately expelled and given yet another black mark on his already blemished political character. With this on his record, it meant that he couldn't get employment anywhere.

Our tiny income was suddenly halved and Viktor was unemployed for the next two years, not allowed to teach, and only able to compose. Thanks to Viktor and my mother, though, I was never too depressed about my poverty because I knew that there were worse things that could happen in life. We also somehow always had the hope that we would eventually make it through perseverance and talent.

After two years without work, one of Viktor's former students who had become a high-ranking communist and a director of Prague Radio contacted him. 'Are you still gnawing on the poverty bone?' he asked. When Viktor confirmed that he was still unemployed, the man offered him a post as an editor of music broadcasting for children at Czechoslovak Radio. He would be working with a children's choir and helping to plan all the programmes. His former student told him, 'I need somebody there who really understands what he is doing.' It wasn't the job Viktor had wanted, but he accepted gratefully.

The communists never stopped trying to get us to join the party and many people told us that our lives would be much easier if we did, but we couldn't. We were not trying to be subversive; it was a matter of principle. I told the officials who continually badgered me, 'I am an individualist and I will never obey commands and rules.'

Then they tried to get friends to influence us, people who would promise us, 'They would make you a prominent official and you could help us so much with your backgrounds and your story.' I'd laugh and tell them, 'Can you honestly imagine me in a procession shouting, "Long Live Stalin"?'

They had to admit they couldn't.

Quite a lot of Jews came back from the camps and joined the Communist Party. They thought of the Russians as our friends. The English and the French had let us down in the war, but the Soviets insisted that they had liberated us. We knew many people who joined and who believed passionately in communism until the end, but our refusal to be political drove a wedge between friends and families and meant that we could no longer consider each other true confidants.

With Viktor it was even more risky. At one time he started to receive dangerous reviews about his music, articles which admitted that he was a master of his profession but said he was 'too influenced by Western music' and suggested that it would be better if he could understand the mind of the worker and perhaps spend more time in the factories or the mines. I was terrified for him, which only exacerbated the nightmares I'd had since the camps, in which I would wake up crying, believing that someone was threatening or mistreating us. Viktor was always so kind and so patient, holding me in his arms until my tears dried.

The next three compositions he wrote were deliberately influenced by Czech folklore, which was the only way not to be criticised. After the third I told him, 'That's enough now, Viktor. Don't stick with this.' If he had I would no longer have loved his music and our marriage would not have been so harmonious. We respected each other's honesty enormously and were grateful that we could be truthful with one another in a climate where everything else was secrets and lies.

Still the party tried to lure him. One minister in government offered him a wonderful new job and tried to hand him American cigarettes, but he turned down both. As a so-called 'White Jew', his name had already been sent to every institution to be blacklisted and the official offered to lift the ban and open up the world to him as a composer but still he refused, as did I. It was too high a price to pay for freedom and I'm convinced our lives would have been just as difficult because we'd have been such bad party members and almost certainly expelled. Exasperated by their harassment, I eventually told one official, 'Comrade, if I sign up you will regret it forever because you will only ever have difficulties with me.' In the end they somehow accepted that and didn't bother me quite so much.

The only time they really put pressure on me was a little later when the composers' union arranged a three-day visit to Salzburg in Austria with tickets for a concert, and Viktor and I were both elected to go. I went to the authorities to apply for my passport, not sure if they would allow me to have it, and was immediately asked to follow an official to a different office. They sat me at a desk in a small dark room and – just like in the movies – a bright light was shone directly into my eyes. It was so bright that I couldn't see anything beyond it. I could only hear a disembodied voice.

'So, you want to got to Salzburg with your husband?' the official said.

'Yes, Comrade,' I replied, squinting.

He shuffled some papers and said, 'Well, we know that you and your husband have a good marriage. You even live with your mother-in-law and your family is reasonably content. But your salary isn't very high and you are not living in a big flat, so when you both leave and someone approaches you in Salzburg and offers you a much higher salary and a much better flat, what will you do?'

'Come back,' I replied.

'Why?'

'I love this country.'

'That's what they all say. Then they cross the border and start to feel free.'

I started to laugh inside. 'You don't understand,' I said. 'I have had many other possibilities to stay abroad, but I really do love this country. This is my home, and my mother is here.'

He let out a long sigh. 'I had a similar conversation with a cellist recently and – guess what – he defected.'

'I can't help that.'

He sighed again. 'The problem is I have my summer vacation starting now and if I let you go, I won't have one peaceful night for fear of you and your husband staying in Austria.'

I tried to suppress a laugh. 'I am sorry for you,' I told him truthfully, imagining how difficult the authorities must make the life of a low-ranking official whenever someone slips through the net. 'I'll tell you what, I really don't want to spoil your holiday so just let my husband go on his own this time. I will go to Salzburg another day.'

I heard the sound of his chair scraping against the floor as he pushed it back and stood up. He paced the room beyond the light for several minutes before finally sitting back down. I found it all quite ridiculous – this little imp afraid of losing his position and worrying about whether we'd return or not. I actually pitied him.

Finally, he stamped my papers and cried, 'Go. I think I'll risk it!'

I could hardly believe it. We had a marvellous time, travelling there by bus with fellow Czechs. The problem was that when we got there we were in another ridiculous situation because we had little money. We were not able to afford tickets for the main performance and we were very thirsty. We went to the kiosk and asked for the cheapest lemonade they had and the kiosk seller laughed and asked us, 'Why do you ask me that when you have such quality cameras?" He couldn't understand why we would have no cash. We, in turn, looked at the old Leicas we'd brought with us and were astonished that someone in the West would value them so highly.

Viktor was determined that we should see all the concerts we had come to see and, being a good negotiator, he went to see the conductor and told him of our plight. Kindly, the conductor allowed us to sit in on the rehearsals. Afterwards, I recall standing on the bridge in Salzburg and telling Victor how beautiful it was and how tempting it would be to stay.

We both knew it was out of the question. My mother was in Prague. His father was in Bohemia. They would have suffered terribly.

In all the years under the communist regime, Viktor and I were only allowed out of the country together five times – twice to Salzburg, twice to Zurich when his works were being performed there, and to Moscow because one of his quartets was being played.

I never dreamed that Viktor would want to go to the Soviet Union, so when he accepted an invitation there I was shocked. Having been to Moscow many times for Pragokoncert and since,

I knew Viktor would be absolutely lost in that city. His panic would begin when he discovered there was no one to meet him at the airport and he had to wait at least an hour because of the Russians' unique sense of time. I had a study visa for the Soviet Union at the time because I'd been invited to take harpsichord master classes for some Russian music professors – and, because there was no chance of us ever defecting to Moscow, the authorities allowed me to go with him.

Whenever I went to Moscow I always had a so-called translator, who was really a minder in the pay of the government. Some were rather primitive, but some were well educated and intelligent and I usually became friendly with them and asked them their stories. Similarly, I was very open if someone asked me questions I could answer. One woman who was good to me and who gave me a gift of amber (which I love) seemed unhappy with her work and deeply suspicious of me so I asked her, 'Either you are in the secret service or you think I am, so which is it?'

She relaxed immediately and told me her story. She said she was from a family where her father and grandfather had been sent to Siberia for crimes against the state. 'If I end up there too, what can I do? I am bored by my life so I applied for this job so that I can at least meet interesting people like you.'

We became instant friends.

Viktor and I had another wonderful guide, a young man who had studied dramatic arts in Prague. The first thing he said when we arrived in Moscow was, 'I have tickets for the Bolshoi that I'm supposed to take you to, but I won't. I want to take you to a smaller progressive theatre instead. I think you will prefer it.'

He also took us to an exposition of photographs and chatted to me endlessly about everything – from life in Prague to the musical culture of the concentration camps – as he showed us around the real Moscow. I remember he accompanied us to the home of one of my Russian professors, who invited us to eat some blue cheese with him and his family. They were all radiant about it and so excited. We didn't tell them that blue cheese was one of the things we could get quite easily in Prague.

Even though Viktor's concert was a huge success in Moscow and he was very popular at the international symposium of composers he attended, he still found the place too oppressive for his taste. They invited him to return the following year but he was quite frank and declined the offer, telling me, 'I just want to go home.'

Being that close to the heart of Stalinism and the root of all our troubles was a step too far for my kind, sensitive Viktor.

6

Terezín, 1942

The morning of our departure for Terezín arrived cold and misty. Mummy, Tata and I got up in in the dark and dressed in silence. None of us had slept. Cumbersome in so many layers of clothing, we trudged to the assembly place, our hearts and suitcases heavy.

The Nazis favoured early starts so that people wouldn't witness their evil but many were awoken by the unhappy sound of our boots on the cobbles. Most of the people of the town cleared from the streets during such events and hid in their homes, but several friends and customers emerged tearfully from the mist to wish us luck and bid us farewell. There was also a service held by the archbishop in the church of St Bartholomew during which there was a large procession of people who prayed for us.

Once at the Sokolovna we were treated very rudely as we were pushed into lines to wait with thousands of others to be registered. Herded with shouts and sticks we stood for hours and eventually an SS officer came forward to count us. My father looked at him in such a way that he was immediately smacked hard across the face; he had been unable to hide the contempt in his eyes. Tata never once flinched or seemed afraid. I had never seen anyone do anything like that to my father before and my heart shrank with fear.

There were three main transports from Plzeň in early 1941, each made up of around a thousand people. We were following several hundred young, male 'volunteers', skilled craftsmen from Prague who'd been selected to go ahead and prepare the dilapidated ghetto buildings for new arrivals. In return these volunteers were promised better conditions and exemption from further transports, all of which proved to be false. They were named the Aufbaukommando (Construction Commando) transport, known as 'AK'. Thereafter every new transport to Terezín from around the country was labelled with a relevant letter between A and Z, so the three from Plzeň were R, S, and T.

Our 'T' transport was sent to Terezín on 26 January 1942. My number was T345, which was written on a tag I had to wear around my neck. My parents were T346 and T347. From that day on whenever we were summoned or accosted by the SS, we were supposed never to say our names, only our numbers. The gradual stripping of our identities had begun.

It took several more hours before we were ordered to march to the railway station and then crammed into cattle wagons for the town the Germans insisted on calling Theresienstadt. I was terribly ill on that train. I don't know if it was nerves or something I'd eaten but I was so tired and so sick. Trying to stay calm, I played Bach's sarabande over and over in my head, singing it to myself quietly and thinking of the last time I'd played with Madame.

The music in my head was more important to me than ever then. It didn't weigh anything and the Nazis didn't even know it was there. They couldn't steal it from me and it was mine, and mine alone.

When we arrived at the station, three kilometres from the garrison, everyone, including the young, old and infirm, was ordered to walk – a silent procession of ghosts in the grey dawn. It took two hours before we reached the gates of the fortress town laid out in the shape of a star and surrounded by a moat, grass-covered ramparts, and high brick walls.

The ghetto had its own government run by Jewish elders but overseen by Czech police, the Gestapo and the SS, the latter operating out of a building known as the Small Fortress. Under their supervision, we were herded into a huge amphitheatre where we had to stand and be counted – again – and that is when I fainted.

When I came to, I saw the face of a young man looking down at me with kind eyes who asked my parents in German, '*Was ist los mit diesem kind? Ist sie krank?*' ('What is the matter with this child? Is she ill?')

My father told him in Czech that I was just tired and assured him they were taking care of me. As we sat on our luggage waiting to see where we would be put, my paternal grandparents, Jindřich and Paula, were taken away to the old people's barracks. Fearful for them, we embraced and were told we could see them in a few days. I was comforted that my grandfather was unusually healthy and looked considerably younger than his eighty years, thanks to a lifetime devoted to physical exercise. My once lively 'Babička' already had a hopeless look in her eyes, however. At the age of seventy-one, she bore no resemblance to the vital woman who'd enjoyed holidays in the French Riviera or taken me to concerts and operas, festivals, and shows. I feared she wouldn't survive in a place like Terezín.

Over the next few hours, men were separated from women and children, and all of us were directed to one of eleven huge barracks that had each been named after German cities. It was horrible seeing my father escorted away, not knowing where he was and if he'd be safe.

My mother and I were eventually billeted in the barracks named after the city of Hamburg, along with many other women and children, all in one dormitory. It was immediately oppressive. The allocated space for each prisoner was 1.5 square metres in a filthy damp room. There were no wooden bunks as they had in other barracks, just straw mattresses laid on the dirt that we moved around and doubled up with blankets in the daytime to sit on. A small stove sat in the corner that everyone fought over, and a single kerosene lamp hung from the rafters.

Within hours, the atmosphere was stifling and there was not enough air to breathe. Everyone was forbidden from leaving the room. Women were weeping at being separated from their men, and several became hysterical. Quarrelling broke out between those who wanted to cook something. Sensing the fear and despair, the children started crying too. My mother, the eldest, was appointed dormitory overseer and tried to organise everyone, but the noise remained unbearable and my head throbbed.

I felt so dreadfully ill.

Like some sort of vision, the beautiful man who'd previously asked after my health walked into our barracks and instantly made everything better. His name was Alfred 'Fredy' Hirsch, a 25-year-old athlete from Aachen in Germany with a broad grin and a ready laugh that endeared him to everyone.

Fredy stood tall and erect with a muscular physique and a most elegant manner. He had been such an accomplished sportsman before the war that he would have been on the German Olympic athletics team if he hadn't been Jewish. The writer Arnošt Lustig once said of Fredy that if he'd been blond with blue eyes he'd have made 'the perfect Aryan'. Even in that place, he seemed cleaner and better dressed than the rest of us, with his hair slicked back. I didn't know it then, but he was someone who would become crucial to my survival.

From the moment he arrived in Terezín in December 1941, as part of the AK transport, Fredy – a medical student and pioneer of the JPD, a German-Jewish scouting group closely allied to Maccabi Hatzair – devoted himself to the service of children. A man of great dignity who conversed with the Nazis in their own Hochdeutsch or 'high German' and knew how to handle them, he used his charisma and charm to persuade people into doing what he wanted. As soon as any new transport arrived, he hurried over to see how he could help.

The first thing he did for us was to arrange for the older children to take care of the younger children. He had them escort the little ones to a courtyard to play so that the mothers could compose themselves. Even though it was snowing he taught the children some games and made everyone jump up and down and do exercises to keep warm. Nobody was allowed to move beyond the building or the courtyard without a special pass because the regular population of the town still lived in homes there and were forbidden from having any contact with Jews.

Having moved the children out, Fredy came back to check on the rest of us and when he looked at me again he immediately appreciated that I was more than just tired. He went to the ghetto doctor and returned with some medicine that he administered himself. From that moment on, Fredy Hirsch became one of the most important people in my life.

Everyone was assigned a job over the next few days, but because I developed my first lung infection in ages I was unable to work outside in the agricultural labour force with my friends. Once I was better, though, I was assigned to help Fredy arrange places of safety and learning for the other children. He'd found an old attic full of cobwebs in the Hamburg barracks that he wanted to turn into a playroom, so he enlisted teenagers to help him clean it up. It was cold up there, but not as cold as outside and that little attic became a godsend, a safe haven from the oppressive atmosphere below. We had some lessons from a painter who was apparently famous, and a very good singer. Then Fredy rounded up some of the teachers he had already enlisted to his 'Youth Services Department' and arranged for us to have classes with them, or with the *madrichim*, the youth leaders and counsellors. Fredy placed twelve children in my care, which meant I could join in with the art and poetry lessons, singing, dancing and lectures. Those in charge also ran competitions for neatness and exercise, and others for cleanliness – anything to keep the children busy and to occupy the long days.

Left on her own in the overcrowded barracks, my mother's emotions finally got the better of her and she collapsed with some sort of nervous complaint. Thin and frail, she suffered a series of fits or panic attacks and was admitted to the so-called ghetto hospital, which had few facilities and no medicines. The prisoner-doctors didn't know what was wrong with her, but they warned me she was very ill. In the end they diagnosed a weak heart. Almost every day after that I was called out from the children's group to hurry to my mother because she was dying. The prisoner-nurses looked so grave each time, I was terrified. But Mummy somehow pulled through and was eventually considered well enough to be put to work.

Once I'd accepted that she wouldn't die, my biggest problem was the hunger that gnawed at my shrunken stomach constantly. Having been thin and fussy about food throughout my childhood, I was suddenly ravenous all the time. (How I regretted refusing to eat that bowl of buttery noodles back home.) I was fifteen years old and entering puberty and my body needed all the food it could get. What was on offer simply wasn't enough.

Breakfast in Terezín was a piece of bread and some black water they called ersatz (artificial) coffee. Lunch was thin soup made from crusts or vegetables – never meat – and then we were given bread and 'coffee' again in the evening. On Sundays we might get dumplings with a little sugar and occasionally we were given a cooked potato with a little margarine. Anything else we ate had to be stolen or bartered. There was a busy black market, but my mother and I were not well versed in the ways of illegal commerce so we usually went hungry.

Mummy volunteered to peel potatoes for the kitchens in the hope that she might be able to steal some or at least the peelings to make a more substantial soup. She did, but it was a high price to pay. Her job involved being up to her knees all day in wet peels in a cold, dark, damp cellar. It broke my heart to see my dear, elegant mother who'd once had her clothes handmade and had always held herself with such poise reduced to that. Later, she managed to secure a job as secretary to the ghetto dentist, which was much more suitable, even if it meant we didn't get extra potatoes.

To take my mind off being hungry all the time, I worked as diligently as I could for Fredy and continued with my Zionist studies in the Maccabi Hatzair group, to which I still belonged. Our Plzeň young leaders Tilla Fischlová and Karel Schleissner had been transported with us, so we reformed our original Kadima group and recruited two more so that there were five girls and five boys. Within our group we set up a *kvutza*, or communal collective, with a strict socialist discipline in which we were supposed to share everything – food, clothes, music, and books. I was always so afraid of spoiling others' belongings. Nothing was private and all property was in common to prepare us for life in a kibbutz. I didn't much like it because I was an individualist and not accustomed to sharing. Besides, I was never a person to be told how to behave.

I had a friend the same age as me who was also called Zuzana. Her surname was Heller and we completely understood each other immediately. She became my closest friend in Terezín. Her father was a doctor in the ghetto. We two were the rebels in our group because we thought some of the communal rules were silly, especially the so-called 'critic sessions' where everyone was encouraged to speak their thoughts about everyone else. As I was always being criticised for not being a good enough member of the collective, I was fast coming to the private conclusion that kibbutz life in Palestine wouldn't suit me at all.

More and more people began to arrive in the ghetto, which became intolerably overcrowded. Epidemics were rife and disease and infection killed hundreds, especially the old, the very young, and the sick. Wooden carts laden with bodies headed for the crematorium were a frequent and miserable sight, their wheels squeaking as they passed by while we stood and watched in silence.

My cousin Dagmar and her parents had been placed in different barracks to ours so we only saw them occasionally and I missed her. There was another Dagmar, known as Dana, who was in the same room as me and who was terribly nice although two years younger, which seemed so much at that age, and we also became friends. She had been transported from Bohemia with her parents and younger sister, all of whom were eventually killed. Her father was also a doctor, but he'd volunteer to deliver the coal to our barracks just to see his family and we'd all laugh at how black he was from the coal dust.

Once winter was over we started to receive occasional food parcels from people back home. When that happened, it was a good day. There might be a tin of sardines, a cake or some biscuits, and we tried to be fair and share everything out. Another good day became Sundays because that was the day Fredy had agreed with the SS that he could take all the children out onto the fortress ramparts, a wonderful treat. He was determined to keep us healthy and taught us that the main objective in Terezín was to stay alive, so he made us all line up along those grassy ramparts every Sunday morning and do gymnastics and other exercises.

It was quite a sight to see hundreds of children bending and stretching and running on the spot each week as he called out instructions. It felt so liberating to stand up there in the fresh air, our first in three months, looking across green meadows and burgeoning orchards to the purple-tinged foothills beyond. This was a new freedom and gave us something to live for.

I couldn't help wondering, though, as I watched life carrying on as normal for those beyond our walls, who might come to save us.

On Sunday afternoons we were allowed to visit our families. Mummy and I went straight to see my father in the Magdeburg barracks where he lived, or he would come to us. It was so good to see him and to learn that he'd been given a job as a ghetto policeman in the Ordnungsdienst (Order Service). My uncle Karel was in the same barracks and had found a position as a fireman. He and my father had always been close and were relieved to be together, but the atmosphere in their barracks was most solemn because they'd been told that several of the younger AK transport men caught smuggling letters to loved ones had been publicly hanged a week earlier. The hangman was a German pimp named Arno Böhm who had been imprisoned in the ghetto because he'd murdered one of his prostitutes in the St Pauli district of the city of Hamburg. This unsavoury character was someone we were destined to meet again. These hangings, and others that he carried out later, came as a dreadful shock to everyone in Terezín. Once we had settled into ghetto life and realised that, though hard, we could survive it if we managed to avoid disease and infection, none of us thought that the Nazis would actually execute people there, so now we all became depressed.

On Sunday afternoons we would also visit my grandparents in the old people's barracks – a shabby attic. Grandfather had organised a Sokol group in his room and he woke them every morning and made them wash in cold water, just as Fredy did with all of us children, even though we always complained. Personal hygiene in Terezín, both insisted, was of vital importance to keep disease and the lice at bay, especially when we could only wash our clothes every six weeks.

After their cold wash, the old men were taken outside by my grandfather for some vigorous exercise, so determined was he to keep them healthy. My grandmother, however, was not. She was sick all the time, and although she was pleased to see us, she seemed to have given up because of the hunger and the cold and the dirt.

By June 1942, all the remaining civilian residents of the eighteenth-century garrison town just beyond our barracks were evacuated to make room for the thousands of new Jewish prisoners arriving. The little terraced houses and larger public buildings were requisitioned and carpenters worked day and night making bunks, as well as coffins for the rising numbers of dead.

Fredy quickly reserved two of the vacated buildings for children's homes or *heims* – one for boys and one for girls. The Council of Elders agreed that those aged between ten and sixteen could be relocated there from the adult blocks. In the end, I think Fredy managed to arrange for ten of these *heims* to be established to cater for the hundreds of children arriving every day.

I was worried about leaving my mother in the airless Hamburg barracks to move into the girls' home, known as 'L410 Heim', but I soon came to realise that it was better for us both that I was gone. Although Hamburg reeked and there was constant quarrelling amongst the women, she instantly became calmer without having to watch me go hungry every day, which had been a torment. For me, too, it was a kind of liberation because of her frequent panic attacks.

My cousin Dagmar was also moved to a *heim*, but she wasn't in my room and went to work every day with the animals on one of the nearby farms. I didn't see her much at all because she'd also acquired a nice young boyfriend named Arci Yigal with whom she was very much in love.

Thanks to the unhygienic conditions and the lack of food, I developed pneumonia again and was too unwell to work for a while. When I was a little stronger, Fredy found me a quiet job in the youth care office, a dingy little room where I had to sort administrative papers and file the names of new arrivals. I was bored with nobody to talk to and not enough to do, which only made me pine dreadfully for my parents and our former lives. Thinking of Madame and my piano, my books and my music, only made me more miserable. I couldn't even allow myself to play music in my head because it was too painful.

The highlight of my day was when I had to pass messages between the Jewish Council of Elders, who ran the ghetto from the Magdeburg barracks, to Fredy and his team of helpers. Once I found him I'd hang around and help, picking up news from those who had a better idea of what was going on in the world. There was always someone with a radio who reported the latest developments and the Czech civilians who worked in the ghetto smuggled in all manner of contraband wrapped in newspapers, which we could then read.

The bulletins from beyond our walls, however, were rarely good, and there continued to be so much suffering inside Terezín. First of all hunger, then physical exhaustion through hard labour. There were plagues of lice and bedbugs, fleas and rats that brought epidemics of typhus, meningitis, jaundice and encephalitis. Our skin itched permanently and was red raw from scratching. Old people and the mentally ill were kept in their quarters with little or no medical care. The overcrowding became so bad that the transports 'East' began to accelerate, which became the new, big, dark cloud hanging over us all. We still had no idea where 'East' was exactly, although most suspected Poland or Germany. We'd never heard of Auschwitz or the so-called 'Final Solution', but there were so many horrible rumours of death camps and slave labour that no one wanted to go, wherever it was.

One of the most sadistic things the Nazis did was to force the Council of Elders to decide who should stay in the ghetto and who should leave on the next transport. Fearing the worst, they tried to save the children wherever possible, and they also tried not to send people whose families were still together. This meant that if you lost someone you had the added distress of moving higher up the transportation list.

Strange postcards started to arrive back in Terezín from many of those who'd already been transported East. The official stamp said 'Birkenau', which no one had heard of either. The plain cards were written in German capital letters stating that all was well but were composed in a formal and unnatural way, as if they'd been censored whilst being written. Random words of Hebrew meaning 'bread' or 'danger' kept cropping up too, which only added to the rumours.

I had a lovely Maccabi friend called Margaret Winternitz from Prague, who was one of the first to be sent East with her entire family, having been given just two days' notice as before. We were all afraid for her – such terrible fear – but what could we do? We wept and we hugged and we helped her pack and then we escorted her to the block known as the 'Sauna' where people were deloused and prepared for the transports before walking the three kilometres back to the station. I don't know what happened to sweet Margaret but as far as I know neither she nor her family ever returned. As was the way in Terezín, another girl quickly took her empty place in our barracks, and in our group.

Then a transport from Dobříš arrived in the ghetto bringing members of the rest of our family, including my first love Hanuš, along with his brother Jiří, their parents, my Aunt Hermine and Uncle Emil. We were so excited when we heard the news, until we learned that the Dobříš Jews were to be kept in a holding area and not allowed into the main ghetto because they were to be sent East almost immediately. Determined to see Hanuš for what might be the last time, I somehow managed to get him out – I don't even remember how – and I took him to meet Fredy.

'Please can you try to get my cousin taken off the transport list?' I pleaded, but Fredy didn't even try to lie and told us flatly that there was nothing he could do. Hanuš thanked me for trying and calmly claimed that he would rather remain with his family. Before we parted, we spoke fondly of our happiest summer days running through the castle meadows in Dobříš and promised to keep in touch when we could. Like me, he hoped to emigrate to Palestine one day, where he planned on becoming a professional footballer.

'See you in the Promised Land!' Hanuš told me cheerily as we said farewell and he returned to his train.

It was years before we discovered that he and his entire family – those happy aunts, uncles, and cousins who'd gathered noisily around my grandmother's table for feasts and holidays – were all sent to Belarus in the Soviet Union to be shot dead and buried in a mass grave in the Maly Trostenets death camp near Minsk.

As my parents and I remained in our colourless, airless ghetto, waiting for we knew not what, what little spare time we had when not working was filled with educational or cultural events. With so many intellectuals among us, Fredy and others saw to it that we older children continued our high school education, so we learned everything from Czech poetry to languages, the history of Rome, the geography of Bohemia, drama and the finer points of trigonometry.

I attended everything I could, probably more than the others in my group, and especially those events organised by Fredy.

For a while I joined a communist group and went to some marvellous lectures on Marxism–Leninism given by teachers who once again assured us that communism was the solution to everything and an end to anti-Semitism. When I met my father at the weekend and told him what I was studying, he listened respectfully as before but then he said, 'Maybe your generation will have a different view on these things but I am afraid that it won't be as you hope. Think about this if you will. Think about a dictatorship of the proletariat. Think about it very deeply.' And I did. After that, I started to hear those lectures in quite a different light.

I also attended Hebrew lessons. The classes were well attended by some of the older members of Maccabi, including a handsome teenager from Brno named Hanuš Austerlitz, who became my first proper boyfriend. He was a very coveted boy, the kind who had the girls excitedly whispering, 'He's coming! Hanuš is coming!' each time they saw him approaching. Ours was a sweet and childish affair, we just kissed and held hands, but it was the first really good thing to happen to me in Terezín. He and I also set up a little group where we each recited what we remembered from stories and plays as there were so few books.

We also decided to learn Latin and Greek together and found a linguist and professor of oriental studies from the University of Vienna called Professor Israel Kestenbaum, who agreed to teach us in return for half our weekly bread ration. That was not at all easy because we didn't get much to begin with and bread was something we really depended upon to stave off our hunger.

We were eager to learn, though, and he taught us quite a lot. With his help, we could read and understand the Book of Samuel from the Bible, and then we started on *Caesar's Commentaries on the Gallic Wars*. The professor was a strict scholar who told us we were wrong to say Caesar like 'See-tsar' and insisted that it should be pronounced 'Kai-ser'. There were many times as my tummy rumbled during his lessons in the attic that I regretted the sacrifice of my bread, which seemed too great. Still I couldn't wait for those classical language studies, which reminded me so fondly of the *Odyssey* and the *Iliad* that my father had read to me as a little girl. I never fell out of love with all those fantastical stories of gods and sea monsters. Neither did Hanuš.

Almost every house had an attic where something was going on. Karel Ančerl, who later became the chief conductor at the Czech Philharmonic, was one of our cooks in Terezín but also an inspirational musician. It was he who dubbed we teenagers his 'little rabbits' and always fished around in the bottom of the soup pot to give us an extra potato or piece of vegetable because we were so thin. When he wasn't feeding us physically, he was feeding our souls with music. In another attic there was a string quartet complete with instruments, some of which had been smuggled in piece by piece.

As more and more trains disgorged their sorry human cargo, Terezín welcomed some renowned tutors and musicologists who immediately started playing and giving lessons in the darkest of places and the strangest of circumstances. The Nazis officially forbade most of these activities, but they didn't intervene because it kept us all busy and – as far as they were concerned – we were all doomed anyway. Later on the 'Administration of Free-Time Activities' was formally set up to coordinate events.

The man in charge of the musical life of the ghetto was a young Czech pianist and composer named Gideon Klein, who was very kind to me. He gave me lessons and harmony exercises. He was a fantastic personality. He worked alongside a talented composer called Hans Krása who had written a children's opera called *Brundibár,* based on a play by Aristophanes, which had a hidden political subtext. Krása was adapting it from memory for the children of Terezín and I was chosen as a member of the choir so, as well as my classical studies, I had rehearsals twice a week. Although I learned all the words, I never got to sing in the premiere, sadly, as I was transported out of the ghetto a few weeks before it happened. Nor was I aware until after the war that Krása, Klein, and most of my fellow singers and performers were later all murdered.

I was also selected for the choir of *The Bartered Bride*, the opera written by the Czech composer Bedřich Smetana, which my aunt Vlasta had famously performed in Paris in 1928. The comedy of true love prevailing despite a scheming marriage broker was accompanied by an old harmonium played by the musician and conductor Rafael Schächter, who worked in the ghetto with the Czech opera singer Karel Berman and went on to arrange some powerful performances of Verdi's Requiem, whose rehearsals I also saw and which moved me deeply.

Schächter, Krása, and Klein were remarkable and inspirational young men, none of whom survived the Holocaust. All these composers, conductors and musicians managed to achieve so much in the ghetto in spite of the fact that they, their choirs, and their soloists were repeatedly being pillaged for the transports East.

Fredy also played his part, working with a choreographer to create a wonderful show out of the German novelist Stefan Zweig's drama *Jeremiah*, in which several of us dressed up and danced like little flames in an expressionist ballet.

Jeremiah is a satire on the fascist state and was so sustaining. It says we have always through the centuries suffered and been beaten or put in prison. But still we are living and those who have beaten us have perished and we are still alive. This message was so important in Terezín.

The ghetto had a number of extremely talented pianists and only one or two pianos, so everyone had to take their turn. In our district the only instrument had just two or three legs, as I recall, and, propped up by boxes, it sat in an attic – unlike the harmonium in the basement. I was able to play it a few times when Gideon Klein asked me or offered to give me lessons in harmony, but then all these incredible pianists arrived so he was too busy and it was no longer possible for me to play.

I didn't mind so much. My heart wasn't really in it. In spite of Gideon's encouragement, I didn't feel the music in the same way that I had when I was with Madame. I wasn't able to play it in my head somehow or translate my thoughts to the keys. Playing that old piano in the attic only reminded me of happier times and that made me very sad.

I had every reason to be sad in the coming months. First Tilla Fischlová and Karel Schleissner were sent East on the next transport, along with some of our other friends from Plzeň. We bade them farewell and promised to meet them in Palestine. Then my grandfather Jindřich died unexpectedly of prostate cancer in October 1942, followed by my grandmother Paula from pneumonia six months later. There were no proper funerals in Terezín, just a brief sort of ceremony. The bodies were cremated and their families given little cardboard boxes containing the ashes, which had to be thrown into the river Ohře that meandered its way along the tree-lined fringes of the ghetto – a place we were never normally allowed.

I sobbed as I walked with my father down to the river carrying that little box containing the remains of my grandmother. I had loved my 'Babička' very much. I would never forget her returning from Nice with gifts of violet creams and dried lavender, or how much she enjoyed the opera at the Plzeň Spring Festival as we sat in our family box, where I was too excited to breathe.

Mummy was too ill to go to the funeral that day so my father held my hand as he threw the ashes into the fast-flowing water while we stood on the riverbank and said goodbye. Drying my tears, he pointed to a beautiful apple tree in full bloom just a few metres away. 'Look Zuzka!' he exclaimed. 'Don't cry. The ashes of your grandmother have gone into the river and the water from the river is feeding this tree. Soon dear Babička will be in the blossom.'

I looked at the tree and couldn't help but smile. My darling Tata was such a wise and wonderful man. We each had so many duties and demands made on us in Terezín that we didn't get a chance to be together as much as we'd always been, but the few things he told me there were so poignant and necessary for my whole life.

I went back to work after the funeral, but my job in the office of youth care had been abandoned and, as I was feeling physically stronger, I was assigned to agricultural work. All children over the age of twelve had to work, usually in the vegetable gardens of the ghetto or in the farms beyond its walls, which was considered a privilege. We went to work every day at 5 a.m. and came home by 8 p.m. It was February and bitterly cold, but it was still nice to be away from the ghetto so this was a relatively happy period for me.

To begin with I worked in the fields, unloading cow dung from the back of a tractor with my bare hands. It was extremely heavy work and I was not at all used to it. We worked nine to ten hours every day and I worried all the time about damaging my fingers, which were stiff and sore, but I didn't have a choice. The dung was heavy and it smelled awful but so did we, yet somehow I was lighter of spirit because I was back in the world. I saw nature for the first time in a year. I could see the whole of the heavens and trees and flowers – things we could never see inside the Terezín ghetto.

When we came back from the fields we were so tired that we usually just washed, ate, and went to bed. I had never slept well in the ghetto but physical exhaustion finally made me sleep like a baby.

Then we were transferred to the vegetable gardens and that was even better because we were supervised by a Czech gardener – not by the Nazis, for whom all the food was destined. Our job was to manage the positioning of the heavy glass frames that were placed over long beds filled with seedlings. There were potatoes and tomatoes and cucumbers and I loved to watch the little seedlings thrive. Each morning we lifted the frames out of the way to weed and water the plants. It was extremely physical work and, as well as the frames, we had to haul heavy watering cans – around fifty of them – to and fro which was very exacting, especially for someone who wasn't robust. My hands burned from gripping the metal handles and my fingers became increasingly stiff. At around 3 p.m., when the sun started to get lower, we had to carry the glass frames back and put them in place for the night.

My friends tell me I used to help keep their spirits up by singing to them from the operas while we worked, telling them the stories and then singing the arias, but I don't now remember doing that. I do know that every song, every poem I recited, and every opera I recalled was another means of escaping from the terrible reality.

The best part about working in the gardens was being able to steal some vegetables, especially when I had my arm in a sling because of a swollen lymph node in my armpit. That week I managed to hide some spinach and a whole cucumber, which I took straight to Mummy. She couldn't believe her eyes.

One beautiful spring day in May I was out in the garden working as usual. The sun was shining and I felt healthy and was sitting on the ground weeding, surrounded by vegetables and those beautiful flowers. I felt unusually happy. I began to hum a tune from my childhood, letting music seep back in.

Then a messenger boy appeared from the Magdeburg barracks and sent word for me to return to the ghetto immediately. 'Zuzana Růžičková should go back to Theresienstadt because her father is dangerously ill.'

I hurried to the hospital and when I got there I was horrified to see Tata vomiting and in excruciating pain. He was suffering terribly. He had been in perfect health the last time I'd seen him at the weekend but had suddenly collapsed. They took him to the doctor and then they tried to get him into surgery but it was impossible. We learned much later that he was suffering from volvulus, a bowel obstruction in which a loop of the intestine twists and causes necrosis and often death, but the doctors thought it was an infection and, in any event, they had little or nothing to treat it with. He needed to be operated on immediately, but there was no one available to help him.

It was so distressing to see him in that much pain and I wanted to stay by his side, but the doctors told me to leave. I stood outside the door for a while and then I went back to work. I had no idea that I was seeing him for the last time. My mother remained by his side until the end. It took four days. When she sensed that he was dying, she clasped his hand and told him tearfully, 'I hate all Germans! I will avenge your death.'

My father could hardly speak by then but he told her, 'Don't hate, Poldi … Hate is something that poisons your soul … Leave the revenge to God.' Those, his final words, were so significant to me, because he was an agnostic. They have remained with me always.

Jaroslav Růžička, my darling father, died on 13 May 1943. He was forty-nine years old. Aged sixteen, I was so shocked that I didn't even weep. I never did until many years later. I somehow buried the pain too deep.

My head was full of so many lovely memories of my Tata – of singing together as a family, of hiking together in the mountains with our trekking poles, of listening to him read Homer by the fire. I could remember the fresh smell of his skin after he'd shaved, and the way he'd scoop me into his arms when he came in from the shop. I tried to recall his fine baritone voice and the words of some of the songs he sang me. To my increasing distress, I found that I couldn't conjure up his face as clearly as I would have liked. Nor could I remember the precise colour of his eyes. Now it was too late – too late to see them again and too late to ask Mummy.

In that ghetto, where my father and I had been forcibly separated for the previous sixteen months, I had only been able to see him briefly, once a week, little knowing how short our time together would be. If we had been back home in Plzeň, he would almost certainly have survived. Mummy would have summoned the family doctor we knew so well, who would have had my father operated on immediately and then she would have cared for him during his recovery with the attention she had so often lavished on me.

The Nazis had murdered him just as they had murdered the 33,000 other Jews who died in Terezín from starvation, disease, cruelty or execution, and the 88,000 who were deported from there to the death camps. I was too young to want to seek the revenge my mother had spoken of, but I completely understood what my father had said about hatred poisoning the soul.

My father was cremated and his ashes were cast into the fast-flowing river, but I don't remember witnessing that or taking any comfort from the apple tree. My mother was too devastated to offer me any solace and became so desperate that she soon resolved to kill herself. She announced, 'I cannot live without my father, without my husband. I will not be able to survive that.'

It took repeated visits from my Uncle Karel to persuade her out of it. 'You mustn't abandon the child,' he insisted.

I was desperate too. I felt deserted by Mummy as well as by my father, because I knew she was planning to leave me there on my own. It was a double loss, because I felt I'd also lost her love. I was far too young to fully understand her grief. I went back to the children's home and only saw her once a week, but each time she was the same.

Fearing for my mother's sanity, the Council of Elders assigned me a guardian or 'foster father', a 27-year-old senior member of the Maccabi and a friend of Fredy's. Egon Redlich, known as Gonda, was one of those who helped Fredy care for the children. The hope was that, with such a person as a guardian on my records, my name wouldn't be put on one of the next transports East. Like my mother, though, I was so stricken by the loss of our darling Tata that I didn't believe anything could save us.

We knew.

We both knew that we would have to go.

My boyfriend Hanuš and all my other friends were extremely kind to me. But I lost all hope for a while and felt so abandoned by my mother. Was I not enough reason to carry on living? I had no inner strength. I was desperate. I wasn't even able to get up from my own bed. I kept lying there in some sort of coma. I was not even able to weep.

Uncle Karel did his best to convince me that Mummy would recover, but I wasn't sure. I don't know how he did it, but in the end he did persuade her to live for my sake and somehow life went on.

Then something new and terrible happened. In the autumn of 1943, when it looked as if the Axis forces might lose the war after the Battle of Stalingrad and their flight from North Africa and Sicily, a transport of some 1,200 Jewish orphans arrived in Terezín from Białystok in Poland. They were assigned a number of adult carers – most of them doctors and nurses, including Ottla Kafková, the youngest sister of the Czech writer Franz Kafka.

As was the norm in what had become a well-oiled machine, the new arrivals were taken to the processing centre to be disinfected and deloused. Unusually, though, these children were kept in isolation and all communication with them other than by their carers was forbidden.

Fredy, anxious for their welfare, managed to make contact with those in charge, but he was caught. His punishment was immediate imprisonment and a sentence that he would be sent East with the next transport of 5,000 Jews. Those of us who worked with him every day felt as if we'd been beheaded. There was worse to come.

Before Fredy left Terezín in a packed cattle wagon on 6 September 1943, he told his friends that he'd discovered why the Białystok children had been kept apart. The Swiss authorities had been showing an interest in the Nazi labour camps and were threatening to visit. The children from Bialystok were supposed to be part of a negotiated deal that would exchange them for German POWs in Switzerland. When they arrived in Terezín and were led to the showers to get clean, however, the children became hysterical and started screaming, 'Gas! Gas!' Huddled together, they refused to shower or even remove their filthy, lice-infested clothes.

That was the first time any mention of gas or gas chambers had reached Terezín and the news sent seismic shudders around the entire population. I heard it from those closest to Fredy and I half-believed it but I half didn't. I couldn't allow myself to accept that an entire race was being exterminated in its thousands. From that day onwards the atmosphere in the ghetto was incredibly tense.

The Białystok children's hysterical response to the Terezín showers cost them their lives and the entire group was later sent back to Auschwitz to be executed, along with their hapless carers.

Life seemed so hopeless then. Fredy disappeared and my father and my grandparents were dead. One of my father's sisters, Aunt Jiřina, went on the same transport as Fredy, as did my lovely friend Zuzana Heller and her family, including her doctor father. My mother was still very depressed, so all I had was Hanuš. Feeling isolated and vulnerable, I gradually grew away from my Maccabi group, even though I was meant to be one of its leaders. I didn't like its politics anymore, not least because there was so much infighting for influence and power, even for keeping people out of the transports.

I was so idealistic and always fought to do the right thing. I believed that any new information needed to be shared and that everyone should be told everything, whereas others felt that the leadership should know more in order to control the rest. In the end, I got out of politics and started to think for myself – just as my father had always hoped I would.

A severe epidemic of encephalitis broke out around this time. Many people died. None of my family and friends were affected at first, but then I got it. I developed terrible headaches and dizziness, and every time I stood up I fell over or tilted dramatically to one side. There were enforced neurological tests to see who might be suffering, but I didn't want to take the test and I didn't want to go to the hospital because I was afraid I'd be sent East or put in quarantine, which meant that I wouldn't be able to see Hanuš.

He and some of my friends tested me repeatedly to see if I could stand up straight on my own. 'Go to the left even if your head tells you to go right,' they suggested, and after much practice I somehow managed to trick my brain into standing straight – most of the time. When it came to the test I succeeded in keeping upright right until the German doctor deliberately dropped his pencil on the floor and told me to pick it up. The moment I bent over, of course, I lost all balance and fell over.

I was in the ghetto hospital for six weeks during August and September, which was torture, although it may have saved us from the September transport as the elders wouldn't have sent my mother without me. In quarantine, I couldn't see Mummy or Dagmar or Hanuš, although Hanuš would come to the window each day and wave. Fearing for my health, Mummy rallied and, when I was released, she helped me recover. I was grateful for her support and relieved that she had re-engaged with the world, even though I still believed that she and I would be sent East to face a dreadful death.

Suddenly there was a big change in Terezín. The Swiss Red Cross had expressed even more interest in visiting the ghetto along with representatives from the government of Denmark, who were especially concerned about the fate of almost five hundred Danish Jews there. The Nazis panicked and began their '*Verschonerung*', a beautification programme to transform the ghetto's filthy disease-ridden streets into something suitable for a possible Red Cross inspection. Not long afterwards, on a bitter November day, and having been notified two days earlier about a so-called 'census', the entire inhabitants of the ghetto were marched to a valley at gunpoint in order to be counted.

As we trudged down country roads to a vast open field, everybody was wondering what was going to happen. Few believed it was just to be counted, because they could easily check the paperwork and count us in the ghetto. Were they planning to kill us all somewhere where nobody could see? Did they only change their minds because they realised they would have to deal with all our bodies? None of us knew, but we feared that we were going to our deaths.

What actually happened was that we stood there for a whole day – all 40,000 of us – a swaying mass without food or water; people had to relieve themselves where they stood. It was very difficult, especially for the old. Some died. We teenagers from the Maccabi group each had one old person to care for and mine was an old lady who was frail. It was windy and cold and we were standing outside for a long time afraid of what might happen.

It was past midnight before we were finally allowed to go back to the ghetto, by which time we were all extremely tired and hungry. Guiding my old lady back across the muddy field in the dark I twisted my ankle, which made an already deeply disagreeable experience even worse. We were never told what the purpose of our ordeal was that day, but the Nazis continued with their beautification programme, setting up little shops full of goods we couldn't buy with 'Theresienstadt money' that they handed out but which wasn't real. They cleaned up the pavilion in the central square and had Karel Ančerl conduct chamber music concerts there. Everyone was suddenly given more freedom than before and encouraged to walk around, socialise, and play football. They wanted people to get a healthier colour to their pallid skin as they planned to film the entire visit for propaganda purposes.

With almost fifty thousand people in the ghetto at that time, the Nazis needed to make some space before the Red Cross came so new notifications were sent out to 5,000 people ten days before Christmas 1943. Just as I had dreaded, my mother and I received our draft ticket. After almost two years in Terezín watching others come and go, we were finally on the list.

Several people in my Maccabi group immediately assured me that I could be exempted, so I went to see Gonda Redlich, my 'foster father', to ask if that was true.

'I can only save you, Zuzana,' he told me. 'I am helpless to prevent your widowed mother from going on this transport.'

'Then I shall go with her,' I declared, refusing all his arguments as to why I should save myself.

I not only wanted to stay with my mother, I had to. Up until 1939, it had been my parents and me against the world. We had enjoyed such a close relationship and so many happy years, never suspecting that our lives would end this way. I was especially fearful for Mummy who, at forty-six years old, would probably be considered too old to work. Gonda insisted that my father would have wanted me to live, but I knew that Tata also wouldn't want us to be separated, and I prayed there might be something I could do to save her.

I spent the next few days in a tearful daze. We had been afraid for so long, seeing others leave, packing for them, getting into the routine, but it was terrible leaving the life we had built for ourselves there, even under those conditions. I was saying goodbye to all of that, as well as my friends and my 'sister' Dagmar. I was leaving sweet Hanuš, and the final resting place of my father and grandparents.

Incredibly, Mummy was suddenly completely calm and did all she could to help me. She was so strong for me, but I was not strong for her then, or later. I still have a bad conscience about that. We marked a mock Christmas together in Terezín, for which friends somehow managed to find a few little things to give us as gifts – a book or an item of clothing. We all did our best to pretend that we might get to use them.

With my mother's encouragement, I began to pack as my friends and family helped. My Uncle Karel urged me to be strong and to remember my proud father. My Aunt Kamila tried hard to be brave too. Dagmar and I said goodbye, embracing and promising to find each other 'when it's all over'. Hanuš said goodbye too, although we both wept. He wished me happy birthday, as in a few weeks' time – on 14 January 1944 – I would be seventeen.

My friend Dana helped me with my case, but when she saw all my musical notes she said softly, 'Don't take all those, Zuzka. They're needed here.' Mummy agreed.

I knew they were right, although I was very sorry to lose them. Sitting on my bunk, feeling strangely resigned to my fate, I sifted through the sheets and decided to copy just one page, the opening of Bach's touching sarabande to his English Suite No. 5 in E Minor.

It was the last piece of music I had played with Madame – a beautiful, soothing piece and one I'd always loved to play for her. Even though I knew it by heart, I found a scrap of paper and wrote down the first few chords to take with me.

'This will be my talisman,' I told my mother, attempting a smile. 'As long as I have this, there will still be some beauty in this world.'

7

Munich, 1956

Each time I played the harpsichord I felt more in tune with Bach and more out of tune with the piano. The harpsichord not only sounded completely different, it required an entirely different technique. For a time I managed to arrange some combined concerts so that I'd play the Bach concerto on the harpsichord and then the same piece on piano to illustrate the difference.

Whenever I did this, though, I had trouble with Bach's music especially, for it no longer sounded quite right to me on piano. The more I considered that he had only ever composed for organ, clavichord, or harpsichord, the more I knew I would soon have a difficult decision to make – which instrument would I favour?

It was quite a dilemma, for I could tell from the reaction of my audiences and the number of bookings I was getting that I could have a good piano career ahead of me, if I wanted one. Playing harpsichord exclusively would limit me tremendously at a time when every kind of music excited me, especially the new compositions – not least my husband's. I would also miss the many wonderful pieces written for piano, particularly Beethoven's sonatas, that would be impossible on the harpsichord. Not to mention the fact that no one was composing for the harpsichord anymore. It had fallen out of fashion and I was frustrated by how little sheet music I could get my hands on. It was such a shame that

Janacek didn't write anything for it, or Prokofiev or Hindemith or Bartók. I would so love to have had music by them.

I was also starting to make a name for myself as a recording artist, working with the flautist Václav Žilka and the Vlach Quartet performing the works of Couperin, Byrd and Rameau as well as many of the French and Italian baroque sonatas.

My problem was that Johann Sebastian Bach had stolen my heart when I was nine years old. He had become my philosophy and my confession. It was Bach's music that was embedded in me and which had saved me during the darkest days of my life. I wanted to know everything about him and his early music, so I read all the literature I could get my hands on, which was quite difficult at the time as so many books were forbidden. I had to order them from the National Library, and they took weeks or sometimes months to come.

The more I read about Bach the more I realised how much he had endured in his lifetime, and how much we had in common. His two constant companions were music and death. At the tender age of eight, he lost both of his parents and, soon afterwards, his beloved uncle – his father's identical twin. All of his siblings eventually died, and then his first wife, after the deaths in infancy of four of their seven children. Having remarried, Bach went on to father thirteen more children, eight of whom did not survive childhood.

His unbearable grief at these multiple tragedies is expressed in so much of his music, such as his Chromatic Fantasia and Fugue in D Minor. One whole passage of the fantasia is of despair, with chromatic chords going down and down. It's really a human being despairing of life, despairing of every hope. Then he starts with the fugue and that is above human suffering. It's about order. It's about law. It's about something more than human. For me, it always reaches the depths of suffering but then there is something above you, above your individual faith, and above your individual suffering. You always feel in his music that God is present somehow.

Bach also expresses his defiance in pieces like the *St Matthew Passion*, a sacred oratorio. That to me is the defiance of someone who has little or no control over the hand dealt by Fate. I, too, knew that feeling. Bach tells us that there is something above us, or near to us, which makes absolute sense. He tells us: don't despair. There is a sense to this life. There is a sense to this world. Only we don't always see it.

Almost involuntarily, I began to think in every situation, *What would Bach do?* How would he have handled the train journey to Auschwitz or slave labour in Germany? Which of his works would have best complemented the cultural explosion in Terezín? What would he have made of post-war Europe?

Playing Bach on the harpsichord made me think about him in quite unorthodox terms. In many ways I was a heretic, although the early-music movement of the 1950s and '60s still moves me and means so much because it opened so many doors. To begin with I was fascinated by the idea of him, but I realised that Bach was becoming a kind of ideology for me, and I hate ideology. So whenever I listened to CDs of his music or on the radio I found myself wondering if Bach would have played it like that. Then I began to question why anyone should play it just as he did. Why couldn't we have fun with it? Why couldn't we mess around with the music as a pure form, beyond any restrictions or rules? It is more than three hundred years since Bach was alive and there might be something in his music that even he didn't appreciate.

I think about those beautiful Roman statues that archaeologists now tell us were originally painted in garish colours, whereas we have always praised them for their pure white marble. Which was right? Does it matter? Everyone can have their own opinion and their own interpretation, based on their own experience; Viktor taught me that. An excellent composer and pianist and a very good conductor, he was always so generous about sharing his own music. He would play it in a certain way, but whenever someone else played it slightly differently, he would never be upset. Instead he would tell them, 'I had a different idea, but I love what you are doing.'

Similarly, I sometimes found in Bach's work things which he may not have meant or didn't even know, but which he would have eventually discovered through listening to the interpretation of his music by others.

Bach had always resonated with me, but the more I played his music on the harpsichord after the war, the deeper that resonance felt. And it wasn't just Bach that made me want to concentrate on the harpsichord alone. In 1955, I recorded two harpsichord concertos by Czech composer Jiří Antonín Benda with the Prague Chamber Orchestra and felt completely at home.

Not that playing the harpsichord was easy. I didn't have my own instrument and if I was requested, say, in Brno or Bratislava, I had to borrow one, find a tuner, go to a garage, find a driver with a truck and ask him to transport it for me. 'Please would you take me, my harpsichord and my tuner?' I'd plead. 'I don't know if I can pay you enough, but would you just do it for me?' It was really pioneering work.

In 1955, my good friends in the Smetana Quartet – whom I often accompanied together and individually – alerted me to a leaflet they had come across on one of their tours advertising the fifth annual ARD International Music Competition for young musicians.

'It's next September and it has a category for harpsichord for the first time!' they told me excitedly. 'We think you should apply.' There were also categories for singing, piano, violin, flute, viola and horn.

The thought of listening to other harpsichordists from the West playing music I may not even have encountered yet was completely thrilling to me, but the competition was held in Munich, Germany – a country I had a terrible fear of visiting.

Shaken, I hurried home to tell Viktor about the contest and to share my fears. I found him in a familiar pose – sitting in an armchair reading – so I lit a cigarette and sat down opposite and began to discuss the idea with him. Apart from the fact that I have never been a big fan of competitions, as I don't believe one can judge art, I had a strange feeling about going to Germany and never imagined that I would.

It was just over a decade since I had left the camps, and I was still so frightened of meeting some of the SS or the prisoner-functionaries who had treated us so cruelly. Only a handful of them were caught and prosecuted and many continued to live quite openly in Europe and lead regular lives. I knew a Holocaust survivor who bumped into a former guard from Auschwitz completely by chance and the experience was extremely distressing for her.

Viktor and I talked and talked over several days. As always, he listened attentively and then began to debate the pros and cons with me. Eventually, he said, 'Well, you know you are not an entertainer, Zuzana. You are an artist. If you were a mere entertainer I would tell you not to go to Munich. If you do go, however, you will be returning part of their former culture to them. You will be giving Bach back to Germany.'

He went on to press his point further. 'The more I think about it, the more I think that it is really your duty to go there – as a Jewess and as a former prisoner. You will be showing them that somebody who is not German and not an Aryan can play Bach. You will be proving to them that Hitler was not the last word.'

Eleven years after the war, we were still in shock at what such a cultured nation as Germany had done in allowing the Nazis to commit such atrocities. Before the Second World War, we were taught that if you are educated and cultured you will go on to develop a higher morality. Germany was the epitome of that principle and had strengthened our faith in the idea that mankind can improve through the arts and sciences. To regress to such a barbaric level and do it in such an efficient way was something that robbed us of real faith in humanity. It damaged the whole of European culture, and not only because of the Jewish question.

Musically, we still feel the after-effects of the war because we are afraid of big gestures and pathos. We no longer believe in truth. I think there is often too much frivolous playing of music, a belittling of it in some ways, without the reverence it deserves.

The more I pondered what Viktor had said, the more I thought to myself, if I refuse to go to the land of Bach then where else should I refuse to go – France or England? How about all the other countries that knew about the Holocaust and did nothing? They too were culpable, but if I took that view then I wouldn't be able to go anywhere.

I realised then that it was my moral duty to put aside my fears and – if I had the chance – to play Bach in Munich and to play it well.

First, though, I had to get permission from the Academy of Performing Arts and from the Ministry of Culture. I had to play before a committee that would also look into my political character and then I had to pass the ministerial selection procedure before entering the qualifying round. I believed I was probably good enough to enter the competition, but never for one moment did I consider that I might stand a chance of winning any prize. All I wanted was to hear other young harpsichordists play, because there was nothing in Prague. I had only those old records of Landowska, so I knew nothing about the contemporary harpsichord interpretation and there was no one else apart from my professor playing this instrument in my country.

I was lucky, because when I sought permission to leave my musical director, Magda Reichlová, was already an admirer who attended all my concerts and she said, 'Why not?' Magda was a very brave woman. She was disabled and died quite young but she was the one that helped me the most to get to Munich. She also gave permission for two flautists – Jaroslav Josífko and Jan Hecl – and a pianist, Mirka Pokorná, to accompany me so that they could try to win their categories too. Jaroslav was a professor of flute, so they trusted him to oversee us and make sure that we didn't try to escape.

The authorities did more than just trust us, though. They were very well informed, chiefly because our neighbour could hear every word we said. They knew whether Viktor and I really loved each other as much as we professed, or at least enough not to defect. There was also a street committee, comprised of the concierges from each apartment block who spied for the state and had the power to give every citizen a good or bad reference as a political character.

One time I went to the passport office near the Old Town Square to collect my documents for another trip organised by the ministry,

zana's mother, Leopoldina

Zuzana's father, Jaroslav, in WWI

Zuzana and her mother

Zuzana's grandparents, Heinrich and Paula

Zuzana with her cousins and playmates, Hanuš and Jiří, in Dobris

The Růžička toy store in Plzeň

gmar and Zuzana: like sisters

Zuzana and her parents, Jaroslav and Leopoldina

Zuzana's first teacher, Madame Marie Provazníková-Šašková

Thin and sickly, but still practising

Zuzana and her beloved parents

Zuzana and her parents on a hiking holiday in the mountains, before the war

zana, third from right, at Bergen-Belsen, with some of the medical staff who saved her life

Zuzana as student at the Academy

but when I got there they told me, 'You have a problem. You don't have the permission of your street committee to leave the country.' This was the first I had heard of any such committee.

I went to see my neighbour and asked if he knew anyone on the committee that I could speak to. He claimed ignorance, but at 9 p.m. that night there was a ring on our doorbell from someone we'd never previously met.

'Hello, I'm a neighbour,' he said. 'I would like to get better acquainted. Could I get a glass of wine?'

I knew exactly what he was there for, so I invited him in and let him look around our two rooms so that he could see that our bags weren't packed and we weren't about to flee the country. The next day I heard that I had approval from the committee and could collect my passport after all.

Viktor and I learned early on in our marriage that we had to develop a secret double life – a public one in which we spoke and behaved in a certain way, and then a private life where we could express ourselves freely. This was how we lived for more than forty years – in a permanent climate of secrecy and fear.

Although I was up against some impressive competitors from all over the world for the Munich competition, including Karl Richter, a German harpsichordist who I was convinced would win, I was rather amazed when I passed the first round of auditions and then the second.

Astonishingly, I then made it to the finals where scores of competitors would be judged by – among others – the German composer and former First World War soldier Carl Orff, the Hungarian Jewish conductor Georg Solti, the anti-fascist German composer Karl Amadeus Hartmann, the French composer and former prisoner of war Olivier Messiaen, and the Swiss composer and harpsichordist Marguerite Roesgen-Champion.

In preparation for our trip, the flautists and I were coached on how to behave in the West and had to promise to contact our embassy as soon as we arrived so that we could be properly monitored. It was the first time I had been to Germany since the war but a lovely young woman called Hannelore, who shepherded us everywhere and referred to me jokingly as '*Zuzana mit dem unaussprachlichen Namen*' ('Zuzana with the unpronounceable name'), met us at the train station and looked after us very well. When she saw that I had a huge edition of the Goldberg Variations, she gave me her own smaller one. We got along so well that we stayed in touch and wrote to each other for a long time afterwards.

As we had no money and were allowed to leave the country with no more than the equivalent of about $10, we could only afford a cheap boarding house in the suburbs of Munich. Soon after we arrived I was informed that I would be playing the very next day – 3 September – in front of an audience at the Sophiensaal, the smallest concert hall of a former Bavarian king's palace. Accompanied by Munich's finest radio orchestra, the event was sponsored by several German radio stations and would be broadcast live. I was to be the first contestant, on stage at 9 a.m.

The obligatory part of my programme would be to perform the introductory aria and the first seven of Bach's Goldberg Variations, a solo piece. For my free selection I had chosen Bach's *The Art of Fugue*, an intellectual piece I'd loved since childhood, and part of Benda's Keyboard Concerto in G Minor which I was to play with the Bavarian Radio Symphony, headed by the Czech conductor and composer Rafael Kubelík. I would be one of twenty-one harpsichord contestants, the rest being from America, Brazil, Italy, Spain, Germany, Austria, Belgium, France, and Luxembourg. Aside from Marguerite Roesgen-Champion, the judges for the harpsichord alone would include Hans Sittner, the president of the Vienna Academy of Music, Eliza Hansen, a professor of piano and harpsichord in Hamburg, Edith Picht-Axenfeld, a German pianist and harpsichordist, and Philipp Jarnach, the French-born composer and founder of the Hamburg Music Academy, who was appointed chairman. They would be awarding points for technical skill, artistic form and personality.

I had never lost my stage fright and – as always – it built up and up increasingly as the performance drew closer until I was in quite a state. The only consolation was that I knew it would drop away as soon as I sat on the stool. I couldn't fight it and in the end I chose not to, as I considered it a natural expression of tension. If I hadn't felt it, I would have believed that something was wrong. Nevertheless, the eve of a concert was always the most difficult to get through and that night in Munich was the worst.

To my horror, and knowing that I was due to play the following morning, I was told that the orchestra would not be attending the finals after all. 'You will have to play without them and prepare your concerts yourselves,' the competition officials announced, without giving any further explanation. We learned much later that the reason for this was that the chief of the orchestra, the Czech Rafael Kubelík who had fled to Britain after the communist putsch, refused to accompany anyone from a communist country. As the other finalists were all from the West, he was refusing to play with me because I was from Czechoslovakia.

I was so upset and angry, because the Benda concerto I had chosen would sound ludicrous without an orchestra. Fool that I was, if I had chosen Bach instead of being so patriotic and picking Benda it would not have been a problem. Kubelík knew that. Other musicians who'd chosen different works might have been able to play all the way through, but I would be playing eight bars and then waiting during the gaps where the orchestra was meant to come in. It would be like a stereo player with only one speaker, or an actor reciting his part without a partner. The entire recital would be painful and farcical.

It was a good thing that I was angry, because I was able to channel that and put it to some use. Determined not to make a fool of myself in front of the audience, I hurried to the Royal Conservatory where the competition was to take place and, offering up my last five Deutschmarks, I persuaded a security guard to let me in with the cleaning lady at 6 a.m. the following morning – just as I had done at the Rudolfinum.

Then I went back to my boarding house with the score and stayed up all night, learning all the orchestra parts of the Benda concerto by heart. There wasn't enough time to learn it all but I managed to memorise the first two movements, which would have to do.

After my dawn practice in the same set of buildings where the Munich Agreement had been signed in September 1938 – a fact that affected me deeply – I tried to find my way back to the guesthouse and got lost. It was a Sunday morning and there was no one on the street to ask. Eventually I spotted a priest, so I approached him and asked for his help. He spoke very nicely and offered to show me the way, but then he asked me where I came from. When I told him that I was from Prague, he made the sign of the cross and ran away.

I eventually found my way back to the lodgings and prepared myself some more. When it was my turn to walk on stage early the next day, I stood in the wings shaking as usual – only this time it wasn't with nerves but with fury. I didn't even have time to wonder if there might have been any former SS members in the audience, as I had previously long feared.

Completely oblivious to the audience, I sat down and started to play the opening bars. Out of the corner of my eye, I noticed that certain members of the jury had dropped their pencils and were staring at me, wondering how on earth I was going to continue without an orchestra.

Summoning up all my powers of memory I played the first movement by heart – including all the orchestra parts – and when I was about to start the second, praying that it would be sufficient, the head of the jury interrupted and told me to stop.

'Thank you, Miss Růžičková,' he said. 'We have heard enough.'

Still furious and determined not to be sidelined, I told him that I would like to be allowed to play the second movement. When one is young, one is a gambler and I took my chance. If they had asked me to play the third movement, I wouldn't have been able to do it because I didn't know it.

The second movement was slower and it went as well as could be expected, so when it was finished I stopped playing and left the stage, relieved that the experience was over but saddened that I hadn't been given a sporting chance.

There was no winner of the harpsichord competition that year – and, strangely, ARD never offered that category again – but I was utterly amazed when the jury awarded me a 500-mark '*Förderungsprämie*' or 'development grant' that was given to the contestant the jury felt was most worthy. My award meant that, as a laureate, I was also invited to play in the prestigious prizewinners' concert at the end of the competition. Their ruling read: 'The jury of the international radio competition awarded Ms Růžičková's prize in recognition of her performances in the harpsichord category. Her excellent technique, her musical intelligence, her strong and distinctive expression gave us the impression of an artistic personality who has great prospects. Her play is fiery and consistent: the harpsichord … corresponds to the fantasy and discipline that adds to her grace.'

Almost more astounding than their verdict were their additional comments, though, which I couldn't wait to tell Viktor. 'The tradition of playing harpsichord is still so young and not yet known that it would be very beneficial if Mrs Růžičková had the opportunity to hear other harpsichords and if she became acquainted with the tradition of organ art in order for her knowledge of style to be expanded and strengthened. We would very much welcome Mrs Růžičková to continue her studies in France or Germany.'

My minders from the Czech embassy immediately seized my cash prize, giving me just a hundred marks of it – but still an enormous sum for me. I didn't mind one bit. That night was one of the happiest of my life. Having spent the day celebrating by shopping and buying three cashmere sweaters for Viktor and two for me, I blew the rest of my prize money on oysters and champagne to enjoy with my fellow Czechs, the flautists who had not won their category.

We drank the champagne but had to discard the German oysters, which were horrible and not at all fresh. I didn't care. Nothing could spoil my happiness. I was twenty-nine years old. I had been honoured in a most prestigious competition for playing the harpsichord, the instrument I decided there and then would be the one I would dedicate the rest of my life to. I was so in love with Viktor, and finally able to feel the kind of joy again that I had known as a child.

As with everything in my life, though, there was hope and then there was a loss of hope.

After Munich I was invited to play in several socialist countries, including Hungary, Poland, and Bulgaria, although when a new director of the Soviet equivalent of Pragokoncert was appointed in Bulgaria, I wasn't invited so much as he was an anti-Semite. He once complained, 'When I look at the programme, it is one Jew after another here,' adding: 'So I reserve Zuzana Růžičková from Prague and she's yet another Jew!' What he didn't understand was that running a concert schedule without Jews was quite difficult, because they would have had no one else other than the Soviets: David Oistrakh, a violinist, and pianist Emil Gilels.

With my new status, I was even allowed to teach abroad – which was a great irony, as I wasn't allowed to teach Czech students the piano or harpsichord because of my refusal to join the Communist Party. Not only was I forbidden from teaching anything but piano to composers, but the harpsichord wasn't even on the curriculum of the academy, as it was still considered a religious and feudal instrument. It wouldn't be included until 1984.

The authorities would ask me, 'How can you educate young people when you have no Marxist–Leninist education yourself, and you have to explain the court of Louis XVI or Bach, with all the religion in his sacred music? You are not ideologically prepared to teach students this instrument.' It was another black mark against me and one I didn't have an answer for. Thankfully, other countries felt differently. The Germans, Belgians, and Swiss invited me back repeatedly and I was able to perform Viktor's two-part canonic inventions at the Third International Harpsichord Festival in Switzerland.

After Stalin died, followed just days later by our first communist president, Klement Gottwald, we seemed finally rid of all these terrible dictators. Nikita Khrushchev, who came to power in the Soviet Union, claimed he would remove 'the stain of Stalinism', and began by freeing thousands of political prisoners and exposing the worst of Stalin's cruelty. He allowed more freedom in the arts and curbed many of the illegal activities of the security agencies. It really felt like a wind of change blowing our way from Moscow and we lived in a much better atmosphere. We were not quite so afraid anymore.

Then in 1957 the composer and harpsichordist Marguerite Roesgen-Champion, a devotee of Wanda Landowska, followed through on the Munich jury's incredible offer for me to continue my studies in the West by inviting me to Paris for a six-month scholarship. She said I could study with her and give classes to her students while listening to other harpsichord players and experiencing something of French culture. I feared it wouldn't be permitted, not so much because it was in the West, but because it would mean that I couldn't be earning anything for the state.

Oh, but I so wanted to go. I was originally meant to study under Wanda Landowska in Paris as a teenager, but Hitler had put an end to that. The city had held a kind of mythical allure for me ever since. I would never forget how excited my father had been at the thought of accompanying me to the French capital, chattering excitedly to Mummy about how she could join us and what fun we'd all have.

Viktor was thrilled for me too and insisted that I should go if the authorities allowed it, even though we would miss each other terribly for the six months that we'd be apart. Having been denied his doctorate and his professorship from the academy, he was still working in the children's music department of Prague Radio, trying to make the most of the only position the authorities allowed him. He knew what opportunities this scholarship would give me and how I longed to visit the most romantic city in the world, even if it meant going alone while he stayed behind as a hostage.

My benefactor did everything she could to persuade the authorities to allow me to take up the scholarship. A woman in her sixties and from Geneva, she had lived in Paris since the 1920s, composing for orchestra and choral works, piano, harpsichord and chamber music. She arranged everything perfectly. My musical director also helped me enormously and managed to secure me both permission to leave the country and a small allowance. I couldn't believe my luck.

Once I'd arrived by train from Prague and reported to the Czech embassy so that their spies could keep an eye on me, I went immediately to one of Madame Roesgen-Champion's classes and began to play for her students. It was such a revelation to work alongside other young people as passionate about the harpsichord as I was. I'd been so isolated in Czechoslovakia, where it sometimes felt as though I was the only person left in the world who cared deeply for this instrument, and for Bach. No one was composing for harpsichord, and even if they were acquainted with it, they didn't like to play it.

In Paris, though, I found myself surrounded by enthusiastic musicians as eager to hear my interpretations of baroque works as I was to hear theirs. I discovered that, in most instances, my way of thinking was often different to theirs. I tended to think of music as pure sound that opened up vivid visualisations in my mind, as opposed to just symbols on a page. Whenever I played Bach I conjured up tales from the Greek classics, and could almost hear my father's voice in the salon of my youth. I might think of a poem by Rilke, or a favourite passage by Mann. The harmonic function of each phrase inspired me and was pivotal to moving me to the next one. As a romantic and a heretic, I didn't feel that there was one historic or 'correct' way to interpret Bach, but rather that we should, as individuals, employ our own artistry and passion and reach the essence of the piece.

I still admired the work of Wanda Landowska very much, especially her musicality, her consciousness of form and her personality. I loved the way she handled the harpsichord, the way she thought about the instrument. She instigated its revival. But I had come to learn that there were two lines of approach to the harpsichord. Landowska's line was to technically combine all the good things that the harpsichord had acquired during its evolution up to the end of the eighteenth century. She saw the harpsichord as a modern instrument that would continue developing. The other line was that of the French musician Arnold Dolmetsch, who had these so-called 'authentic' interpretations and 'authentic' instruments. I still think that the harpsichord will evolve, because at the moment one kind of instrument is used almost everywhere, which, of course, is not very historical at all. It is most pleasant to hear and also not so difficult to build, but if you look at Bach's time, the building of the instruments was so eclectic.

*

My Paris accommodation was in a small room at the embassy near the Eiffel Tower and my schedule was extremely full, but I sent letters home to Viktor every week telling him of my experiences, being careful not to say anything that could get either of us into trouble. Within a few weeks of arriving I was asked to give my first recital, a concert with the singer Germaine Fougier in which I played several solo pieces by Couperin, which received some good reviews. At my second concert I performed more Couperin, but also Byrd, Bach's Italian Concerto, and Josef Mysliveček's Sonata in A Major, a concert I repeated later that year in Bulgaria. More kind reviews followed, so my reputation was growing in a way that I hoped would lead to future international offers. The French students were all so friendly and hosted parties for me in their apartments where we drank French wine, smoked French cigarettes, and danced and sang and talked of politics and art and books with the kind of freedom I had never known before.

The consulate at the embassy was a man named Vladimír who was also kind to me and we remained friends for many years. He told me where to go and where the Czech spies would look for me – especially at Les Deux Magots cafe, a popular tourist destination that was far too rich for my budget anyway. There was an important anniversary of Lenin while I was there and Vladimír was meant to produce something about Lenin's time in Paris, so he took me to the Café de la Rotonde in Montparnasse, where Lenin used to go, and asked if there was anyone there who remembered him. We were told that an old waiter was still alive and they gave us his address, so we went to his tiny apartment and asked him about Lenin.

The old man shook his head and said he couldn't recall anyone by that name. Inspiration then came to Vladimír. 'What about Mr Ulyanov?' he asked, wondering if Lenin might have used his real name, rather than the revolutionary *nom de guerre* he'd adopted as homage to his exile in Siberia at a place near the Lena river.

As soon as the consulate mentioned the name Ulyanov, the old man's face lit up and he said, 'Oh yes! Whatever happened to him? He was very nice to me.'

I had so many plans for my half-year in that lovely city. There were so many places I wanted to see and so many museums I wanted to visit, especially the Louvre, which had been emptied of all its treasures during the war to keep them from the Nazis and then gradually restocked. I spent all my spare time at the Louvre, wandering from room to room in awe, when I should really have been studying French music. I also hoped to attend as many concerts as I could, and to improve my French conversation with Madame Roesgen-Champion and her students.

My allowance was extremely limited, the equivalent of about £10 a week as well as whatever my mother had been able to give me, and I was hungry all the time. I packed salami and sardines and ate them during my breaks as I sat somewhere along the banks of the River Seine. I bought French bread and butter – and oh, what butter! I had never tasted anything so heavenly. Every now and again a colleague with money would invite me to dinner and I would devour everything in sight. I always made sure that there were a few francs left over each week for some wine or a coffee and a cigarette in one of the famous street cafes.

I loved those cafes and I loved the culture. I loved the jazz and the pop music and the clothes and the art nouveau Métro stations. The women were beautiful and so well dressed and the men very handsome. Everything was a surprise to me. There were so many cars, unbelievable cars, and so many beautiful places to see. I couldn't help but compare it to Prague, where there were few vehicles and the buildings, although grand, seemed uniformly grey and drab.

Walking the streets of the French capital I fell completely in love with Paris. I was extremely realistic about the West and never for one moment thought it was Paradise. Far from it. But I revelled in the psychological freedom of Paris and was envious of the Parisians' ability to do and say as they liked. The time I spent there was, without doubt, one of the happiest of my life.

My marvellous dream was unexpectedly interrupted, however. In my absence, a famous French conductor and composer by the name of Manuel Rosenthal had been invited to Prague by the

League of Composers to hear some contemporary Czech music. Rosenthal had been chief conductor of the National Orchestra of Paris as well as conducting all over the world. The son of a Russian Jewess, he had fought against the Germans, was captured and sent to forced labour, then escaped and worked for the French resistance until the end of the war.

Monsieur Rosenthal was introduced to Viktor both as a composer but also for his work at Prague Radio. When he heard Viktor's Woodwind Quintet he was immediately interested in him. 'What else have you written?' he asked, so Viktor told him of his Concerto for Violoncello, Op. 8. After he heard that played at the academy, the conductor immediately offered to perform it with the Orchestre de Paris and the renowned cellist Jacques Neilz at the art deco Théâtre des Champs-Elysées in Paris. This was the most marvellous opportunity for Viktor and a chance for him to establish himself as an international composer for the first time. He immediately agreed.

'You must, of course, come to the concert,' Rosenthal insisted.

If we had lived in any other European country at that time, my husband's crowning achievement would have been one we could have joyfully celebrated together as he joined me in Paris and we attended his debut together. From the moment he told me of Rosenthal's offer, though, we both knew that, if Viktor was allowed to leave Czechoslovakia, then we would have to swap places.

There was nothing for it. The authorities would never permit us to be somewhere as 'dangerous' as Paris at the same time. Abandoning my scholarship and all my Parisian dreams after just three months, I packed my few belongings and said goodbye to my fellow students.

With tears in my eyes as I wondered if I would ever see that beautiful city again, I caught a train to travel home and allow Viktor his moment of glory, which was – naturally – the most wonderful success.

8

Auschwitz II-Birkenau, 1943

Hell began immediately. Leaving the Terezín ghetto on 19 December 1943, hundreds of us – men, women and children, young and old – were crammed into wagons like human cattle so that we could only stand, no one could sit. It was bitterly cold. It was dark. We had one bucket between fifty of us and we were not able to do our necessary hygiene. The journey took three days, as we mostly only travelled at night. There was no dignity.

We had just one window, high up, and only a few could see out as we crossed the foreign flatlands heading East. We didn't get any food and we didn't get anything to drink. We were so very hungry, but the thirst was worse. Our tongues were swollen with thirst.

We finally arrived somewhere late at night, and the doors were thrown open only to have horrible white light shone in our eyes. We were pulled out of those wagons onto the snow in a dreadful state. Immediately, there was shouting – '*Raus! Raus! Schnell! Schnell!*' Dogs barking. SS barking. Guards kicking, shoving, and cursing. All the time that hard light in our eyes.

I have never been so frightened in my life.

Mummy and I were momentarily separated in all the noise and confusion, as men were parted from women and children and mothers cried and babies howled. Disorientated and terrified, I had no chance to reach for Mummy's steadying hand as I lurched forwards with everyone else, clouds of steam rising from our stinking bodies in the cruel night air. It was all so fast and efficient and terrifying, as we were pushed and prodded and shouted into line by the SS and by men in striped uniforms bearing sticks.

Mercifully, Mummy and I found each other again in a long line for the open-backed trucks that were waiting to ferry us deeper into the vast camp. Standing numbly in the bitter wind, arms wrapped around ourselves, heads down, we remained glued together, puffing steam and avoiding eye contact with any of the guards, just as my mother had drilled me to do.

In my right hand, numb with cold, I still gripped Bach's beautiful sarabande from the English Suite and I looked down and read it to myself because it was somehow essential for me at that moment to keep it in my head.

The first truck was almost fully loaded by the time I was next in line to be pushed onto it. Hands reached for me and I was pulled up to join the other fifty or so watery-eyed souls. As soon as I regained my balance, I turned to reach for my mother too.

To my horror, the guards suddenly barred her way with rifles and one of them banged the back of the truck to let the driver know that he could move away. The soldiers shoved Mummy and the rest of the prisoners backwards, knocking several over like dominoes as a second vehicle pulled alongside.

My mother's strict instructions that I should never do anything to attract any attention to myself abandoned me completely then, along with all my reason. We had been together in the ghetto for two terrible years. I'd volunteered to go with her to this place in the belief that it would be better to die together. Part of me hoped I might even save her, but I could only do that if we remained together. Hysterical, I began to scream and call out to her above the wind as she grappled with the guards. My hands stretched out to her plaintively while my fellow prisoners clung on to me to stop me from leaping off the truck.

As our vehicle lurched forward, I let out such a wail of distress that my mother looked up to see my mouth and hands open as my precious scrap of music flew from my fingers and spun away from me in the choking exhaust fumes.

Breaking free from her guards, she rushed forward to rescue my snippet of hope as shrill voices rang out behind her. She was the only human being in the world who knew what that piece of music meant to me. Sprinting like a woman half her age, she somehow plucked the score from the air and ran to our truck, offering it up to me inches from the tailgate. Her only thought was to return my talisman to me in what she must have thought would be her final, parting gift.

Desperate, I reached for my mother only to be pushed aside as others from behind me stretched out and snatched hold of her coat. Hoisted upwards by her shoulders, arms and lapels – anything they could grab – my dear, sweet Mummy was pulled unceremoniously into the back of the truck with me, her hands outstretched and her expression as astonished as mine.

Stunned, I looked back at the mayhem she'd created as guards chased after her, shouting and waving their rifles. Numb, I watched as the fragment of Bach's sweet sarabande that had almost certainly saved her life flew up into the air to swirl and dance triumphantly in the inky darkness.

We became mere numbers in Auschwitz II-Birkenau on our second day. Mine was 73289, tattooed neatly into my left arm by a pale Polish woman with a sunken face who refused to make eye contact. Whatever identity I'd had up until that moment was eradicated by the point of her needle, which scratched at my skin and drew more than my blood.

The previous night Mummy and I, along with the rest of our unhappy group, had been pulled off the truck after it stopped deep inside the camp and funnelled through long corridors of barbed wire. There was no moon and the only light came from the searchlights and the red flames leaping three metres high into the sky from two infernal chimneys in the distance. Filling the night air was the smell of singed hair and burned meat.

Pushed along by silent prisoner-functionaries in striped uniforms supervised by a handful of SS, we were marched in close formation in groups of five. We had to cross a bleak, snowy plain punctuated only by the long, low shapes of hundreds of wooden blocks, each with its own chimney, as far as the eye could see.

Head down again and with a bitter, dry taste in my mouth, I watched my mother's feet in front of me and tried to follow her step, as she in turn attempted to keep time with the woman in front of her. I only lifted my head slightly when I heard the rhythmic crunch of other feet passing close by.

Glancing up warily, I thought I was hallucinating when I spotted Fredy Hirsch in a group of ten men being marched in fives in the opposite direction. He saw me in the same instant. 'Oh, you are already here,' he said, sadly, his face half-hidden by his cap. Then, dipping slightly as if he'd dropped a glove he hissed, 'Tell them you are fifteen!' and then he was gone.

Breathless, almost losing my beat, I half-stumbled into my mother, who gestured urgently for me to get back into line. The moment had passed in a second, but dear Fredy, who must have somehow remembered that I was almost seventeen, had risked his life once more to warn me to claim I was younger and thus save me from being sent away to slave labour.

Deeper into the camp – our section of which was known as BIIb – we were pushed into a huge block in what we later discovered was known as the *Familienlager*, or family camp, a special dispensation for those *Häftlinge* or inmates recently arrived from Terezín. This privilege was granted us only because of the continued international interest in the fate of prominent Jews from Czechoslovakia. Members of the Swiss Red Cross were threatening to visit Auschwitz as well as Terezín.

The family camp was another charade however – something for appearance only. The supposed privilege of being there didn't amount to much beyond not being gassed immediately. The wooden blocks that housed us were never designed for soldiers but for horses. Their chimneys were built to release smoke from fires that were rarely lit and which were supposed to heat the entire block via a horizontal flue that ran through the centre of the building. To accommodate us, the horse stalls had been lined with crude pine bunks, three tiers high, and the only private space was the groom's room at the far end of the building that was reserved for the prisoner in charge of the block. Once we were pushed inside with approximately six hundred others, everyone scrambled for a place, shoving others out of their way. Mummy and I eventually found a bottom bunk, the least popular. There was no room to sit up and with both of us lying side by side it was cramped and unforgiving, with no mattress, just straw. But at least we were together and could keep each other warm in that little pocket.

There was still no food or water and we were so very thirsty, especially the children, who were crying pitifully. Once we were all inside, still reeking from the train, the air became vile – making our thirst even worse – so several people smashed some of the windows on the top tier to suck at the snow from the ledges.

Looking across to the men's block through a broken window, they watched a prisoner venture outside to collect snow for the same purpose. He must have thought the guards had gone, but he only took a few steps before a searchlight found him and a shot rang out. With a collective gasp, we realised he'd been killed.

The next horror was a visit by the *Lager älteste*, the elder in charge of our part of the camp, who marched into our block with half a dozen guards, made us all line up and shone his torch into frightened faces before selecting the prettiest young women. This *älteste* was a hideous creature whose name we later discovered was Arno Böhm, the German pimp who'd volunteered to hang the young men in Terezín. Sobbing quietly, the hapless girls were ordered to follow him to his nearby block.

Within minutes, we heard the sound of music being played badly on poorly tuned instruments by what I later discovered was the camp orchestra. It was coming from the *älteste*'s block and as the night wore on, the discordant cacophony could no longer drown out SS voices rising in drink and the occasional cries of their victims. I recognised the music as the 'Marinarella', by the Czech composer Julius Fučík, a rousing and popular march composed for a military band.

It was to become my most hated piece.

*

Dark rumours flew around our block like bats on that first terrible night. The prisoner-functionaries in charge of us were veterans of the camp who informed us we were in Auschwitz II-Birkenau in Poland and that the guards could do as they pleased with us. They then confirmed that there were gas chambers after all and that the flames from the ovens lighting the skies and the pervading smell of overcooked meat was the grisly residue of bodies being burned.

I was still only a child and the shock and horror of what I learned that night paralysed me emotionally and physically. It was no longer possible to believe that the Nazis would allow us to live and it seemed probable that we'd be treated most cruelly before we were murdered. The doubts that had been clawing at our minds were all confirmed. To see the fires from the furnaces and smell burnt flesh in the air, to realise that one man can liquidate another in such an inhumane way, brings about the collapse of any faith in humanity and in mankind. It was a loss of all hope and I lost control of myself then.

All I could do was curl up in my mother's arms and cry, 'I don't want to die, Mummy – I want to live – I so want to live!' I will never forgive myself for the way I behaved that night and most nights afterwards, which must have been unbearable for my mother. In less than a year, her mother had committed suicide and she had lost her parents-in-law. She'd watched her husband die in agony. She feared that the rest of her family from Dobříš had perished because they were nowhere to be found in the family camp. She must have been in her own private hell with nothing she could do or say to comfort or protect her only child – the last surviving member of her family.

What shattered us most was how perfectly thought out the whole thing was. If people kill in times of war or out of spontaneous emotion or passion, even the wrong emotion, then that is something different. This was intentional genocide, organised to the last detail and planned so precisely by representatives of a nation we had always held in the highest regard. That was something so heinous that none of us were really able to express how we felt about it, and we are haunted by it, even now.

My mother and I hardly slept, but at dawn we were rudely awoken by shouting and banging before being driven outside into the morning fog. It was roll call, known as the *Appell*, held in the muddy open ground between blocks. The methodical counting of the thousand or more new prisoners took at least two hours and was accompanied by the camp orchestra playing that ghastly 'Marinarella' again. There was an accordion player named Otto Fröhlich and two string players and that was almost all they played.

When the *Appell* was finally over and we were dismissed, we turned to hurry back to the block to try to get warm but were instead screamed at to form a new line and follow the guards. Fearing the worst, we stuck close together as we staggered and stumbled through deep snow to the 'Sauna' building in the woods at the furthest point of the camp.

Once inside, we were divested of all our clothes by expressionless fellow prisoners, and our precious belongings immediately carried off, no doubt to be picked clean. Stripped naked, we were then deloused, pushed under the cold trickles of water that passed as showers, and tattooed, but not shaved or gassed – a fact that surprised us, even in our state of shock. We didn't even mind the painful tattooing, which was done so neatly by the Polish women, as we prayed that it indicated we'd be expected to work rather than be executed.

Standing embarrassed in the nude, we felt subhuman. We were thrown clothing from a huge heap of old clothes and then we were ordered to dress. The garments the prisoners tossed us were ridiculous and random. They were just rags really – items too old or shabby to be wanted by the Germans. I was handed some odd underwear, a pair of oversized men's boots, a woollen cap with a strange widow's peak, and an emerald green bathrobe that swamped me. I looked like a scarecrow. Thankfully, I was allowed to keep my glasses. Mummy was given a dress, a thick black coat and shoes, but just a thin scarf for her head. Little did we know we wouldn't have a change of clothing for months.

For reasons that have never been explained to me, we were then pushed towards desks manned by Nazi officials who asked our names and ages. In answer to questions fired at me I replied that I was born in 1928, not 1927 – just as Fredy had told me – a lie that remained on some of my identity papers for the rest of my days. We were then forced to endure some kind of mock trial in which we each read our 'confession' in German stating that we'd been arrested and tried for crimes against the Third Reich, and that all our possessions had been confiscated. There was never a proper trial and it was never made clear what our so-called 'crimes' were.

Our sentence was listed inexplicably as '6SB'.

We had to sign and date the documents to indicate that we accepted what was effectively our own death sentence. It was all so rational and conscious – as if there was some legality to what the Nazis were doing. When there is nobody left who lived through this and who can be asked about the details, it will be easy to believe that it was not possible. Because it's unbelievable, it sounds impossible. And yet, it happened, and our papers had to be rubber-stamped and in perfect order before we could be moved on to whatever the next terror might be.

All 5,000 of us from Terezín remained separated by gender and were crowded back into our rows of parallel blocks to be kept in quarantine for a week. At last some food was brought to us. Each day we were given a little coffee, thirty grams of poor quality bread, and some disgusting soup made of a root vegetable but which was mostly water. We were expected to survive on just that.

To our amazement, one of the women carrying the huge kettles of soup balanced on a wooden yoke turned out to be my Aunt Jiřina, my father's sister, who'd been sent from Terezín a few weeks earlier. It was such a relief to see her alive, but we could tell that she was already altered by her experiences. As she nervously dished out our soup she whispered that she'd try to visit us later that night. This she did, even though it was forbidden, bringing us a little extra soup. 'Merry Christmas,' Jiřina told us wryly, handing us a needle and thread, which was real wealth in Auschwitz. To be able to mend and stitch was an extremely precious commodity in a camp where we had to make do with the clothes we were wearing and any additional cloth or sacking we might find.

Taking it from her gratefully we shook our heads in sorrow and confusion, as we'd forgotten that it was almost Christmas. I couldn't bear to think of all the happy Christmases spent in Plzeň with dear Tata and Mummy, Dagmar, Milošek, and my aunt and uncle. The carp would be kept in the bathtub ready to be killed and fried before being served with potato salad. Emily, our cook, would make delicious *vánoční cukroví,* the traditional sweet Christmas biscuits decorated with icing. Memories like that were too painful to contemplate.

Aunt Jiřina came to visit us frequently and we were always pleased to see her, not least because we were so very hungry and grateful for the extra soup. The rations in Auschwitz were even worse than in Terezín and there was little chance to steal anything, unless it was from your neighbours – which many did because a piece of bread could mean the difference between life and death. I continued to privately berate myself for being such a fussy eater as a child.

To my dismay and that of many others, several of the women in our block who must have been as hungry as the rest of us sat around discussing recipes every night – dreaming up lavish banquets of cakes and meats, breads and rich desserts until their mouths watered. I couldn't stand to hear them and would press my hands to my ears so as not to conjure up images of things that only made me even hungrier.

It was bread I craved most of all – warm bread fresh from the oven like the soft, plaited challah my grandmother used to make for Shabbat in Dobříš, or the warm poppy-seed rolls, or the rich Christmas breads Emily made for us in Prague.

I didn't even have any work to distract me from my hollow, aching stomach, as I'd had in Terezín. Instead, I spent my days half-hidden at the back of our bunk on my mother's instructions, keeping out of sight to avoid attracting any attention in case Arno Böhm or one of the guards singled me out. We'd heard dreadful stories from the girls who were taken to his block each night and forced to have sex with SS officers and visiting 'dignitaries' from the area. In return they received better food, clothes, and other privileges and some even formed emotional attachments with a few of the guards. We never judged them, but we were afraid that we might become one of them.

The loneliness and fear was often overwhelming, so I was relieved to discover that my friends from Terezín, Dana and Zuzana Heller, were in the same block as us with her mother, which meant that we were at least able to spend time together in the hours when the guards rarely came. It was wonderful that they were still alive, although Zuzana's father had been enlisted as one of the prisoner-doctors under Dr Josef Mengele, which was a difficult and dangerous position to be in.

My mother, as one of the oldest women in the block, was given a job of *Entlausung*, or delousing, to check and remove the ever-present lice from hair, clothing, and bedding. If she found any she immediately had to shave the infested head and use petroleum to wipe down the bodies and clothes of those affected. There was never any shortage of lice, so she did this all day and it was emotional, exhausting work as the women who lost their hair wept bitterly over this final loss. One privilege of being in the family camp was that we never had our heads shaved as others did and we were grateful for the extra warmth and dignity hair provided. To lose it only added to the sense of lost identity, as all those who were shaved suddenly looked the same.

Every morning and evening we had to attend the roll call, heralded at 5 a.m. in the dark by the shrieks of a young woman in charge of our block. As *älteste* she had special rights and privileges, including more food, a coal fire, and a small room to herself at the far end of the building. It was her job to get us all up and out to the communal latrines and washrooms before being lined up to be counted by the guards by 6 a.m. She would do this by shouting at the top of her voice and running through the block with a whip and a stick, beating anyone who was slow to rise. Sometimes she almost beat them to death. Although my mother and I always made sure to be ready and keep out of her way, the woman with the whip was hated by all for her unnecessary cruelty.

While the infernal 'Marinarella' played on and on, we were forced to stand out in our flimsy clothing in cold, wet mud so well trodden that it never froze and could suck the shoes right off our feet. Shivering, wretched, we continually kept our heads bowed so as not to stand out in any way.

Sometimes the *Appell* took an hour. Sometimes two.

In mud, snow, and ice.

Those who were sick, old, or exhausted often passed out and were immediately carried off. They had what was known as 'the Auschwitz disease' that affected far more men than women, in which the whole expression and especially the eyes would be dead. There was a sort of utter resignation to one's fate, a kind of philosophical slump, which left them unable to regenerate mentally. In such cases, the light in the person died and there followed a collapse of the perception of the meaning of life. Once that happened, we knew that this person didn't want to live and that he wouldn't live. He didn't have to commit suicide or walk in front of a train. There was instead a complete physical shutdown – the collapse of a principle. These prisoners, male and female, were called '*Muselmann*' in camp slang, which is thought to have referred to the prone position of Muslims at prayer.

The rest of us who were still hopeful of staying alive waited to be counted and sometimes inspected by Dr Josef Mengele and the *Lager älteste*, a man I understood to be Obersturmführer Johann Schwarzhuber, who was always accompanied by other SS officers. Under their command the *Appells* became worse and worse, especially for the men lined up in blocks a little further down the camp. Several of the SS guards, mostly those drunk on vodka, started to make a sport of the most exhausted, sick and emaciated prisoners, forcing them to do gymnastics in that vile, sticky clay. Kicking at the legs of these doomed individuals, the guards would push them to the ground and order them to do dozens of press-ups or make them run on the spot, perform squats, or jumping jacks until they collapsed. We were forced to watch men feeble with heart disease, starvation, or other problems struggle to keep going until they gave up or even died.

Roll call was such a humiliating and frightening experience, endured twice a day. Every time I heard the band strike up the opening bars of that horrible march, I would be filled with new despair at another day of hunger, fearing death in that living hell. The things that we saw were unimaginable in their horror and cruelty. Each of us knew that it could be us next. All of us were helpless to prevent what was happening or save anyone else.

Yet the human spirit is remarkably resilient. Just as some of those men managed to keep going and survive another day, so we were able to block the horror of what we were witnessing and keep focusing on our own survival. In this way, we grew accustomed to even the most dreadful of circumstances and were somehow able to endure a little bit more every day.

After a few days there, I began to lift my chin and look around a little to get my bearings. Just like Terezín, Auschwitz I and Auschwitz II-Birkenau were part of a large former military camp not far from the Polish town of Oświęcim, seventy kilometres from medieval Kraków. The almost two hundred-acre site beyond the red brick garrison of Auschwitz I was a barren no-man's-land surrounded by fields and birch trees. *Birken* is the German word for birch trees. In that miserable camp there was not a flower or a blade of grass. There was nothing but mud.

There were thirty-six blocks in our area, each numbered, either side of the main dirt pathway or *Lagerstrasse*. The evil *Lager älteste* Arno Böhm lived in Block No. 1. Beyond that were the stinking latrines we were marched to once a day and forced to do our business as guards leered. Then there was the so-called health block supervised by medical staff including Dr Mengele and his colleague Dr Fritz Klein. We didn't know it then, but it was there that wicked experiments were done on children, especially twins, or pregnant women. Next door to it was Block 31, which Jiřina explained was the new children's barrack in which those aged eight to fourteen could spend their days – a concession insisted upon by Fredy Hirsch who ran it ostensibly as an 'improvement for morale and discipline'.

Someone like me was forbidden to go there – or anywhere else in the camp – but I was determined to get to Fredy somehow. Before I had a chance to memorise the route and make a plan, though, roll call would be over, and the woman with the whip leapt into action again to bully us all back inside.

It was several days before I finally got a good look at her face and when I did, I almost fainted. I could hardly believe it was Tilla Fischlová, our beloved Maccabi youth leader from Plzeň, who'd taught us so diligently with her boyfriend Karel Schleissner. She spotted me just as I spotted her and the recognition was instant, although I couldn't believe how much she had changed in the three months since I'd last seen her in Terezín. The pretty girl who had always been so kind to us had turned into a hard-faced woman who was collaborating with the SS to keep us in order.

Leaning in so as not to be overheard, Tilla whispered in my ear, 'Come to my room tonight.' My blood turned cold. Mummy and I looked at each other and back at Tilla but she was already gone, wielding her stick against the weak and the infirm.

I approached her room that night with the greatest trepidation. The last thing I wanted was to come to the attention of anybody in Birkenau, least of all someone who worked for the Nazis. Tilla's little room was gratifyingly warm, though, and I noticed that she had a proper bed with a proper mattress, not just straw. She closed the door behind me and gestured for me to stand in front of her. Before I could stop myself, I blurted, 'What happened to you, Tilla?'

It quickly became apparent to me that she was not the same person I'd once known and was having some kind of mental breakdown. She started rambling, almost incoherently, about Karel and how she couldn't bear to think of him and what he was doing. I couldn't make much sense of it at first. She said we were all going to die anyway so she had every right to take a career posting and get herself better treatment until that day.

'Sing to me,' she suddenly instructed. She must have heard me sing a hundred times at the Jewish lake with all our friends, our skin tanned and wet as we sat around laughing and sharing songs and stories, oblivious to what was to come.

My eyes filled with tears at the thought, and my throat became too constricted to make a sound. Frustrated, she barked, 'Recite me a poem then.' Too upset and frightened to remember any, she reached for a book of Czech poetry and handed it to me. My hands shaking and my voice tremulous, I stood before her reading lyrical poems by Jaroslav Vrchlický and Vítězslav Hálek as she lay on her bed with her eyes closed. When I'd read her enough, she dismissed me and I hurried back to my mother to try to warm her body with mine.

Reading and singing to Tilla became my nightly chore from then on and, in time, I learned more about why she had become so deranged. Karel, her one true love, had been put into the Sonderkommando, comprised of Jews forced – on threat of execution – to dispose of the bodies of all those who'd been gassed. Sometimes they would come across the bodies of their own family members, and the only way to avoid this grisly task was to commit suicide. They were kept in isolation, but their work came with exceptional privileges, including their own block, as much food, drink and tobacco as they wanted, and no need to attend the group *Appells*. Each new Sonderkommando unit was replaced every six months to a year, and the next group tasked with disposing of their predecessors' bodies.

The thought of what Karel did every day and the idea that he could be gassed any minute filled Tilla with such pain that she took it out on us, waking up each morning full of violent, angry thoughts. She went completely insane, and her humanism flipped over to the other side so that she became entirely evil. I used to ask her, 'Why are you so mean?' and she would tell me that she couldn't help it. 'It's a reaction. I feel so angry with all the world.'

Every now and again she was somehow able to see her beloved Karel, but that only made her angrier as she told me that he was losing his mind. Because I knew Karel before the camps and could talk to Tilla about happier days, she became quite dependent on me. I was the only one who witnessed her inner torment, but each morning she would be different again – full of hate and hated in return – although she was never cruel to my mother or me.

My daily encounters with Tilla, the interminable *Appells* and the ghastly music made me all the more determined to find Fredy. To my mother's horror, when my Aunt Jiřina came to see us one night I asked her to lend me her coat. She had a number sewn onto it that identified her as being from the previous transport, which allowed her to move more freely around the camp. Each of us had numbers sewn onto our clothing as well as cloth triangles in different colours to identify which group of 'enemies of the Reich' we belonged to. We were staggered to discover that there were so many categories, and that Jews weren't the sole inmates of the camp. We also had to memorise these colours very quickly as accidentally approaching someone who wore a triangle that meant he or she wasn't sympathetic could mean trouble. Jews had yellow triangles, communists and political prisoners had red ones, prostitutes, murderers and asocial prisoners had black, criminals and saboteurs wore green, gypsies brown, Jehovah's Witnesses purple, and homosexuals, rapists and paedophiles wore pink triangles.

Praying my aunt's coat would protect me, I left her with my mother and slipped out to hurry to the children's block. The shock of walking into that building for the first time will never leave me. It was like stepping into another world.

Our block was dirty and cold. It stank and the inmates were full of disease and despair. The women squabbled constantly over everything from food to personal space. People suffered from diarrhoea and angry rashes from the lice and hacking coughs that kept everyone else awake. All possessions had to be fiercely guarded from thieves and there was violence and mayhem every day. But Fredy had done something absolutely miraculous for the 700-plus children in the family camp by persuading the Nazis to let him remove them from all that. He'd successfully argued that unruly youngsters would only cause chaos and spread disease. In their new block, where several teenagers I recognised from Terezín were helping to supervise the youngsters, the drab green walls had been whitewashed and painted with flowers and birds and scenes from *Snow White and the Seven Dwarfs* by a talented teenage inmate named Dina Gottliebová. The transformation was astounding. Being so dexterous, Fredy had also made little tables and benches from offcuts of wood so that the children could sit and have lessons, just as they had in Terezín. I saw it all in a moment and I will never forget the scene, though at first I thought I was hallucinating.

Fredy came out of his *Jugend älteste* quarters – the little groom's room that had been painted to look like a gingerbread house. As before, he looked cleaner than the rest of us and better dressed. He was wearing riding boots and breeches with a blue jacket bearing the pink triangle that singled him out as a homosexual, something I'd suspected in Terezín but never thought much about. What shocked me most though was that, in the space of just a few months, his hair had turned completely grey. I almost didn't recognise him.

He sat down with some of the children, looked up at me with a sad smile and said, almost casually, 'Hello, Zuzi. Well now, what are we going to do with you?'

Resisting the urge to run to him, I pleaded, 'Couldn't you somehow arrange it so that I can work with you again?'

'You mustn't be here,' he replied, suddenly serious. 'Your block is still in quarantine. Come and see me again when that's over and I'll see what I can do.'

At that moment, a senior SS officer walked in. I froze, believing that this was the moment I'd be discovered and killed. Hoping not to be noticed, I dropped to my knees and pretended to pick up something from the floor.

To my amazement, Fredy stood and said to the Nazi nonchalantly, 'So, who have you robbed and murdered today?' He stared into his eyes like a circus tamer looking into the eyes of a tiger. I was absolutely white with fear, convinced that the high-ranking SS officer would pull out his pistol and shoot us both.

Instead, the Nazi laughed, reached for his other pocket, pulled out his cigarette case and offered one to Fredy, who shook his head. That was really something so unbelievable, especially in a place where tobacco was a currency worth more than gold. It reminded me of my father stubbornly refusing a cigarette from the *Treuhänder* who took over our shop in Plzeň.

Still laughing, the officer said, 'I just came in to see how you were getting along today.' I later learned that the officer worked with Dr Mengele and was one of several Nazis who visited the children's block because it felt like the only place they could breathe.

When he finally left, Fredy gave me a signal to get out, so I quickly ran back to my mother – who'd been in a state of high anxiety the entire time I'd been gone. Even though I could see the fear in her eyes about me being out of her sight, I told her the good news and started counting the days until I could get back to Fredy and remind myself that there was still some good in the world.

As always, Fredy kept his promise. As soon as quarantine was over, I hurried to see him in my aunt's coat and was delighted when he was able to secure me a pass to work alongside him again. I was too young and inexperienced to be classified as one of the teachers he'd selected from the intellectuals in the camp, so he made me one of the *Hilfsbeträuerinnen* or teaching assistants. This meant that I could be a helping hand with the younger children and enjoy spending time with my friends Zuzana and Dana.

Working together under Fredy's guidance we were able to keep up some sort of normal life in Birkenau. I was put in charge of a group of little ones aged four to seven, but the seven- to twelve-year-olds joined us sometimes too. I'm sure some of the older children had an inkling that we were in a place of great danger but most were in pretty good shape mentally. They believed we were all waiting together to be sent to a work camp somewhere in the East. They longed to play outside but that was impossible, so we did everything we could to distract them, telling them fairy tales and singing songs and nursery rhymes together. I taught them canons such as 'London's Burning', just as my father had taught me. They also learned a few German songs and the French 'Alouette, Gentille Alouette'. We danced and drew pictures, supervised and educated the children, just as we had done before.

There were few books, but each of us had some favourite poem or piece of prose we remembered by heart so we would recite those, and whenever Fredy was able to get hold of any pencils or paper we wrote them down. He was incredibly resourceful. We gave lessons from memory on history and geography and recited satirical pieces by the popular Czech playwrights and actors, Jiří Voskovec and Jan Werich. We even managed to put on a recital of *Manon Lescaut*, adapted by Czech poet Vítězslav Nezval from Abbé Prévost's novel, after someone smuggled in the script.

Fredy arrived in the block every afternoon around 4 p.m., having done a full day's work somewhere else in the camp. Although he must have been exhausted, he was always pleased to see us and seemed to remember all the children's names, even though there were so many. Often he would pick up his recorder and begin to play a tune. Each day he taught the children a new song in Czech, Hebrew or English – all different, many of which I memorised. That was our feast of the day and something we all looked forward to.

One of the best things Fredy did was to create a musical of *Snow White* using some of the popular songs he'd taught us. He had written it in German so he was the prince, of course, and a beautiful and talented young soprano took the role of Snow White. The little children played the many dwarfs and the mean people in the story were depicted as the SS. We all knew that. The premiere was quite dramatic, a big event, and several guards came to see it along with Dr Mengele who applauded most enthusiastically. For the SS too, I suppose the children's block provided a welcome glimpse into another world.

Part of Fredy's negotiations in getting the Nazis to agree to his demands was that the children should learn German to better understand orders, so he taught them a few key sentences along with some songs and poems they learned by rote in case any senior SS walked in and demanded to know how much they understood.

Being in that block saved my life, and my sanity. Every day it allowed me to escape to another world, although I still had to face the *Appells* morning and night and live on the same disgusting food as everyone else. My skin was soon tight with dirt and sore from scratching. We had such limited washing facilities and only ever in cold or lukewarm water, which meant that our clothes always smelled and so did we. I coveted the crisp, clean skirts and blouses of the SS women. I longed to be clean.

Once a month we were led to the Sauna, that building where we'd first been processed and tattooed, and told we were to take a shower. Nobody was really sure what was going to come out of the showerheads – water or gas – so it was another horrific experience. There would be attendants sitting there and we would ask them, 'Are we really going to have a shower?' They used to laugh and say, 'You will see!' We were given a towel and a small bar of soap and herded naked into the shower where water really did come out, although never much and never for long enough. The suspense was terrible.

Working with the children beneath those cheerily painted walls gave me a strange double existence. In that little piece of heaven where we taught the children about everything from dinosaurs to the Romans, I was allowed to play and sing and laugh and have some sort of a normal life, in spite of all the hardships.

Fredy had also somehow arranged for better food for the children – a little margarine or marmalade as well as bread and soup – diverting some of the packages sent by the Red Cross or by relatives of those already gassed. This meant there was usually some extra bread, salami or tinned fish to supplement our diet.

Of course, we still lived in the shadow of death, our nostrils filled with the stench of it and our throats choked with the ashes of the slaughtered. The flames from the chimneys burned night and day and we witnessed cruelty on a daily basis. We talked about it all the time, especially amongst people the same age. Some even joked about it. We spoke of the fires incessantly, especially on the days when the fresh supplies of gas didn't arrive. This was something we were all most afraid of because that was when they threw people into pits and poured gasoline over them and burned them instead. It became a perverse hope in the camp that the gas wouldn't run out.

Each night I'd return to my mother, wrung out by the day, as was she after hours of shaving and cleaning off lice. We would both be exhausted, but once we slid into our bunk side by side and fell asleep, I'd have terrible nightmares about the gas chambers and wake up screaming and crying again.

'I don't want to die, Mummy!' I'd sob, as she cradled me in her arms and let me weep. My mother stayed strong for me. She had such character. I didn't have the intelligence to know that I was only adding to her pain, but I couldn't help it and was deeply afraid all of the time.

Alarmingly, the impeccably dressed men responsible for this genocide continued to saunter into the children's block frequently, bearing smiles and looking for their next victims. As always, Fredy maintained his dignity and behaved as if he was an equal in every way to their class, breeding and intelligence.

The first experience I had of this was when some doctors arrived to measure the children's heads. They had special callipers and tools and started taking precise measurements of the little ones lined up terrified before them, writing the data down with forensic fascination. They were testing the racial theory that Jewish heads were a different shape to those of Gentiles – inferior somehow – and could be physically proved in the face of any verbal denial.

When Fredy walked in and saw what they were doing as we teenagers looked on powerless, he scolded the doctors severely. 'Stop that!' he told them. 'Aren't you ashamed of yourselves for believing such nonsense?' Then he sent them away.

Dr Mengele was another daily visitor, smiling as he chatted to the children, sat them on his knee, and encouraged them to call him 'Uncle'. I told Viktor years later that if he met Mengele in any other circumstances he probably would have enjoyed a glass of wine with this good-looking, educated doctor, and had wonderful conversations about music, medicine, or books. It was the same with Mengele's deputy, Fritz Klein, who was in his late fifties with a marvellous head of thick hair. He looked like the kind of man who would listen to Bach or discuss Goethe with you, but was a vehement anti-Semite. That was one of the worst things really. One might expect this kind of cruelty from a primitive person but not from an intellectual. That is why I can't regard them as human.

Dr Klein used to arrive with chocolates – such a luxury during the war and something the youngest children might never have even tasted. I hadn't eaten a chocolate in at least five years and would have loved one too. We always declined, though, and warned others not to accept them either, because any child who took those delicacies from the doctor was doomed and would usually disappear within twenty-four hours.

'See what happened?' we'd tell the children. 'Andrej took a chocolate and now he is in prison.' We didn't say what the 'prison' was or where because we didn't know if the child was dead or alive, being experimented on, or at the beck and call of other sinister characters. Unfortunately, some of the children so missed the sugary treats of their youth that they succumbed and took the sweets anyway.

Fredy did his best to help us overcome our constant hunger. He was one of the first people I ever met who spoke about mind over matter, as he taught us all to concentrate on breathing deeply and to use self-hypnosis to imagine that our bellies were full of food. 'Even if we are hungry we can tell ourselves that we are full,' he insisted, before making us close our eyes and repeat, '*I am not hungry. I am not hungry. I am full.*' Occasionally, it worked.

The SS didn't always cooperate with Fredy and sometimes he'd return from trying to demand something very badly beaten. Brushing aside our concerns, he'd limp to his room to recover and tell us afterwards that he'd probably been too cheeky with his requests. Needless to say, he was determined that we should do our utmost to enjoy what time we had and make the children's lives as pleasant as possible under the circumstances.

One day he caught me sitting on the flue reading a tattered old book about Freud that had been smuggled into camp, probably from the hospital block. I badly missed the beautiful library of my youth that I devoured anything I could, even Freud's *Introduction to Psychoanalysis*. I had not even read the first chapter when Fredy's hand came from behind me and snatched the book away with, 'Now, what are you reading here?' Examining it, he frowned and told me, 'This is no literature for a young girl! You need to enjoy your childhood.'

He confiscated my book and I was angry with him at first but then I realised that being without it was liberating. Suddenly it felt as if I was at home with my father taking care of what I was reading and deciding if it was appropriate. I fell out of favour with Fredy for a few days after that, so I threw myself into writing songs and poems for the children instead, which was much more fun than Freud.

In spite of Fredy's efforts, every day brought a new fear – even in that little piece of heaven. Another of our frequent visitors was the dreaded Arno Böhm. He was a man who'd beat someone to death for not standing in line at *Appell* but, perversely, seemed to adore children and had also fallen in love with one of the girls in our block. She was very beautiful, and he gave her the moon – gold jewellery, nice dresses, everything.

Böhm, on the other hand, was unusually ugly. Aside from the black triangle that marked him as a murderer, he had the kind of look that would terrify most – extremely primitive with dreadful scars on his face and a misshapen back that gave him the appearance of Quasimodo. With his twisted smile, he'd walk in and sit down to play with the younger children as if he'd known them all his life. We didn't like him being there and we teenage girls always kept out of his way, but there was nothing we could do or say to stop him.

Aside from fearing men like Böhm, we all had a morbid dread of becoming ill in case it hastened our entry to the gas chambers. In the unhygienic conditions of Birkenau, though, it was impossible not to suffer from dysentery or typhus, which we were all afflicted by at some time or other. One day I woke with a badly swollen tongue. My friend Zuzana arranged for me to see her father, the doctor, and he gave me some medicine that gradually reduced the swelling. Another time I became seriously ill with dysentery and was sent to the camp doctor, a fellow prisoner who asked me for my medical history. I blushed and told him, 'I won't tell you because you'll think I'm crazy.' In the end I admitted to everything from pneumonia and pleurisy to encephalitis and typhus, and then he understood what I meant.

It is a mystery how I was able to survive so many illnesses after such a sickly childhood, but my theory is that it was my mother's intense coddling of me in Plzeň that gave me the strength to resist death time and again.

In early February the September transport that came to Auschwitz before us – which included Fredy, most of the children, and Aunt Jiřina – were ordered to write postcards to their families still in Terezín. They'd been in the camp almost exactly six months.

They had to write in German, keeping their messages to less than thirty words, and send assurances that they were working and in good health. They then had to post-date them to the end of the month on the grounds that they'd need to be censored in Berlin before they could be mailed. We didn't realise the significance of that until much later and prayed that the cards were an indication of something good.

As soon as everyone had written their messages they were informed that they'd soon be sent to a Nazi labour camp at a place called Heydebreck. The Germans were clever in their deception as there was a genuine subcamp in Poland by that name, a town with a chemical plant. The departure of this transport would mean being separated once more from Fredy, Jiřina, my friend Zuzana, and so many other loved ones, perhaps never to meet again. It was such a horrible thought, but we were helpless to protest and still so very afraid.

Fredy's birthday was on 11 February, and we organised a surprise party for him in the children's block with a few treats and some tiny gifts. Unusually, he arrived late and when he came in he was covered in blood. He'd been badly beaten again by the Germans, but he wouldn't say why. Something was troubling him terribly and we could tell over the next few days that he was becoming more depressed. We all noticed it, but believed he was fretting about the impending move and concerned for those left behind. He had already appointed his successor, a man named Hugo Lenk, who would be helped by others, but Fredy still worried about how we'd all fare without him.

The seventh of March is a day of national celebration for Czechs because it is the birthday of our first president, Tomáš Garrigue Masaryk. Not that we were even aware of the dates but it was the following day, coincidental or not, that the SS arrived in force with a convoy of trucks. They woke us up shouting in the middle of the night, beating people with clubs and ordering everyone from the September transport outside. One was a neighbour in the next bunk and she did as she was told, although we heard later that some people committed suicide rather than go with them.

It was always terrifying when the guards arrived unexpectedly and especially after dark, so we waited and watched and listened in silence as they loaded everyone up and started to drive them away.

Weeping for our fellow Czechs, whose imminent gassing we feared and whose departure pointed to our own fate once our six months was up, we stopped to listen to the sound of singing from the departing trucks – it was our national anthem 'Kde domov můj' being sung by those about to die. The opening lines are, 'Where is my home? Where is my homeland?'

We heard later that in the gas chambers some of the 3,792 men, women and children who were about to be murdered bravely sang the Jewish hymn 'Hatikvah' – ('The Hope') – until, one by one, their voices faded, including that of my kind, brave Aunt Jiřina. After they'd left the family camp, all the blocks fell quiet. I'm ashamed to admit that when we could no longer hear the trucks, we fell back to sleep, beyond exhaustion.

The next thing I knew I was being roughly shaken awake. It was my friend Zuzana crying, 'I'm back! I'm back!'

'What? How come?' I asked, blearily.

'Dr Mengele insisted that he couldn't manage without his doctors, so they sent all the medical staff and their immediate relatives – including us – back to the family camp,' she explained. After a pause, she added, 'The rest all went to the gas.'

I sat bolt upright, and so did my mother. Even though we'd half-expected this, we were both in shock.

'What about Fredy?' I asked. 'Did you see Fredy?'

She shook her head. 'I don't think he was among them.'

We all had to go to *Appell* as usual, but afterwards I ran straight to Block 31 to find Fredy and make sure that he was safe. Instead I found the block full of strange men who were all talking at once in a very heated atmosphere. Nervously, I huddled in a corner with the other teenagers who'd also hurried there for news until we were finally told that Fredy had taken some poison. They were trying to help him and somebody suggested that a glass of milk might save him, so people were running around trying to find some, but then we heard it was too late.

It was several days before we found out the awful truth. As soon as the September transport had been instructed to write their postcards, members of the underground resistance in the camp knew this meant they would be gassed imminently. Their time was up, as they were considered too weak to work after six months in Auschwitz. The idea of the cards was that if anyone later accused the Nazis of the wholesale slaughter of Jews, they could protest and say, 'But look, they wrote these at the end of March. They were still alive when they wrote these.'

However, the system ran like clockwork and the six months from the arrival of the September group had expired, which meant that their '6SB' sentence could be carried out as per the confessions we'd all been forced to sign when we first arrived. The letters 'SB' signified the German word *Sonderbehandlung* or 'special treatment' – Nazi code for extermination without trial. The '6' stood for six months.

The spies in the camp had sent a respected Slovak prisoner named Rudolf Vrba to Fredy to warn him what was about to happen. But Fredy didn't believe them. He countered that the Nazis would never have kept them alive and let him run the children's block for all that time if they'd intended to murder them all along. Vrba argued that even if he was right there should be a contingency plan. They had smuggled in some guns and said if enough people staged a revolt just before entering the gas chamber they could at least kill a few of the SS. Some might even be able to escape and inform the world what was happening. Because Fredy was so revered, the underground members insisted that he was the only one with the authority to lead what would almost certainly be a suicide mission. The plan was that he would blow a whistle to signal the others to open fire.

According to Vrba's accounts after the war, Fredy was appalled. 'But what about the children?' he asked. 'How can I leave them to be butchered? They need me … They trust me!'

He wasn't afraid to take action, but he didn't want to be a part of anything that would frighten the children and was determined to die alongside them if necessary. Besides, he still held on to his hope, as he'd had a promise from those SS he regularly negotiated with that he and all of the 500 children in his block would be spared. He argued finally that even if he could bring himself to orchestrate such a thing, everyone left behind in the family camp – including the remainder of the children – would surely be exterminated in revenge.

Although he repeatedly refused their request, Vrba and others kept pressing him. I will never forgive those older men for putting such a kind young man in an impossible position.

In an agony of indecision, desperate and fearful for those in his care, Fredy eventually asked for one hour to think it over. It was the morning of 8 March 1944. Vrba returned an hour later to find Fredy unconscious in his little gingerbread house. He had taken an overdose of the barbiturate Luminal, a drug to stop seizures in epileptics. I personally don't think he killed himself, as I don't believe Fredy Hirsch was the kind of man to have taken the easy way out. One rumour was that he was murdered, another that he went to the doctors and asked for something for his nerves and they gave him the Luminal. For whatever reason, he swallowed all of the pills and fell into a coma.

Either way, he died because he was being forced into doing something that he couldn't do. I think he was at the end of his tether and that if they hadn't pressed him he'd have lived because the SS would have sent him back to the blocks with the doctors.

Even if they hadn't and Fredy had blown the whistle, then the entire September transport would have perished – including the doctors and their families who were saved by Mengele. And it is entirely possible that our transport would have been murdered immediately too after such a rebellion.

I owed my life to Fredy Hirsch that day – again.

Fredy passed away in his bed as those he had striven so hard to help for years were beaten and pushed into the gas chambers amid heart-wrenching screams and cries.

Poor Fredy. I still grieve for him. He was such a beacon of light. After the death of my father he became a second father to me, and the one man who had the greatest influence on my time in the camps.

We all learned hope from Fredy – that even in the most desperate situations you can rise from the dead. As long as a person has a spark of hope inside them, they can still live. He was such a dignified young man, someone with strong ethics who was rejected by his own family because they were Orthodox Jews and didn't approve of his sexuality. Those who knew him said he kept fighting his instincts and his friends tried to help him. He even tried to date some of the girls they pushed on him, but he wasn't happy about it and it never worked out. In the end, he had a boyfriend who was with him in Terezín until that friend found a girl and got married. And then he had another steady boyfriend in Auschwitz right up until his death.

Everyone in the camps knew and I had heard rumours in Terezín. I didn't really understand what being homosexual was and I remember asking my father about Fredy and he told me, 'Never mind about that. You can put your trust in him. He is a good man.'

His family should have been proud of Fredy Hirsch, for he was the spirit of morality in these camps. It was Fredy who taught us not to lie, cheat, or steal in a place where people could be killed for a piece of bread or a ladleful of soup. He showed us how to develop friendships and tolerance. He was an ideological figure who kept us in another world, separate to the horror, a place where humanity and decency were still important.

I remember once when extra bread came into the children's block and there was some left over. Even though I was very hungry, I didn't eat it. Instead I took it to Fredy and asked what I should do with it. He replied, 'You keep it, Zuzana, because you are so decent.'

Coming from Fredy, that was the highest praise.

After I appeared in a documentary about Fredy, a former child prisoner now living in America wrote to me and told me that he was tasked with handing out the soup in the children's block and would be so hungry that he would lick the spoon from time to time. Eventually Fredy went to him and said, 'You know you shouldn't do this so we'll probably let someone else lick it now.' He could suggest that something wasn't right quite beautifully. Approximately thirty per cent more of us from that block survived compared to regular prisoners in Auschwitz, because we had different rules.

Years after his death, the communists tried to put a stop to the legend of Fredy Hirsch and promoted some nasty articles about him in the state press. They announced that he was gay and had collaborated with the Nazis. They cited the fact that he taught the children German words and German songs – but I know he only did so in order to keep the children's block operational. He did not collaborate. He was German – he spoke impeccable German – and was always so refined in his manner that the Nazis trusted and respected him. His whole mentality with them was of open contempt, but he was able to persuade them to allow things they would never have agreed to with anyone else. He was a negotiator, not a collaborator.

A once-ardent Zionist, Fredy changed his views completely in Auschwitz. This handsome young man who was such a great speaker – someone who could move masses – gradually shifted from his former beliefs in that camp. Furthermore, he carried me, and many others, with him.

One day, he gathered all the surviving teenagers from the Maccabi groups and said, 'Look at all these people in the camp with their heads shaved and in prison clothes. Can you tell a rich man from a poor man, a Zionist from a communist? Do you know their political views? No. They are all just men and women, each as miserable as each other.'

Taking a breath, he declared, 'I am no longer a Zionist. I am no longer political and will never join any party. I am a humanist. The only true philosophy is humanism, as advocated by our first president Tomáš Garrigue Masaryk. If I ever get back to the world, I will go to Prague and study Masaryk. I urge you to do the same.'

That speech made such an impression on me – the concept that we cannot tell which race or class anyone is from, and that it doesn't matter anyway.

Fredy's wise words have remained with me my whole life and were instrumental in my decision never to join any political party – a decision that would have serious consequences later on.

9

Paris, 1965

When I was forced to leave Paris in 1956 after Munich so that Viktor could have his moment in the spotlight, I wept bitterly. On several occasions thereafter, I would wake with tears in my eyes after dreaming of that gilded city and say to Viktor, 'I would so like to go back to Paris one day.'

That didn't seem likely, although we did consider the possibility of emigrating around that time because Viktor's mother had died and his father was happily settled with relatives in the country. It would have been difficult getting my husband and my mother out of Czechoslovakia while I was abroad but not completely impossible at that time. I could maybe have given one of my Eastern bloc recitals and slipped into the West by train instead of coming home. At the same time Viktor could have gone to the country with Mummy where friends could have helped them cross the border. The possibility of living and working in London or Paris was very tempting and Viktor too had received offers to stay when he was in France.

Immediately after the war we had also considered moving to America. A doctor friend in Dobříš, who was close to President Beneš, warned us, 'Get out. The communists will come and they won't let go until they have made *muzhiks* (Russian peasants) out of all of us.' He was right.

Mummy wrote to her sister Elsa in New York to see if we could join them there and she immediately replied yes and suggested that I complete my studies at Juilliard, which was kind of her, but I wasn't in any fit state at that time to pass the exams for such a notable arts school. They sent the application papers for Juilliard anyway, along with US government questionnaires – so many forms. I started to fill them all in but stopped when I came across the column which asked me my 'race'. I was so revolted and angry that I immediately tore up the forms. Living behind the Iron Curtain, I didn't understand the serious racism problems in the United States or how it would lead to the formation of the civil rights movement. All I could think of was the Nazis and their obsession with 'racial purity'.

'I will never live in a country where I will be asked about my race!' I declared to my mother.

'Well, if you really feel that way,' she said, a little uncertainly, but she already had misgivings and was worried how her sister and brother-in-law could provide for us too when they were not yet prosperous and were struggling themselves as immigrants. She feared we would have always been considered the poor relations, a burden on their resources, and we both knew that I would have to earn a wage and couldn't have afforded the fees for Juilliard anyway.

It was my concerns for my mother that stopped Viktor and I fleeing in the 1950s. She was approaching her sixties and I couldn't imagine her adjusting to life in the West or being happy anywhere else other than the country our Tata had felt so passionately about. In any event, life under communism was less oppressive after Stalin died and the sense of living in constant fear had lifted.

My professional career was just beginning to take off too, with all sorts of doors opening to me. I had underestimated the importance of winning the ARD competition because not long after returning home with those cashmere sweaters I was inundated with requests to give recitals, record the most wonderful works, and travel widely. Viktor and I were even allowed to go to the Brussels World Exposition in 1958, not together of course, but separately. This kind of freedom was more than I'd dared hope for.

Even though time was running out for my biological clock, there was never a time when I thought I should take a break from music to have children. It wasn't just that I knew that Viktor didn't really want them, I wasn't sure that I wanted them either. It was all too soon and I still felt I was catching up with the six years I had lost.

My health had never been especially good and the medical legacies I was left with after the war conspired to undermine me repeatedly. I had suffered pneumonia and pleurisy, encephalitis and typhus, as well as repeated breakdowns of my immune system. Somewhere along the way, I picked up malaria too, which affected my kidneys and liver, so I fell victim to every infection. I'd always been small for my age and couldn't imagine carrying a child or giving birth.

Viktor and I were so happy together and I didn't want to do anything to risk that happiness. I'd seen so many of my young musician friends get married and have children and the effect it had on their careers and relationships. I absolutely knew that if I held my baby in my arms I couldn't leave it and would then be permanently torn between my child and my music. I didn't want to be so conflicted.

My mother had also made it clear from the start that if we ever had children, she couldn't be expected to take care of them. 'It would be too much work and too much worry,' she told me with her usual candour.

I never regretted not having children. After all, I ended up having so many children, grandchildren, and great grandchildren with my students over the years, as well as contact with the schoolchildren I spoke to about the Holocaust. So many of the young musicians I taught grew up to have children of their own and then sent them to me for lessons as well.

It has been a kind of motherhood.

In 1957 I was asked by the French recording company Véga Gramofon to record some of Bach's Brandenburg Concertos for them – a great honour. I hadn't truly studied these complicated works, though, and they wanted me to complete the recording within three weeks when I already had a full schedule, so I reluctantly told them that this was impossible.

The following year they asked again and this time they offered quite a substantial fee, so I was able to fulfil the brief and record the Brandenburg Concerto No. 5 in D Major with the Ensemble Instrumental Sinfonia conducted by Jean Witold, which was a marvellous experience and very important for a soloist. Witold was an interesting person, Polish by birth and an incredible Bach musicologist who published a book on the composer. I treated him terribly because he just couldn't catch the tempo, so before we went onto the stage, I tapped the tempo on his arm. He wasn't even mad at me.

The concert was well received and I still have one of the reviews, which reads: 'Great success of a Czech artist in Paris. Led by Jean Witold, she played the concerto for the harpsichord by Jiří Benda. All the Paris critics highly valued her performance. As the expert French reviews confirm, she's a great hope of the Czech nation and she'll surely be ranked among the leading world virtuosos.'

Immediately afterwards, Witold invited me to a recording of the Fifth Brandenburg Concerto for Véga – in three weeks' time. I didn't know it; I didn't have it on repertoire, so I told him that I wouldn't be able to learn it in three weeks. Then I went to sleep and in the morning I woke up with a pillow wet with tears. I had a dream about Paris and how I missed it so much, so I called Witold back and said that I was coming.

A strange thing happened while I was preparing for it. I was with Viktor in our flat and had just started to play the piece I'd be recording and, before I knew what was happening, Bach was in my head and I no longer needed Viktor to turn the pages. I had this feeling that I already knew it by heart and once again asked myself, *What would Bach do?*

Viktor was astonished and so was I, but I carried on and played the entire work until the end.

The next few years saw me travelling and recording, performing and teaching in a way I could never have imagined. I was even able to perform my wedding gift, Viktor's beautiful piano concerto, in Prague – one of the few occasions when I agreed to relinquish the harpsichord for my former instrument. In 1959, on the one hundred and fiftieth anniversary of Haydn's death, I was invited to the Haydn Music Festival in Budapest where I not only performed Haydn but Bartók and Benda. I also had my first experience of appearing on television there. In the summer of 1960, Viktor and I went to the country to rest and for me to prepare for a four-week course on the interpretation of early music for teachers in Sofia, Bulgaria. In 1961 I was invited to Scotland for the first time, as part of an international cultural exchange programme where I performed Purcell and Handel in the Ayrshire town of Cumnock. Two years later I performed my debut at the Wigmore Hall in London, a place I returned to six years later to play the Goldberg Variations, about which reviewers said I showed 'huge vitality and momentum', as well as 'a touch of wantonness'. All of these recitals were arranged by Pragokoncert, which had become the official state agency for bookings and was still sending me on cultural visits to places such as Kiev and Romania.

Wherever I was sent, the audience response was gratifying. The Soviets were the most gifted of listeners, and in Dubrovnik they showered me with so many roses that I had to stop playing and have the petals removed from between the strings. The English gave fiery and enthusiastic speeches – not at all cool and restrained despite their reputation – and in places like Paris and Austria concertgoers listened so attentively that they often asked me why I had played a piece at a different tempo from the previous time or from the recording. Perhaps most of all, though, I appreciated the responses of the Prague audiences, who treated me as one of their own. It gave me special satisfaction to play to those who were discovering the harpsichord for the first time through me.

Although I was so happy to be working and in demand, the years between 1959 and 1962 – after a decade of political terror – heralded a newer and bleaker time for us. It was the height of the Cold War and then the Cuban Crisis when another war suddenly seemed imminent. Viktor was working at the radio station where preparations were being made for the war to begin. He was terribly depressed and in 1961 he began to compose his Symphony No. 2., Op. 18 – his Sinfonia Pacis (Peace Symphony) – as a plea for peace. He didn't want it to be called that to begin with because 'peace' was a word used profanely by the communists when complaining about the West as 'war mongerers' while they arranged 'peace conferences'. In the end, he specifically stated that his symphony was not about peace for one group or another. It was peace for all people, notwithstanding their race, nationality or social position. The first movement opens with the tinkling sound of the radio signal from the Soviet Sputnik satellite, the launch of which in 1957 precipitated the Space Race.

The message was that humanity was ready to go into the cosmos but was still so primitive that we were on the brink of war. Then after a very vigorous *scherzo* there was a third slow movement that was really an elegy for a burned world. It led to the funeral march and repeated itself again and again and then the fourth movement started with a simple children's song, took us to the theme of a fugue and then ended optimistically with bells, before the theme of the fugue was repeated. This symphony is Viktor's profound and stirring musical reaction to the threat of war and it perfectly reflected our mood at that time.

The communists, of course, objected strongly to his new symphony, which scored another black mark against him, but it became a very important work in his career because it was played almost all over the world. In Durban, South Africa, the performance had to be repeated because it was so well received. There was a similar response in Australia and all over Europe, where it was performed with some of the greatest conductors. Sergiu Celibidache, principal conductor at the Berlin Philharmonic, called it 'one of the greatest symphonies of the twentieth century'.

After that, he wrote his String Quartet No. 2 for his father, who was dying – a powerful and expressive piece. Ironically, this was a very happy time for me musically because in 1962 there was a new fashion for early music in Czechoslovakia, a movement that had crept in from abroad. Many new chamber orchestras were being formed, including the Prague Chamber Soloists, with whom I performed often, and the Slovak Chamber Orchestra featuring violinist and conductor Bohdan Warchal, always a great experience. To be in such collectives was beautiful and I enjoyed playing with chamber groups as much as I enjoyed performing solo. In both regards, I was becoming quite well known as a concert artist, with attachments to two separate chamber groups with whom I travelled in England, Germany, and Austria.

I was not actually a very strict early music performer. I had my own ideas about performing it and used to play on a modern instrument. I liked what we harpsichordists call the colours. I didn't feel so much at ease with those small French instruments and longed for a sixteen-foot harpsichord, like the ones Handel and Wanda Landowska used to play. Sixteen-foot, like eight-, four- and two-foot, are all octave pitch relationships and not lengths. (Almost all harpsichords made before 1958 were equipped with a sixteen-foot set of strings that sounded an octave lower than the eight-foot pitch, which is now the norm.) I was never orthodox. Nor did I object, though, when given the opportunity to play on something historic. The Dutch keyboard player and conductor, Gustav Leonhardt, was critical of me for that. I never attacked him, but he wrote to one of my students that only a 'primitive' could think of using a sixteen-foot register in Bach. He was a puritan about what he thought was historic, but we now know the sixteen-foot was authentic after all. Karl Richter used to say that anyone who had listened to the *Qui Tollis* in the B Minor Mass would never say Bach didn't have a sixteen-foot stop.

I was amused to be presented as a romantic, a sort of Slavonian from the far woods, not knowing anything about early music. It was quite the opposite. I knew when I went to the West that my students and I would be regarded this way, so I was quite particular that they should be in touch with all the early music developments. Maybe I was too punctilious. I once recorded some Purcell, including a little march that ended with a dominant chord. I was not sure whether to play it da capo or not, so I wrote to the musicologist professor Thurston Dart at King's College, London, to ask. I got a funny reply. He said he thought it would be all the same to Purcell if he heard me playing. I was very moved by this.

By this time I had a manager in Munich who handled all my bookings and liaised with the Czech state. He secured me an engagement in a castle in Germany called Schloss Langenburg, which belonged to the Hohenlohe family, relatives by marriage of Prince Philip – Queen Elizabeth II's husband. The former Prince Gottfried had been a huge music lover who owned a Steinway piano and an ancient harpsichord and invited musicians from all over the world to play them both. After he died his eldest son Kraft took over the estate and, although he was not especially musical, he wanted to keep up the tradition. The castle was high on a hill in a beautiful part of Baden-Württemberg so I was happy when my agent arranged for me to go for three days and give a recital of early music.

I liked the young count. He was very pleasant. When I arrived he met me in person and I asked him, 'How should I address you please? Your Highness?'

He smiled. 'What would you call me in Prague?'

'Comrade,' I replied with a shrug.

He laughed so hard and we got on well after that.

He was a medical doctor and his wife was a librarian, I believe, and they had led a relatively normal life until they had to move to the castle when he inherited the title. They did not appear to be especially wealthy and the castle was extremely cold, so he lit many big fires. He had no airs and graces and welcomed me into his family. I even helped him to bathe his babies.

We had a lovely dinner, where he sat me on his left and we talked and talked. Halfway through the meal he noticed the number on my arm and he asked about it so we spoke about that too. He didn't try to hide that he knew all about the camps and was extremely open. A lot of Germans were appalled and claimed not to know a thing about it. One of the dinner guests was Princess Andrew of Greece and Denmark, the elderly mother of Prince Philip, who was deaf and almost blind but also very friendly and she showed me a beautiful doll's house she'd played with as a child.

After I gave my harpsichord recital in the main hall of the castle there was a reception where I was surrounded by people who came forward to thank me and asked me to sign autographs. One man pushed to the front to hand me a small box, wrapped in paper. 'This will bring you luck,' he said, cryptically. 'Think of it as the gift of a German who feels very ashamed of what happened.'

There was no time to respond, so I thanked him before he melted into the crowd.

When I went to my room later that night and opened the package I found that the box contained a heavy gold signet ring with a noble heraldic emblem deeply engraved on it, as if to use as a seal. My immediate thought was that I couldn't possibly accept it, so I hurried back to the reception to try to find the man again, but nobody could tell me who he was or where to find him. It remained a mystery until some years later when Viktor showed me an article that claimed that the prince's father Gottfried had served in the German army during the war but had later been dismissed after joining a plot to assassinate Hitler in 1944.

It made me think then that the young count had probably sent the man who gave it to me. I have worn the ring ever since and consider it my lucky talisman.

The talisman seemed to work because not long afterwards I met a violinist named Josef Suk who had a remarkable musical pedigree. Two years younger than me, he was the great grandson of the composer Antonín Dvořák, and the grandson of Dvořák's favourite pupil, the composer Josef Suk. He and I were approached by Czech television to appear on a programme they were making about promising young artists. Strangely, they dressed me in a ball gown and took us to a castle where they balanced the harpsichord at an angle on a slope overlooking a river and asked us to play. We both laughed so much that we soon formed a bond.

Then we started to play Bach together and the chemistry was immediate. We didn't even have to practise. It worked so wonderfully well that I came up with the idea of working with him and a flautist, but the flautist turned me down as he was by then a soloist with the Czech Philharmonic. In the end we decided to form a chamber music duo instead, which was the beginning of a thirty-five-year partnership that took us all around the world.

Josef was a delightful colleague and we understood each other completely. He was gallant, sociable, and humorous. He'd been suspended from the Prague Academy in the 1950s for objecting to being forced to dig trenches for fear it would ruin his hands, and was punished with two years' military service playing violin. We were not in the same class but we immediately loved each other, and his wife Marienka and Viktor felt the same so we became a close foursome. Viktor wrote a concerto for Josef and a sonata for us both. My husband was never jealous and understood that we were just musically sympathetic with each other.

The same year I met Josef Suk I was invited back to the United Kingdom, this time to the luxurious country home of a man named Robin Bagot, who was a great lover of baroque music and especially the harpsichord. He designed, built, and played several of his own instruments. His home was a beautiful manor house called Levens Hall in the Lake District. Robin had inherited the house as a boy and spent much of his life renovating and restoring it. I was welcomed most warmly by him and his family and my recital was a great success.

Later that night, after I had retired to my chamber with its four-poster bed, I was awoken in the night by a little black dog running happily around my room. Sleepily, I wondered how it had gained entry, as my door was shut, and went back to sleep.

When I went down to breakfast the following morning, I was met by the Bagot family and their many dogs. 'Where's the little black one?' I asked, innocently, and they all stopped talking and looked at me.

'Did you see it?' Robin asked.

'Yes,' I said, laughing. 'It was in my room playing all night.'

I subsequently learned that the phantom dog was one of Levens Hall's many ghosts, which included a 'Grey Lady' and a ghostly figure playing the harpsichord – a detail that pleased me greatly.

*

Most of the time I was living an ordinary life and not dining in castles and great halls at all, but grabbing something to eat from a street kiosk in between rehearsals or performances. I was so busy there was hardly any time for anything else.

On a day in 1964 I was called to the Ministry of Culture and told that I was going to teach some English students who were arriving for a year on a cultural scholarship from Oxford and Cambridge, organised by the British Council. One of them was a young man named Christopher Hogwood.

My first impression of Christopher was that he was a rather strange fellow. He immediately told me that he was only in Prague because of me and said that he didn't want to see or hear anything of a communist city. 'I am just coming to the musicology department to have lessons, and that's it,' he declared. Of course, it didn't take long for him to fall in love with Prague and we became good friends. The next time he came he told me he couldn't bear to stay away so long.

Dear Christopher could have been a great soloist, but he already knew that he was a Renaissance man, wanting to focus on his conducting, editing, and scholarship. He became an eminent conductor, harpsichordist, and musicologist who founded the Academy of Ancient Music and became a leading figure in the early music revival. He and I became close and he often came to visit me. After he died, aged seventy-three, in 2014, his brother wrote and said he always spoke about me.

The same year that I started teaching Christopher I was invited by the violinist Henryk Szeryng to perform at the Dubrovnik Festival. I was also asked back to Berlin by conductor Helmut Koch, who selected me along with fellow harpsichordists Hans Pischner, Hannes Kästner and Linda Köbler to perform Bach's concertos for four harpsichords and orchestra, a real thrill. Then the Czech record company Artia approached the authorities to ask if I could record the Goldberg Variations for export.

Within a year of its publication and subsequent reception, Michel Garcin, a producer with the Erato record company in Paris, came to Prague to make me an extraordinary offer. It was a ten-year contract to record the entire keyboard works of

Bach on harpsichord, a total of forty playlists across twenty-one discs. Astonishingly, this vast body of work had never been recorded in its entirety to include the peripheral works such as the four-movement Sonata in D Major, a number of minor fugues and preludes, the sonatas for violin and harpsichord and viola da gamba and harpsichord, as well as transcriptions of Vivaldi concertos, and the Triple Concerto in A Minor and the Brandenburg Concerto No. 5. Michel was an enthusiastic young man tasked with building up an original catalogue of baroque works with a specialisation in French music for the ten-year-old label. Best of all, the recordings were to be in studios, concert halls, and churches throughout Paris.

I could hardly believe my luck.

The kudos of having a Czech musician go down in history as the first person ever to do this must have been too great for the state to resist. I'm sure the fee was lucrative too. It wasn't an easy negotiation, though. They asked that the contract give the Czech record company Supraphon the rights to the Eastern bloc while Erato kept the Western world. It was a tense time while they considered the position, but in the end they came to a compromise.

Erato did everything they could to help me complete my mammoth undertaking. They paid for me to have French lessons and they arranged for me to play a range of instruments in Paris, including some heavier 'Revival' harpsichords manufactured by German companies such as Ammer, Sperrhake, and Neupert. These modern instruments incorporate some latter-day piano technology such as steel wire to update the sound, which purists believe detracts from that intended by the composers, but which I try to exploit to the best of my ability.

I was also fortunate enough to be allowed to play historic and original double manual harpsichords made by Henri Hemsch in 1754 and 1761 – two of only five left in the world. These had been restored by the French harpsichord maker Claude Mercier-Ythier, who had recently opened a shop in Paris – *À la corde Pincée* – specialising only in the harpsichord. I could never have imagined such a resurgence of interest in my beloved harpsichord that it could warrant a shop all to itself in the middle of the Swinging Sixties.

I had never played on such a venerable instrument as the Hemsch and immediately noticed the difference. The sound was better and the keys lower than the twentieth-century harpsichord built by the German Jürgen Ammer that I usually played for my Supraphon recordings.

Then the record company chose some remarkable soloists for me to perform with, not least Josef Suk and Pierre Fournier, but also the French flautist Jean-Pierre Rampal, and some historic places for me to record in – usually at night when there was less noise. Among the most memorable were the beautiful churches Notre-Dame du Liban, and the German Evangelical Church, as well as the tiny Salle Adyar theatre in the shadow of the Eiffel Tower. It is so artistically inspiring to work in somewhere like an old chapel. I would always focus on some detail within it such as an angel or a painting and create a visual theatre around it in my head as I lost myself to the music once more.

Michel Garcin was a marvellous producer and extremely patient with me. There was also a deputy director of the company and his wife, as well as a capable technician. Our collaboration worked very well and our efforts produced the volume of work of which I will always be most proud.

Not that it was without its frustrations, the chief one being that I was watched everywhere I went and the Czech authorities would only allow me to be in Paris for three or four days at a time. This meant that I had no time to listen to what had been recorded with the engineers, and tell them which ones to keep or have the time to correct technical mistakes. The editing was done elsewhere, later, and without me.

Under such pressure to get the work done within the time allowed, things often felt rushed and I had absolutely no time for myself – just a few hours in the morning and then another short break in the afternoon. I also had to learn to respect the relationship between the harpsichord and the microphone, and subordinate my technical expertise in order to adjust the dynamics and change the pace – shortening breaks between sentences and so on. The highlight was being taken to some wonderful French restaurants after work where I once again marvelled at the heavenly butter and the bread and often ate so much of it that there was hardly room for anything else.

I missed Viktor terribly of course and barely had any contact with him at all when I was away because we still didn't have a telephone at home – we had applied but it took more than ten years before it was permitted. This enormous project to create the complete recordings of Bach began in 1965 and ended in 1974, a pivotal time for our country, whose political turmoil was reflected in how often I was allowed to travel to France or sometimes Switzerland, and when the Erato team had to come to Prague instead. I felt more at home in Prague but I was happiest in Paris.

It was whilst preparing for one of those trips to Switzerland that I behaved in a most cowardly way. I wanted my mother to go with me and it would have been possible then if Viktor had stayed in Prague as hostage. I got her a passport and she was almost issued an exit permit when I realised what a shock it would be for her to find out that the world she knew during the First Republic still existed out there, beyond our borders. She had reconciled herself to the world as it was and I was afraid what would have happened if she saw the freedoms of life elsewhere. In the worst-case scenario, I imagined her as depressed and uncommunicative as she had been during the war and I knew then that I didn't have the strength or the energy to cope with that. Once I realised how she might react I never took her anywhere with me, out of respect for her feelings – and for my own.

During the more lenient years, I had a standing visa to France, so every time I was ready to record I would contact Erato and they'd arrange everything. The ideal rehearsal period for me before I recorded any work was about eighteen months. I practised and practised in my spare time between performances and on holidays and then I tested my interpretations and concepts in front of an audience, paying detailed attention to my own evaluation and their responses. I'd return to the piece six weeks before the deadline, re-practising it and thinking some more about the concept. Then I was ready.

These were some of the happiest years in my musical life, because I was studying Bach all the time. And every time I sat at the harpsichord I discovered more and more about him and the depth of his creation. Bach really became the philosopher of my life. In his music he created complete images of the world. He searched for life's meaning and he found it. His message was as clear to me as day or as a starry night.

It was even better when some of the recordings took place in Prague, because then I had Viktor helping me and working with me. I really had my hands full because of all my other commitments too, and I couldn't record without having concerts because that was a necessary part of my recording contract.

The set was released in 1975 on black vinyl as twenty-one records, and won the prestigious Grand Prix de L'Académie Charles Cros and really opened me up to the world. Fans of the harpsichord around the globe were able to buy the recordings and listen to my interpretations and so I became more and more in demand. After Bach they asked me to record all of Scarlatti, but it would have been the same amount of work and I already had so many concerts booked, which I needed to do to sell the CDs and to keep the state happy. Then Erato signed a contract to release the CDs with the Japanese and that's when I became famous in Japan, which in turn led to me recording the whole of Purcell.

By this time I was quite free to play as I liked. I could use my own repertoire. I have always changed my repertoire frequently to take in new things, including twentieth-century music, so during this period I was enjoying more freedom than I had ever known.

Sadly, I was still not allowed to teach Czech students, only foreign ones. This hurt me very much because it had always been so important to both Viktor and I to pass on any expertise or knowledge that we might have had. In many ways I lost the best years of my life as a pedagogue because in your thirties you really start to discover things that you want to share with your students.

There was still a lot of state anti-Semitism which I only became aware of when I tried to do something unusual.

Under the more relaxed regime, the ban on the Czech composer Martinů was lifted, so I planned to give the first hearing of his harpsichord concerto, which had never been played in Czechoslovakia before. Viktor, my mother and I were friendly with Karel Ančerl who was the chief of the Czech Philharmonic. He had been in Terezín with us and survived. It was Karel who called the skinny teenagers his 'little rabbits' and gave us extra soup. He didn't remember me among the thousands he helped to feed, but he was always so kind to me after the war, especially when he knew what we'd been through. He also loved Viktor and especially his work. He called him my 'modest man' because in spite of his mastery of music he remained so humble about his work.

I was excited to be working with Ančerl at last and to be giving this important premiere, but I hadn't appreciated how much the state would be against it. We were all prepared when out of the blue I was informed, 'You won't be allowed to play the concerto. A high party official has said that one Jew in the Czech Philharmonic is more than enough.' I was devastated. A Viennese harpsichordist was engaged for the concert, which was painful for me. After that I was never allowed to play with the Philharmonic under Karel Ančerl during the whole of his tenure. I only ever played under his successor Václav Neumann, and all because 'two Jews in the Czech Philharmonic were two too many'.

Thankfully, right after I played my first concert with Václav Neuman we knew that the chemistry was there, and so we started our own chamber orchestra group. It is usual that the conductor and the soloists get together before the concert to know what each wants from the other. Neumann didn't feel the need for that and said, 'No, no, no. You know I am quite an intelligent person, and, and besides, I hear you think.' It was like playing tennis. He'd get one ball from me and give it back in another way. It was really extraordinary and we formed a steady group, like with Josef Suk. I loved the way we collaborated together.

Neumann and I had a rather amusing experience at a concert of Handel and Benda in Prague in 1960. The concert was a great success and having played my part, I stood to bow to the audience only to realise that I had screwed my green silk gown into the stool when I'd adjusted my seat. To much laughter all round, Václav Neumann and my fellow soloists came to my rescue and eventually released me.

Rather marvellously, Viktor's music started to be performed by the mainstream orchestras in Czechoslovakia too. He was asked by Ančerl and Neumann to write works for the Czech Philharmonic, and was becoming increasingly well known. The problem was that the state press frequently harassed him. Every poor review he received was dangerous because that really could have sent him to the mines, but Viktor was always quite calm about it.

One night after his piano concerto was performed all the composers and the reviewers were invited to discuss his work and find whether there were any 'ideological faults'. There was one strict and much feared reviewer who announced that he really didn't like the work. He claimed it was too idealistic. Viktor responded that our next-door neighbour liked it and added that this meant there were two opinions and he would prefer to accept the one from our neighbour. It was of course a cheeky answer, but also quite risky.

In spite of his insubordination, as I was becoming quite profitable for the authorities, they chose to overlook my marriage, my race, and my dubious political character and began to afford me the kind of VIP status that allowed me to travel more and more. I was finally allowed a telephone so that I could receive new offers and check my diary before going through all the formalities with the state. It was a common line shared with others in the building and we knew that every conversation was listened to.

Whenever I was offered a particularly good contract I was encouraged, or rather instructed, to play because the state was eager for my earnings and the prestige to their reputation. The authorities based their decision on whether I could go or not on the terms offered and how that country stood with us politically.

I wasn't usually aware of the requests until they'd been approved. Nothing was ever said, but I would often learn whilst abroad that an invitation had been denied. I couldn't go to America, China, or South Africa, and I never went to Greece for some reason. Nevertheless I had bookings for so many concerts that some of them were years in advance. My mother despaired. 'You are crazy. None of us know what will happen tomorrow and yet you have diary engagements ten years ahead!"

This was partly due to the baroque music revolution in the 1960s that was sparked by popular bands incorporating classical instruments into their songs to create an orchestral sound. I was suddenly in such demand that I think I must have visited almost every European country, even if I often didn't know where I was going until the last minute. Sometimes, the authorities would issue me with my passport and only tell me the night before that I had to report at the train station or the airport at 9 a.m. the following morning. Once there I'd be met by an official, who would only then give me my itinerary for Holland or Germany, the Soviet Union or Yugoslavia.

They believed that by giving me such short notice I wouldn't have enough time to make contact with anyone politically subversive or to arrange things so that I could defect. And of course I was never allowed to go to the United States until 1985 when I was invited to play at the United Nations in New York for the three-hundredth anniversary of Bach, an invitation the Czech government couldn't refuse. The concern was that I had family in New York and could easily have stayed, but they also knew of my devotion to Viktor and my mother, so they decided to risk it.

With each new booking, I often had to guess where I would be going and whether I'd need to pack warm clothing for, say, Siberia, or lighter clothing for Armenia. The only clue I had was that I knew the working harpsichords were only in certain countries, and that if I had recently visited a city then I was unlikely to be invited back so soon. Then there were all the places I was told to go that I didn't especially want to go to like Riga in Latvia, where there was real hunger and poverty. I held a master class in Riga once and, afterwards, some of the students put up their hands and said they wanted to ask me a private question.

'Very well,' I replied, 'But all the class has to hear it.'

They looked from one to the other. 'No, we want to ask a special question,' they insisted. Sheepishly, they came to the front of the class and showed me a plate covered in a cloth. Lifting the cloth I found some twenty or so open sandwiches made with mashed carrots, five of which had thin slices of salami on them. They wanted me to have these five special sandwiches while they ate the ones without meat. I was touched and it made me appreciate how rare a commodity salami must have been for them to have chosen it as my treat.

By contrast, parts of Siberia were luxurious – especially Novosibirsk, a famous city that's home to many of the best Russian scientists, and a major stop on the Trans-Siberian Railway. It had some wonderful buildings and my accommodation was always of the best quality. When I first went there in the 1960s, I travelled with my own harpsichord because no one knew what a harpsichord was. The audience responded so enthusiastically that the city's orchestra quickly acquired its own and trained some excellent tuners too.

Whenever I had to travel with my harpsichord, which had to be transported on the same train as me, it often took hours and hours of travelling. In the Soviet Union this meant crossing thousands of kilometres of land on which there was nothing but birch trees. Sometimes you might see a few cottages, wooden mostly, but no fields, no cows, no horses, nothing. Just birches and more birches. One day, en route to Siberia, I suddenly spotted – in the middle of the birch forest – a massive billboard on which was written in huge letters, 'PLAY BADMINTON'. I started to laugh and my interpreter, who went everywhere I went and kept an eye on me politically, asked me, 'Why are you laughing?' I couldn't really explain it to him. It seemed so absurd. In the middle of nowhere somebody in the Communist Party had this idea to promote sports, so they commissioned this enormous billboard.

The absurdities of life under communism went on in Prague too. Somehow we prevailed, and even managed to keep our sense of humour. Every three months we had a so-called evaluation when somebody from the party interrogated us. One day a senior member said to me, 'It is good that you are getting such critical acclaim from abroad, Comrade, but you are working with holy music like the Passions, with Christ, with religion. What about your political work?'

I smiled before giving him my reply. 'Well, Comrade, I think of politics often. For example, Johann Sebastian Bach was an employee of the city of Leipzig and, as such, he had to write his cantatas for the church. Maybe if Bach lived in Prague today he would be an employee of the city of Prague. Do you think he would have written his cantatas about Lenin?'

I'm not sure he really understood my reasoning, and he didn't know what to say. He couldn't say yes and he couldn't say no, so he let me go. I think my gaze was enough to send him on his way.

10

Hamburg, 1944

After the death of Fredy and the liquidation of almost the entire September transport in Auschwitz-II Birkenau in March 1944, those of us left grieving in the family camp were under no illusions that it would be our turn next.

A six-month rotation from the day we'd arrived would mean that in June 1944, the Nazis would execute us in exactly the same way as our friends and relatives before us. A sense of desperate inevitability pervaded everything after that. No matter how much we carried on living or breathing or working with the children, our hearts were heavy and our minds numb.

Clutching at straws and desperate for any crumb of hope, we girls turned to a fellow prisoner named Klara who knew how to read tarot cards. I have no idea how she was able to keep hold of her cards in that place and she started off reading them just for fun but, in time, we looked to her for answers to some of the questions that constantly consumed our thoughts. For example, there was a woman who was hiding her pregnancy who asked if her baby would survive. Klara laid out the cards, looked at the emaciated young woman and told her, 'Your baby will be sound and healthy.' I have no idea whether that turned out to be the case – and I doubt it – but, increasingly, some of Klara's prophecies came true. Frightened by her own accuracy, she announced that she wouldn't read the cards again. Nothing we could do or say would persuade her. Not until much later when another of her predictions came true.

Fredy's chosen successors took over the children's block and did their best to keep up morale, especially Hugo Lenk, who was a good man. It was hard to play and sing with the little ones, however, when we knew what was in store for them – and for us. There were other reasons to be anxious too. Tilla Fischlová, the block tormentor and my former Maccabi tutor, had been among those murdered in the September transport. I couldn't help but wonder if Karel had been forced to dispose of her body, although I learned later that he was killed shortly afterwards too. Most of our block was happy that Tilla was gone, but we had a new *älteste* in charge of us who could be just as mean, and Tilla's death meant that I could no longer spend an hour in the warmth of her little room each night.

There were other casualties too – not all of them unwelcome. The feared pimp Arno Böhm, who'd fallen for the girl who helped out in the children's block, negotiated with the SS officers who visited his brothel frequently that his sweetheart be sent back from the gas chambers with the doctors. The following morning he found out that they didn't keep their promise.

That night there was a scene worthy of Shakespeare in the brothel. I wasn't an eyewitness to it, but we heard about it later. Böhm invited his SS friends to their normal orgy, complete with the musicians, and when they were at the height of the feast he took a knife and attacked them. He murdered one of the senior officers and stabbed a second before he could be grabbed and sent to the gas chamber. These Greek tragedies were happening around us all the time. As was the way of the camp, his death didn't mean the brothel was shut down. Somebody else just took over the running of it, and so the ghastly music played on and on.

Böhm was replaced by a much kinder *Lager älteste,* though, a German sea captain named Willi who tried to make our lives as bearable as possible and who called us 'my girls'. He wore the green triangle of a saboteur, but I don't know if he really did commit sabotage or if he simply got drunk and neglected his ship. He was serving his sentence in Auschwitz and it was almost over, which made him happy. He used to sing us old sailor songs in German and he even gave us some seedlings to plant, but of course in that vile Polish clay no flower would ever bloom.

There was another young woman who worked in our block who was dating someone from outside the camp. Renée Neumannová was older than us, tall, blonde and very beautiful. An SS sergeant called Viktor Pestek fell madly in love with her. Pestek, who was in his twenties, was the kindest of all our guards and extremely handsome. From the start he came to Fredy and it was evident that the camp and everything that was going on there appalled him. He had helped Fredy as much as he could with food and fuel for the fire. Everyone called him 'Miláček', which means darling.

Strangely, Miláček's older brother was an SS officer whom everyone hated. He was terrible man and we called him 'Mickey Mouse'. The story went that after Miláček was injured on the Russian front his older brother arranged for him to be posted to Auschwitz to keep him safe.

According to accounts after the war, Miláček grew sick of the 'stench of the camp' and came up with a plan to help others escape, including his beloved Renée. In April 1944, he first smuggled out a former Czech soldier named Lederer dressed in the uniform of an SS lieutenant colonel, marching out with him on the day Miláček was due to take some leave. The pair made it to Czechoslovakia where Lederer broke into Terezín to inform them of the horrors of Auschwitz and send evidence of it to the Vatican. Tragically, nobody believed him or, if they did, they didn't act. After trying to get similar messages to the Swiss Red Cross, he fled to the hills and joined the partisans until the end of the war.

Miláček meanwhile spent his leave securing false papers, clothes, and all that he needed to rescue his love – and her mother – from the camp, as Renée refused to leave without her. When he returned to Auschwitz with everything in place, the SS were waiting for him at the train station and he was arrested. They had worked out the whole story and how Lederer had escaped. Charged with desertion and aiding a prisoner, Miláček was savagely interrogated and brutally beaten before being shot. Renée was not implicated in any way so she was safe, if heartbroken. It was a tragic love story.

In May the next transport arrived from Terezín and we knew then that our time was running out. Mummy and I searched for Dagmar, my uncle and aunt, Karel and Kamila, among the throng of new faces, but there was so sign.

Shortly afterwards we too were instructed to write postcards to loved ones which meant that our liquidation felt ever closer. Mummy wrote to family and I wrote to Hanuš in Terezín, signing myself off with the Hebrew word for dead – *Mavet* – so as to warn him what awaited them in Auschwitz. It was years before I discovered that he received it and immediately assumed I'd been killed, which is why he never tried to find me after the war.

With what seemed like the end looming, some of those who'd previously hoped to organise a revolt with Fredy – including Hugo Lenk – decided to try something again. They armed some of the teachers in the children's block with pistols and made themselves ready. We had no idea what was going to happen or when but the thought of it only made us more frantic. I remember one night when we were so afraid that we'd be gassed any day that we pleaded with Hugo to let us stay on in the children's block instead of returning to our cramped and stinking quarters.

'We just want to dance once more in our lives,' we told him, but he turned us down.

'You would dance yourselves to death,' he replied. 'And the SS would take you. Don't worry; you will have many more chances to dance in your lives. Something will happen!'

And something really did happen, because in the early hours of 6 June 1944 – the day that we were led to believe we'd all be gassed – the Allies instigated D-Day with the Normandy landings. We found out later that at 10 a.m. in London the BBC announced the assault so that the Germans would realise the war was finally turning against them. The reaction was one of horror, and there was great panic that morning in Auschwitz. The SS received some new orders and Mengele hurried into the camp where he and the *Lager älteste* conferred for a long time.

We were told that the next day there would be a *Selektion*, the first we had ever experienced, as the Nazis had been ordered to mobilise every man to the front and send healthy women and men to work in Germany. Of the 5,000 in the family camp who were earmarked to be gassed imminently, 1,000 healthy men and 1,000 healthy women would be chosen instead for a slower death by war or by slave labour.

The whole of that night the block was in turmoil and the following morning we were summoned to stand in line outside the children's block where we had to wait for hours in the hot sun. Those ahead of us came out and told us that the sick and unfit were sent to the gas, while those suitable for work were sent elsewhere. My mother and I talked and talked about what we should say, because the SS were asking for prisoners' professions at the *Selektion*. We knew then that whatever we answered could be crucial and help decide whether we were picked or not. It was a terrible and grotesque situation. After much debate, we decided that Mummy would say she was a glove-maker, like her father, and I would say I was a gymnastics teacher to prove that I was fit. My mother had never made a glove in her life, although she had practised making ties in Plzeň, and my father would have laughed out loud at the suggestion that I was a teacher of sports.

Once inside the block, we found the man I knew as Obersturmführer Schwarzhuber in charge but dead drunk, sitting astride the brick flue surrounded by empty and half-empty bottles of vodka and schnapps. We were all instructed to strip naked and step up onto the flue one by one to be examined. Each of us was ordered to state our age and profession. We watched in agony as he selected some to go '*links*' to the left side of the flue, and others to go '*rechts*' or right. Everyone in the camp knew that *links* meant the gas chambers, which meant that *rechts* was for the work detail.

I looked at my mother next in line and gave her a small smile of encouragement. My heart sank at the sight of her, though. Standing there naked, her arm self-consciously across her breasts, she was so thin and looked even older than her forty-eight years. When it was her turn to be interrogated, she said, 'I am forty-six and a glove maker.'

Schwarzhuber just waved his hand dismissively. '*Links.*'

Panicking, I immediately considered leaping over the flue to join her and the older women huddled in a miserable group, but it was suddenly my turn and someone pushed me forward. I stood naked before Schwarzhuber and stated that I was eighteen (I was really seventeen) and a gym teacher. In German, he replied, slurring, 'Very well, show me something!' Hesitating for only a moment, I managed a passable somersault.

'*Rechts.*'

Instead, I stepped to the left. Schwarzhuber looked up and shouted, '*Dumme Gans, wo gehst du hin, du gehst falsch, du gehst in den Tod!*' ('You stupid goose, where are you going? You are going wrong. You are going to your death!').

Pulling myself up to my full metre and a half, I looked him in the eye and told him coldly, 'You already killed my father. You are going to kill my mother. I don't want to live anymore.' I genuinely felt that way and I didn't have anything to lose.

Shaking his head, he looked at me and at Mummy and sighed. '*Aufstehen, geh, du alte Ziege!*' he said, calling her an 'old goat' and flapping his hand drunkenly to indicate she should go with me to the right.

We were both so relieved to be leaving Auschwitz, no matter where we were to be sent. The ones who had been sent left were all marched to a barrack where they were told they'd be put in quarantine. We doubted that we would ever see them again. Although we felt liberated, we couldn't be truly happy because we had witnessed so many terrible things during that *Selektion* – mothers with young children having to decide whether they would go with their children to the gas chambers, or go right and survive. Most of them went with their children, but some didn't, and the look in their eyes would never leave us. I can't imagine they ever got over that.

Once selected, each of us were handed papers that stated we'd be going to work in Germany. I was desperate to know which of my friends had also been saved and where they were being sent, so I hurried to our block to find out. I was pleased to learn that most had been chosen too.

Then a dreadful thing happened. Later that day, while the *Selektion* was still going on, Dr Josef Mengele arrived in the camp. He flew into a horrible rage and chastised Schwarzhuber publicly. There was an awful row. Mengele told the clearly intoxicated soldier that it was not his job to examine the prisoners and that only he, as the doctor and head of the women's camp, could decide who was fit for work. He immediately cancelled the *Selektion* and called for it to be restarted. I was terribly worried then because I knew that what had miraculously happened before with my mother, thanks to a watery-eyed drunk, couldn't possibly happen again.

Somehow in all this upset and confusion, I had lost sight of her. We were all ordered to stand in line, but I couldn't see her anywhere. The day got hotter and hotter and our queue snaked outside the block as Mengele sat inside choosing who should live and who should die. All of a sudden, when it was almost my turn, there was a thunderstorm and a terrible downpour. The SS officers who were supposed to guard us ran away and so did we. My friends and I ran to the latrines and hid.

The rain saved us that day because after that Mengele gave up his grim selection, as it was too much trouble to find everyone and get them back in line. I think he just wanted to make a gesture to his underling. Somebody came to the latrines and told us, 'Mengele has gone. *Selektion* is over!' And I was happy then – the first time I had ever been happy in Auschwitz. The sun came out and I ran around looking for my mother to tell her the good news.

I spotted her walking towards me down the *Lagerstrasse* and I ran to her and cried, 'How lucky we were that the second *Selektion* was cancelled, Mummy?'

'Cancelled?' she replied. 'But I went to it.'

I looked at her, aghast.

'No! What happened?' I asked.

She grinned. 'I passed.' My dear mother was always so disciplined in the camps that she did just as she was told. When she couldn't find me, she went and stood in line hoping to meet me in the block and, for some reason I have never been able to fathom, Dr Mengele sent her to the right.

Was it Fate, or another miracle? We will never know.

Before we could be released from the nightmare of Auschwitz, we first had to endure another ordeal – a period of quarantine in the *Frauenlager* or women's camp. We thought we'd had it bad in the *Familienlager,* but quickly realised that we'd been better off than most.

The main women's camp was so overcrowded by then that they didn't even have any spare blocks, so we were pushed into cellars full of rats. That night was a true nightmare, because we were very afraid of the rats, which were dangerous. We were given no food and the water quickly ran out. It was dark and damp and filthy and we prayed that we would be allowed out of there soon.

Thankfully, after three days we were let out and marched to the railway ramp where the SS handed us over to *Wehrmacht* soldiers tasked with escorting us to Germany. We were so looking forward to getting out of Auschwitz that we hardly paid attention to the soldiers, so accustomed were we to keeping our heads down and avoiding all eye contact. We couldn't help but notice their shock at the sight of us, though. I have never seen people so appalled as those German soldiers when they first set eyes on us. Some of them vomited and many had to turn away from the sight and the smell. They must have had a glimpse of the camp before, and they must have smelled bodies being burned, but I think up until that moment they really had no idea what went on there or how we had been treated.

It made us extremely self-conscious to see ourselves in others' eyes for the first time. None of us had seen a mirror in years. We were so used to everyone around us being dirty and skeletal in ragged clothing, crawling with lice and diseases, that we barely noticed it anymore. These older soldiers, many of whom would have fought for their country in the First World War and lived through the hell of the trenches, were completely stunned.

Immediately, there was a change of atmosphere as they tried to treat us considerately. That, too, was a shock. No one had shown us any compassion in years to the point that many became emotional at the smallest kindness – the offer of a morsel of bread or a drink of water. Although we knew we were still captives of the Nazis, we suddenly had the feeling that we had entered another world. We even received new clothes – proper prisoners' uniforms – thin tunics and tops with dark yellow stripes, wooden clogs, but no cap – and were able to abandon the stinking, threadbare rags that had been thrown at us six months earlier. Then 500 of us were helped into ordinary trains, not the cattle wagons we had come to dread. We were so happy when the train pulled out of Auschwitz. We couldn't believe that we had somehow escaped that hell.

The journey took us the 850 kilometres to Hamburg in two or three days, stopping frequently because of Allied air raids and to allow more important trains carrying soldiers or armaments to pass. On several occasions our train even went into reverse, which was a horrible sensation, as we feared it meant we were being sent back to Auschwitz. Generally, though, we were much more relaxed than the last time we'd been on a train because we had started to lead the life of simple prisoners, not animals.

When we eventually arrived in the Hamburg docks late at night we found them in ruins and still burning from recent bombardments. We were herded into warehouses known as *Lagerhauses* along the River Elbe at Dessauer port, which were all part of the 'Neuengamme' concentration camp system. Incredibly, we had neatly made beds and they were clean, and then they gave us some smoked fish to eat – our first in four years; it tasted absolutely wonderful. We learned later that this was a mistake; the fish was meant for the German workers, not us, but we suspected the soldiers in charge of us had something to do with the mix-up. Somewhat reluctantly, it seemed, they handed us over to an SS captain, so suddenly we were back in the control of the men – and women – we feared the most. Fortunately, they were mostly customs officers seconded to the SS and were older and far less of a threat than they'd been in Auschwitz.

From almost the moment we arrived, the strategic port of Hamburg was regularly bombed – you could almost set your watches by it. At noon the English came, then at midnight the Americans. Much of the city had already been destroyed in a firestorm that killed thousands the previous year. Half of the surviving residents had fled, but the bombers still came to destroy what was left, dropping phosphorous and other bombs until the whole city was ablaze.

Although we'd often seen and heard waves of planes flying overhead in Auschwitz, this was the first time that we had a real sense of the Germans being under attack. That alone gave us hope. We'd stop work to watch dogfights in the skies overhead and cheer the Allied pilots on. We knew there was a chance that we'd be bombed but none of us was afraid. To our minds, there was a big difference in being executed at the hands of the Nazis and dying as a casualty of the Allies. The fact that we died wasn't the problem.

We would have our dignity.

We might be dead but we'd be free.

Our sleeping quarters were on the upper floors of the warehouses and during the night raids we'd see the searchlights and hear the rumble of planes. Looking out, although we weren't supposed to, we'd wait for the brightly coloured flares that indicated a bomb would soon follow. Often we were left on the upper floors while the guards went to the shelters so that we'd be killed first if the buildings were bombed. If there was time, we were pushed into cellars that were open to the river so we all stood in water to our knees. Whenever the bombs dropped into the Elbe or onto the ships – as they often did – the waters would rise dramatically and we feared that we'd all be drowned. So did the rats that frequently joined us.

Our uniforms were made of extremely thin material and we had no coats, so even in the summer we were cold, especially when wet. One of the women came up with the idea that – when we were in the cellars – we should all strip off and huddle together with our uniforms pressed between us, trying to keep them dry and ourselves warm. It's a miracle we didn't all die of pneumonia.

The problem was that I was so very tired all the time that I would quite literally fall asleep, even standing in freezing water, so the other girls would get angry with me and keep nudging me to stay awake lest I dropped to the ground and we all got wet. Some of the women were killed when they were hit by flying shrapnel or the waves wrenched them away from the rest of us.

Being in those ghastly cellars became a nightly ordeal, but we were grateful at least that we were no longer in Auschwitz and were much better fed. We were each given our own metal bowl and spoon and every day there was bread and real soup – not the foul water we'd been given before. Occasionally, we had some fish. Every morning the thirty or fifty grammes of black bread we were each allowed under rationing would be distributed and cut into slices to put in our pockets and eke out during the day. Often I would be so famished that I'd eat the whole lot in one go and my mother would scold me and tell me to wait. I couldn't help it even though the bread gave me no satisfaction. There were times when I almost went mad with hunger and cold from the cruel wind from the north, and we hadn't yet experienced winter there.

The German priority was to maintain the oil pipeline and to salvage bricks and other materials from the rubble of the city in order to build emergency shelters. Each morning we had to get up early and assemble by the river to be inspected by German supervisors from the different local and international companies. One supervisor might ask for five women for building work; another might need ten for salvage, and so on. They would look for older or younger prisoners, depending on the differing needs and on the whim of the SS. It was a matter of luck which group you were chosen for. Mummy and I would always try to keep together for fear of being separated, and because sometimes a whole group of women didn't come back. The worst raid in October 1944 killed 150 prisoners.

Our first job was to help repair any damage to the buried oil pipelines, digging them out so that experts could fix them before burying them again. This was called the *Geilenbergprogramm* and was extremely hard work, and the SS in charge of us on these details were usually women from the Ravensbrück concentration camp, who were the cruellest of them all. They would either favour young girls or be more sympathetic to the older women, so either Mummy or I were always on the wrong side. She would be shouted at as 'an old witch' or I'd be yelled at for being a 'young ne'er-do-well'. We couldn't win.

Mummy was even more tired than I was, and increasingly despondent. We had been under occupation for five years and prisoners for almost three. When would our suffering end? The weather didn't help, as it was boiling hot in the day or freezing cold at night. After a while, the SS gave my mother the nickname 'Oma' or Grandma, and often left her to clean the block out of kindness and respect to the fact that she was twenty to thirty years older than the rest of us.

Going out to work without her was hard, but I hoped that she would at least be spared the arduous labour, which was often brutal. Ships would arrive in the docks and we had to form a line for each vessel and pass salvaged bricks and rubble from one prisoner to another before they were loaded into the hold. That was what ruined my hands finally, as the bricks were heavy and rough and we were not given gloves. In the cold and damp atmosphere our skin was chafed and scored by the relentless passage of wet brick until our fingers split, cracked and bled, becoming extremely painful. It was such tedious, depressing work. The SS would make a bet between themselves which line of prisoners would fill their ship first, so we were encouraged to work as fast as possible on the promise of some extra soup. I remember the day our line won and we were given some delicious pea soup with proper bread.

Incredibly, we never lost our sense of humour and we all understood the need to take our minds off our situation. One day a senior SS officer heard a strange whispering noise coming from our line and sent someone to investigate. He returned to report that we were reciting, '*Danke, Herr Doktor. Bitte, Herr Doktor*' – saying please and thank you as we passed the bricks in a rhythmic motion down the line. It was something to fix our minds on, as our hands were bleeding and sore.

I tended to stick with one group of girls to whom I'd recite poetry, sing arias, or tell stories from the operas and the librettos, just as I'd done with the children in the camps. This was something necessary for my physical and mental health – otherwise I would have gone mad.

The worst work detail I could be selected for was the *Himmelfahrt*, known as the 'heaven commando', in a place called Neugraben. *Himmelfahrt* means ascension in the religious sense and it was our job to ascend 120 metres to the top of the vast gasometers and brush off any shrapnel from the top. Never in my life had I had to climb so high. Placing one foot in front of the other as I made my way up those narrow, fragile ladders I quickly discovered that I suffered from vertigo, which gave me chronic nausea. We were all so terribly afraid of losing our footing and falling off, as some girls did. They never survived.

A couple of times I was so sure that I too would fall that I'd freeze halfway up, and not be able to go up or down. The SS would stand at the bottom pointing their guns at me and ordering me to get on with it. Sometimes I felt it would be preferable to be shot, but then I thought of my mother, who had always saved my life.

I much preferred being at ground level, but one day when I was in a work party tasked with digging out oil pipelines, I picked up a spade from the tool shed without realising it was covered in petrol. An hour into our work I was perspiring terribly and I wiped my eyes with my hands. The pain was searing and I immediately lost almost all of my vision, but the guards wouldn't give me leave to wash the petrol off so I had to stand out under the sun all day working on as best I could.

By the time I returned to the *Lagerhaus*, my eyes and the skin around them were covered in tiny blisters. I asked for the only doctor we had in the hope of a day off to recover and I was taken to see her, half-blind and by then extremely underweight. She took one look at me and told the guard, 'Never mind, she'll die soon anyway,' before dismissing me with a wave of her hand. Mummy helped me bathe my eyes that night but they still stung badly and

I had to go back out into the sun the next day so blinded that I feared I might lose my sight for good.

Unable to see well even a week later, I was standing in the first row at the morning *Appell* but I wasn't perfectly in line because of my affected vision. We had one nasty *Lagerführer*, a man named Spiess, and he was so furious that I wasn't in line that he picked up a spade and hit me across the side of the head with it. My life was saved by my glasses, which took the force of the blow and were lost, but saved me from being permanently blinded. I was in a terrible predicament then because I became the camp *Muselmann*, very thin, almost blind. My mother was far from well, but her health was better than mine at that point.

Our best luck was when someone we knew from Auschwitz arrived in our camp. It was Willi, the German sea captain who'd been jailed for sabotage. He'd served his sentence but had been immediately enlisted to supervise prisoners. Seeing my injuries and knowing that I'd lost my glasses, he found me some replacements and brought us some old clothes and some bread. We didn't see him for long before we were moved on elsewhere, but we were so grateful for his gifts.

The tragedy was that Mummy and I received less food than everyone else, as we were those stupid, strange, clumsy people who couldn't really steal anything. It is human nature to try to better your lot somehow, and there were many in the camps who stole things or went begging to the Germans for food. Occasionally they would leave something for us – a few potato peels or vegetables that weren't good any more. We devoured them gratefully, ignoring how rotten they were, just as we ate clumps of grass whenever we could find them – anything to fill our growling stomachs.

My mother was courageous and sometimes tried to get something, but she was not very good at it. On one work detail we were sent to deliver coal to a manager's flat in the middle of a residential area where ordinary people were going about their lives. It felt so strange to see normality. We hadn't seen anything like that in years. None of the citizens of Hamburg looked at us. To them, we were already dead. We were invisible.

We delivered the coal and when she was down in the cellar my mother grabbed a large lump of it to hide in her clothing, but then she slipped over climbing out and broke a rib. She was in a lot of pain after that and not at all well. She did manage to hang on to the coal, though, which meant that we could sit closer to the fire while it burned.

All of us lived for the brief meal breaks when we could put something in our bellies and rest our aching limbs. The strange thing was that our labour was 'hired' from the SS by the international companies who owned the warehouses and pipelines, so it was they who were officially responsible for providing our food and lodging. Depending on which company we were working for and when, we sometimes received better meals and – on occasion – were even allowed into their staff canteens to eat it. Every time that happened, the repulsion of the civilian workforce at the sight of us was evident. People were so openly disgusted that I often wondered who they thought we were.

One day we were marched into a lovely warm canteen for some hot soup. Cold and hungry, I was desperate to eat, but as soon as I stepped inside I stopped dead in my tracks, abruptly halting the line of equally weary women behind me. Chopin was playing on a loudspeaker. It was one of his Nocturnes. This was the first time I'd heard any classical music since Terezín, and I couldn't bear it. My happiness had once depended on playing music, but since we'd been in the camps, I had blanked it out completely to save my sanity. To hear it again was the cruellest thing. The idea that somebody was playing Chopin out there in the world beyond, and that I was absolutely cut off from it, broke me. That I couldn't get to it or play it and might never be able to hear it again was too much.

Losing consciousness, I collapsed to the floor.

The civilian *Vorarbeiter*, or foreman, helped Mummy pick me up and he carried me to his office to try to revive me. He was kind and tried to give me some water. While he stared into my face waiting for me to come around, he expressed his surprise to my mother. '*Das sieht wie ein Mensch aus!*' he cried. 'That looks like a human!'

He went on to say that I resembled his own daughter and even looked like a little Madonna. 'She really is a human child!'

The Nazi indoctrination was such that the Germans didn't think of Jews or enemies of the Reich as anything more than cattle. They considered us something beneath human. It was just as Freud had said – every individual acts differently when he is in a crowd. The psychology of the masses induces a kind of hypnotic state in which people do anything they are told. Here was a normal man with a normal family from a normal home and every day he went to work with creatures he didn't think of as people.

We were repeatedly moved around from one subcamp to another, all of them under the control of the main Neuengamme camp, which was sited in an old brick factory. In total, more than 50,000 prisoners died under the Neuengamme regime, many of them executed or loaded onto ships in the Baltic that were then accidentally sunk by the Allies. Some two thousand prisoners a month died of starvation and cold during the last bitter winter of the war.

In one of the camps where we were billeted, there were men's blocks adjacent to ours that were mostly full of prisoners of war, some of whom were Czech, so we'd talk to them over the wire. One of my friends ended up marrying a man she met that way.

Some of the women arranged secret rendezvous with the French and Italian prisoners in order to earn extra bread – they could get a whole loaf for having a few minutes' sex. When my friends saw how frantic I was with hunger, they said, 'Why don't you go?' and offered to arrange it.

I was still a virgin and took forever to decide but then the hunger became too much and I agreed. Sneaking out so that my mother wouldn't know, I was led to a small room in which an Italian POW stood waiting for me, but I took one look at his smiling face, panicked, and ran back. I just couldn't bring myself to do it. Nor did I ever tell Mummy.

With winter the weather became colder and colder and the work much harder to face. Our block was heated at least, which was not as bad as Auschwitz, but the north wind was still very cruel. My fingers blistered and went black and then my toes. We were skin and bone after so many years of starvation and badly feeling the effects of hard labour with little sustenance.

Mummy and I were not only hopeless at stealing food but we also never received any packages from the Red Cross, friends or family. The same happened in Auschwitz but that was because of our name. People told us after the war that they had sent parcels but because Růžička was a gypsy name they all went to the gypsy camp. In Hamburg, many of the prisoners received packages containing salami, cheese or little cakes, and then they'd spurn the inedible dry camp bread and have a little party amongst themselves to celebrate. Hoping for the rejected food, I found an easy way to earn it.

Thanks to my glorious childhood, I had a wealth of songs in my repertoire and I also had a passable voice. It's something I have said to young people all my life. When you go to a concert or the theatre or learn a poem or read a book you may think it's just for amusement, but actually it's like having money in the bank that no one can take from you. It is capital. Every poem, every opera that you can act out for yourself or others, offers a means of escape when the world outside is unbearable. If you don't have any experiences like that to draw upon then you are really the poorest of the poor.

The most popular songs in the Hamburg camps were those by the Czech actors Voskovec and Werich who had a well-known political cabaret. Whenever Red Cross or other packages arrived, I would hurry to see those lucky enough to get something and sing songs to them in return for their unwanted bread or soup. That was the greatest education of my life because I learned politics that way. I discovered something that many people don't know even today – that no matter how poor you are, if the society you live in is wealthy, then you can always find a way to be better off because they will go without something they don't care about and you can get it instead. It is primitive social politics and it only works if the community is rich because if the community is poor – no matter what kind of communism you've created – everybody is poor and the poorest are poorer. Mummy and I were truly the proletariat of the camps so I not only learned the basics of economics but also humility and wisdom.

Songs by Voskovec and Werich saved our lives that winter but they also got me into trouble on Christmas Eve, 1944. It was another part of German perversity that they would beat us, starve us, and made us work like dogs, but when Christmas Eve came they would make a small Christmas tree for us and allow us a little extra food. Maybe they did it because they knew the Allies were coming. Perhaps it made them feel like good Christian souls. We hardly knew what day it was but we always knew when it was Christmas because the Germans celebrated it.

On that day we were being supervised by two of the SS guards from Ravensbrück. We finished work a little early and were being escorted back to our hut when I started singing a Voskovec and Werich song called 'Zalezí na nás'. The title means 'It all depends on us', and the sense of the lyrics was that we didn't mind it was Christmas, and we didn't mind our chains because we still had our heads and our freedom was in our minds. Unluckily for me, one of the SS women was Polish and understood Czech. When we arrived at the hut, she kept me back and then she beat me black and blue with her fists. It was the worst Christmas of my life and took me several days to recover. Her name was Eva Maria Goretzka and she was the Nazi I was most afraid of meeting after the war. I never forgot her name.

The air raids increased in intensity and we were frequently caught outside. Some of the girls were killed while working in the industrial areas that were targeted by the Allies. I began to dread being separated from my mother on a work detail, for fear something might happen to her. Being with her through all these difficult experiences was the only thing that kept me going, and the same went for her. My mother certainly survived because of me and I survived because of her – and because I badly wanted to live. I had so much love of life. More women than men survived the camps and I think this is because the men were weaker in some ways – the chief principle of their life was pride and it was hurt by

zana as a bride

Viktor, Leopoldina and Zuzana after the war

zana in the velvet dress that got caught in her seat

Zuzana and Viktor in the Czech countryside

Coming off stage after another recital

Zuzana and her mother, Leopoldina, towards the end of her life

zana on tour in France

ting off on another tour by train

Picking mushrooms in the Bohemian countryside

On tour in Japan

uzana in London

Zuzana with her biographer, Wendy Holden, in September 2017, five days before she died

their imprisonment. In my view, a woman is more practical and survives better because she thinks from minute to minute, hour to hour, and isn't so involved in principles.

As was the way in the camps, we learned to look forward to the simplest of things, taking pleasure from an extra crust of bread, a different soup, or a warmer spot out of the wind. If you got through the day without being beaten by the guards, if you could maybe smuggle a piece of bread, if you got a better portion of soup with a piece of potato, it gave you the same feeling of satisfaction that a normal person feels when he has a successful love affair, is lucky, or wins the lottery. This feeling of libido – to use the Freudian term – is so relative. You cannot survive without getting a certain amount of satisfaction from even the most abnormal situation.

So the little satisfactions start to make life almost normal – you fall in love and have a boyfriend, even though either of you may leave at any moment on a transport. You recite poems. You sing. You live. Otherwise you fall into despair and get the Auschwitz illness – those dead eyes. That is when you cease to get any satisfaction from life anymore, and that is the one aspect that nobody else is able to grasp who wasn't there.

My greatest satisfaction was seeing my mother each night and knowing that she had also survived another day. It was such a blessing that she had been chosen for this work and not the gas chambers, and that we had somehow managed to remain together since the beginning. All that changed for one terrible day and night on my eighteenth birthday – 27 January 1945.

The rules in the camp stated that on a prisoner's birthday they would receive an extra portion of bread. This was really something to look forward to and I had been quite literally counting the days. That rule was nullified, however, if it fell upon a day when we were moved from one camp to another. This is what happened that morning when we were suddenly taken to the Tiefstack cement factory where we would have to move huge blocks of concrete from one place to the next.

My mother and I were put on separate trucks and, although unhappy about our temporary separation, I foolishly assumed that I'd see her at our destination. When I arrived, however, she was nowhere to be seen. I became desperate and risked a beating by asking the guards where she was but one told me she'd been diverted to another camp, Ochsenzoll, to clean and make coffee. They wouldn't tell me where it was and I had no idea if she might be sent on somewhere from there. I cried all night and didn't sleep a wink. I feared that I might never see her again and the despair overwhelmed me.

The following morning at *Appell*, I stood with the other girls trembling and tearful and only looked up when a truck appeared and offloaded a group of about ten women. My mother was among them and she hurried across to join me.

I stared and stared at her but I couldn't speak and I couldn't move. I could hardly believe that she was standing before me. We embraced. We wept and we were very happy. It was the best eighteenth birthday present I ever had. Clinging to her, I was painfully aware that we could so easily have lost each other forever.

Tiefstack was not good for my chest. I developed a horrible cough from all the cement dust. Afraid it might develop into something that could finish me off, I tried to get work with any group detailed elsewhere, being sure to always take my mother with me. One day she and I were sent to work on a house they wanted us to help build in a Hamburg suburb. When we got there the civilian supervisors quickly realised that none of us had any building skills so they ordered us to carry bricks instead.

Halfway through the morning, the air-raid sirens suddenly went off and the planes started to sweep in and many of the girls and the men supervising us ran into the half-built house for shelter. As bombs began to fall, I looked right and left and spotted a little hut in the middle of the building site so Mummy and I ran into that. Once inside, I stood by the small window looking out to see what was happening. Gasping, I watched as a tiny red flare floated to the ground just beyond our hut, indicating that was where the next bomb would fall. The flares came in sequence – first a green one, then a red one, then a bomb. They were like little Christmas trees all lit up.

I grabbed my mother, threw her into the ground, and lay on top of her before a huge explosion covered us in dust and made us temporarily deaf. When we picked ourselves up and staggered outside, ears ringing, day had become night and the air was full of smoke. The house we had almost finished was completely levelled and most of the people inside had been crushed and killed.

In January and February they sent us out to the forest at a place called Hittfeld to dig trenches to hide German tanks, which we then had to cover with turf and the branches of trees. The tanks were supposed to lie in wait for the British soldiers they knew were coming. It was terribly hard work as the ground was frozen in what was one of the bitterest winters in European history. By that time we had already started to hear the artillery guns from the south, in the direction of Hanover, which was frightening but made us hope that the war might really be over soon.

Exhausted and numb with cold, I sat back in the snow for a moment to catch my breath. Looking down, I noticed for the first time that the snow was melting. Gazing up into the trees I could hear birdsong and sensed that spring was coming soon with new life – and maybe new hope.

Hope is what had kept us going for so long.

We'd hoped in Plzeň that the Germans wouldn't invade and that, if they did, our international allies would come to our rescue.

Then we'd hoped that we wouldn't have to leave our home and be transported to a ghetto or camp like so many.

We'd hoped in Terezín that we wouldn't be sent somewhere like Auschwitz.

Then we hoped in Auschwitz that we wouldn't be sent to the gas chambers.

When we heard the guns and saw the planes in Hamburg we hoped that the war would be over soon.

As always, though, hope was crushed.

About a week after I had sat down in the snow feeling that flicker of hope, Mummy and I were rudely woken along with the rest of the female prisoners and loaded into trucks. Like us, the Germans knew that the war was coming to an end and the last thing they wanted was any evidence of their crimes.

In the third week of February, 1945, we were loaded into cattle wagons again for our final 'death march' and transported 120 kilometres south to what would prove to be the worst concentration camp of our war.

If Auschwitz had been Hell, then this was Nether Hell, the lowest part of Hell. Its name was Bergen-Belsen.

11

Jindřichův Hradec, Czechoslovakia, 1968

The night the Soviet army invaded Czechoslovakia is forever etched in my mind. It was 20 August 1968.

It had been a glorious summer and the previous day I'd checked into the room I'd rented from a family I knew in a little town in south Bohemia, where I was to play a concert at a music festival the following day. Viktor had been working on a new composition at his family home in nearby Jindřichův Hradec, but he came to keep me company.

He woke that morning with such a bad toothache, however, that he resolved to drive to Prague to visit his dentist. I offered to go with him, but only a kilometre after we'd set off I changed my mind. 'I'm sorry but I need to work, Viktor,' I said. 'I think I should go back and practise for tomorrow's concert.'

He dropped me back and travelled on to Prague alone. As planned, I practised all day and then I went for a walk. It was a lovely day and I bumped into a woman I knew through Viktor who worked as a moderator at Czech Radio. She told me that she'd only just been able to start her summer vacation because of the important political conference that had recently been held near the Slovak–USSR border between the Soviet leader Leonid Brezhnev and our new First Secretary Alexander Dubček. The talks were designed to hammer out their differences over Dubček's controversial liberalisation plans, which had become known as 'the Prague Spring'.

'The talks seemed to go well,' the moderator commented, 'and now that everything seems settled, I'm taking my break.'

Her mood was light, as was mine. There had been such a shift in atmosphere since Dubček had been elected in January. His surprisingly radical political reforms – dubbed 'socialism with a human countenance' – had brought about changes we would never before have dreamed possible. He'd ordered the abolition of censorship, the relaxation of restrictions on travel, the media and free speech. In theory, this meant that we could travel abroad and speak openly about the government, although – after so many years of political repression – few really dared.

I was much more euphoric about the changes than Viktor, who was sceptical from the first moment. I felt this was a natural evolution and I really believed in socialism with a human face. He had his doubts.

My hopes were bolstered by that year's Prague Spring Festival, which had been especially memorable with the arrival in Prague of world-famous pianist Arthur Rubinstein. He performed Brahms's Piano Concerto in B Major with the Czech Philharmonic and enjoyed the experience so much that the following day he gave an unexpected recital of Chopin. I met him afterwards and found him full of energy and very sociable, an articulate Jewish refugee from Poland who spoke at least five languages.

It was such a strange period in history so soon after the Cuban Missile Crisis, in which Khrushchev and Kennedy had been head to head. The world was at the height of the Cold War and the situation was growing more and more tense. The communist dictatorship in Moscow suddenly seemed less bearable, and that feeling rippled through our country. The revolt began with the cultural and artistic people, most notably the Congress of Writers, who demanded less censure and more liberty. This went on until 1967 when they pressured our then president, Novotný, to resign. Dubček stepped in as a 'safe pair of hands', but he was an enigma. Communist from childhood, he and his family had emigrated to the Soviet Union at one point, but he grew to be a gentle and just man who became the idol of the revolutionary movement of 1968. What he tried to do in Czechoslovakia was extraordinary, but also naive. Sometimes he went too far. I was an optimist, willing to believe that there could be a third way, but Viktor was as realistic as always and never really believed that this could come true.

The Soviet leadership thought Dubček was one of them and were shocked by his proposed reforms. They watched anxiously from Moscow, fearing that his actions were anti-socialist. After expressing their alarm and trying to slow the pace of change, they insisted on the meeting at the border that lasted several days. When Dubček returned smiling and the talks looked to have been a success, we hoped that the Kremlin would leave him alone to pursue his plans. I had already accepted an invitation to tour Australia with Josef Suk, as well as performances in Brussels, Vienna, and West Berlin, and Viktor and I had been discussing where we might go together – if we were allowed.

On the evening of 20 August 1968, I went to bed early and planned to sleep late, something I did rarely and only when Viktor wasn't there. Early the next morning my landlady Mrs Krausová woke me, knocking loudly on my door.

'Mrs Růžičková wake up! Come and listen to the radio. We don't know whether it's a play or whether it's reality. Mrs Růžičková, the Russians have landed!'

I pulled on some clothes and hurried downstairs to hear the radio announce that the Soviets – aided by thousands of soldiers from the Warsaw Pact countries – had invaded Czechoslovakia during the night. My legs gave way beneath me and I had to sit down.

When the announcer added that Soviet tanks were on the streets of Prague, all I could think of was Viktor and my mother, both caught in the city. My mind flashed back to an episode earlier in the year when I'd been invited to take part in a German documentary about the Prague Spring. They wanted me to play one of Victor's harpsichord compositions in front of the Grand Hotel Praha in Old Town Square, but it was raining hard. Every day we turned up but it kept on raining, so in the end the camera crew packed up, saying, 'We'll come back in September when the weather will be better.'

'Yes, the weather will be better,' Viktor agreed. 'But we will be surrounded by Soviet tanks.'

The crew was taken aback. 'What are you saying? That's dreadful!'

Viktor replied, 'You will see.'

The German film crew never did come back.

Desperate for news of Viktor and Mummy, I quickly checked out of my lodgings and made my way to my father-in-law's home in Jindřichův Hradec. There was no telephone there either but the whole family had assembled and we hoped Viktor might get word to us somehow.

We drank strong coffee and smoked cigarettes and sat around the radio or watched television, weeping. We knew so little and we feared the worst. I really suffered then because I had naively thought that life would improve and I never expected this. Soon after the occupation, the Kremlin issued a statement that said the Warsaw Pact troops had been 'introduced to help the fraternal Czechoslovak people'. The Czech government urged the population to stay calm and ordered our soldiers to remain in their barracks.

Shortly before the radio station was taken over by the invading forces with the loss of twenty-two lives, the staff continued to broadcast. They breathlessly announced that thousands of demonstrators were on the streets, using cars and buses as barricades, some of which had been set alight. We switched between Voice of America and Radio Free Europe, which had long kept us informed of developments in our own country. They said the occupying forces were closing in on Dubček and his ministers and that the secret police were arresting people for being 'counter-revolutionaries'.

I shivered. What did that mean? Viktor and I were both non-party members and on the artistic committees of our unions. Did that count? Where was he? Was he safe?

It is difficult to describe the sense of oppression we felt in those first few days after the occupation. Dubček and his supporters were flown to Moscow, we feared never to return. Once again we had this feeling that truth could never win, only brute force. I couldn't believe that there was another regime like the Nazis – so cruel, so stupid, so anti-Semitic. I thought this can't be true.

After two days we still had no news of our loved ones, so I prised myself away from the house and went out to get some fresh air and to buy some provisions while we still could. Who should I meet in the village but my mother? She had just returned from Prague with Viktor, who had somehow found enough petrol to refill the car and drive back to south Bohemia.

'We came as soon as we could get away,' Mummy told me. 'We had to thread our way through hundreds of tanks. For a time a hare ran alongside our car as if it, too, was trying to escape.'

It was such a relief to see them. My mother, seventy-two, told us that when the tanks arrived she went out onto the streets to argue with the soldiers. She asked them, 'What are you doing here? Do you even know where you are?'

Several of the confused young men claimed they weren't even told that they were in Czechoslovakia. They thought they'd invaded Austria or Germany and that the Soviets had declared war. Mummy told them, 'We are unarmed. We are your brothers and sisters. We are not the enemy. Go home.'

Thousands of Czechs took to the streets to protest and hurl abuse and missiles at the soldiers. Many obscured street names so as to confuse them, or painted swastikas on the sides of the occupying tanks. People were advised to wear extra layers of clothing so that if the soldiers or the state police beat them, it wouldn't hurt so much. Viktor went to the radio station where he worked to see if he could help. He found everyone in a state of panic and, while he was in his office, the Soviets broke the door down and burst in. He was lucky he wasn't arrested, or worse. It was only when the Russian military searched the whole building that they realised that the live broadcasts they hoped to stop were coming from somewhere else – a secret location. In addition, several illegal radio stations immediately sprang up to continue to report what was going on.

Viktor and my mother were both very shaken by events and knew they had to get out of Prague. Mummy kept saying that she left our apartment so quickly that she couldn't be certain she had turned off the gas.

We were all so confused and frightened that when there was a knock on the door in our country hideaway, everyone jumped. It wasn't the Soviets or the secret police, though. It was the mayor of our little town who asked to come in. He told us, 'I think you are in danger. Not you especially Viktor, but Zuzana because you are travelling to the West all the time. We would like to hide you. The town has a Second World War bunker. You can stay there and we will bring you food until the danger is over.'

People were so supportive of each other during this dreadful time. We were all of us united by our anger at the Soviets as well as at Hungary, Poland, Bulgaria, and East Germany that had joined forces to muster at least 250,000 soldiers to invade our borders. We thanked the mayor for his offer and hoped that we wouldn't have to take him up on it.

After two more days in which nothing much happened in south Bohemia, we decided it was time to do something. Having lost her previous homes, my mother was still worried about losing our flat so – four days after the invasion and when we heard that the first bus was travelling to Prague – it was agreed that I should go and check that all was in order.

I left with a list of instructions as to what to do and what to bring back. Viktor told me to use our newly installed telephone to call our friends and try to find out what was happening. 'See if they are home, have been taken by the secret police, or have defected.' Mummy wanted me to bring our precious photographs, food, and clothing.

When I arrived in Prague there were tanks and Soviet soldiers on every street corner, as well as burned-out cars and trams. The atmosphere was horrible.

All was well in our apartment and the gas had been safely turned off. I immediately switched on all the lights so that anyone passing would know I was there. I picked up the phone and spent a day calling everyone from Josef Suk to Karel Ančerl but nobody was at home – or at least they weren't answering.

I did manage to get hold of some friends on the other side of town and when they found out where I was, they defied the 7 p.m. curfew and told me, 'You can't stay there alone. We'll come and stay with you.'

When the telephone rang the next morning I was quite taken aback and answered it with care. It was a female producer from ABC, the Australian Broadcasting Corporation radio station, calling to confirm that I was still able to go to West Berlin in two days' time to record a radio interview about my forthcoming tour of Australia.

'Don't you read the newspaper, lady?' I asked, incredulously.

'No. Why?' she asked.

'Then I suggest you do,' I said, putting down the phone because I knew that the Russians would be listening in to everything I said.

The phone rang again soon afterwards and it was Margot Vogl, my second cousin's wife, calling from England. She tried to be discreet. 'Are you coming to London for the tour you planned?' she asked cryptically. 'Do bring Viktor with you. We will, of course, house and feed you.'

I knew she was offering to put us up if we defected but I thanked her and said, 'No, the tour has been cancelled and I will not be coming, Margot, and neither will Viktor.'

After I put the phone down Margot rang again half an hour later. 'I tried to call you straight back,' she said, 'but I was put through to a girl at the post office who said you were not at home. I told them that she was mistaken and that I just spoke to you. The girl told me, 'Yes, Mrs Růžičková is at home and she intends to stay.'

What I was most afraid of the whole time I was in Prague alone was that because people were still protesting and painting, 'Ivan, go home!' slogans on the walls, the Soviet Union might decide to separate the regions to quell discontent, which would mean that people could not travel from one to the other.

If that happened, I would be trapped alone in the city while Viktor and my mother were stuck in the country. Eager to get back to them and still afraid of being caught up in a counter-revolution, I hurried back as soon as I could. Just as she had during the war, my mother made sure that we would be safe, warm, and fed in what could turn out to be another full-scale conflict. She and Viktor's family had stockpiled all that we might need for months under siege so that we were as ready as we could be for whatever might happen next.

Our lives were in limbo then. My concert in Brussels was supposed to be coming up, and Josef Suk and I were due first in Vienna and then on the Australian tour, but we had no idea if we would still be allowed to go. All the most important Czech concert artists had been away on tour during the summer of '68, and many had chosen not to come back.

Those of us trapped behind the Iron Curtain felt completely helpless. I remember Josef Suk coming to see us and being very depressed. He never went anywhere without his wonderful Stradivarius violin, which was on loan to him from the state, and I remember after the Soviets came and we had our first rehearsal, he put it back in its case with a sigh and said, 'I don't see the sense in it anymore.'

We were all afraid to begin and really desperate not knowing anything. The illegal radio stations reported that famous artists and politicians were being arrested. We heard later that their neighbours removed all the names from the houses so that the soldiers wouldn't know where they lived. Then it appeared that they were only arresting those who were politically active, so we hoped that we might be safe.

There was no big counter-revolution in Prague as we had expected, despite the international outrage and condemnation. After the first few wave of protests, in which Soviet flags were burned and several people committed suicide publicly, the population became resigned and rather apathetic. They hoped that Dubček and Brezhnev would come to a compromise, but there was no negotiating to be done. The Soviets insisted that they had no choice but to implement what they called 'a hard hand'. The Czech leaders were threatened with imprisonment if they did not sign a protocol that agreed to a reversal of all the reforms. Dubček signed it, along with most of his ministers. When he returned home he begged that there be no further violence, which he said would be a disaster.

The Prague Spring was over.

In spite of Viktor's joke to the German camera crew, we'd never truly expected it and were still in shock. All we could hope was that Dubček would stay and work out a solution, but that didn't happen either. Within a year he would resign, be expelled from the party, and end up working for the forestry service. His replacement would be Gustáv Husák, brought in to implement so-called 'normalisation'.

There followed numerous purges and expulsions from the party and we all had to sign a proclamation that we were mistaken about the Prague Spring and had been under the influence of Western propaganda. We also had to declare what we had learned from the crisis in '68.

What did we learn? Yes, we did learn something. We learned not to hope.

By September of 1968 it was still possible to cross the borders and some 30,000 Czechs fled, so we spent lot of time thinking about emigrating and discussed it for one whole night until dawn with Josef Suk.

We had a few options. The Australia tour was cancelled but I was allowed to play in Vienna and Brussels. I had another steady musical partner at that time, a brilliant cellist named János Starker, with whom I had performed many times. It was just like with Suk – we played and we played and discovered that the chemistry was perfect. Once again, we said, 'We are a duo. Nobody is going to play with you and nobody is going to play with me.' And we played all over the world. We had a really close personal friendship, and he also asked Viktor to write something for him.

Starker held an eminent position at the Jacobs School of Music at the University of Bloomington, Indiana, but came to Prague in 1968 and immediately offered me a position if we decided to defect. He also proffered invitations to perform at his university and at the Metropolitan Museum in New York, which is another way we could have escaped. I would have taken my mother to live with her sister Elsa in New York and then gone to take up my place as a professor in Indiana. Viktor had a friend who would have given him a job at Vassar College in Upstate New York, so we were sure of our futures in America.

Josef and I agreed that we should at least go ahead with our Vienna recital and play Viktor's Sonata for Violin and Harpsichord, which he had written specially for us. We had already premiered it at the Rudolfinum that year and it went on to be a great success around the world, especially in New York. Josef travelled first to Vienna with his wife and we agreed that if anything really bad happened – such as our friends being arrested or the situation getting any worse – he would send a telegram to say that the concert was off. That would be our signal to go to Vienna too. We hoped the authorities might be lenient and allow us out, and then we could stay in Vienna for a while until we decided what to do.

I had never lost touch with Hugo Lenk, the man who had taken over from Fredy Hirsch in Auschwitz. He had since changed his name to Pavel Ledek and – after a time as a director of Pragokoncert – he had emigrated to Vienna from where he, too, offered to help us but, in the end, we didn't need it. Suk and I played the sonata to almost no audience, and then we came back.

The problem was we had the same dilemma as my father had had after 1939. Like him, we had a strong sense that we should stay with our people in Czechoslovakia. Leaving our country would not have been a very courageous thing to do, even to escape from the suffocating situation. The other realisation I had was that I could probably have stood emigration but not Viktor, who would have wilted without the countryside and the language. He would always have felt a stranger amongst strangers. He might have been able to stand it for a year, but to not be able to come back again, to maybe never see his home and his country would have been too much. The nature in south Bohemia was a great source of inspiration for Viktor, and a lot of that can be heard in his compositions. He would have been terribly homesick and probably wouldn't have been able to bear it. It was the same with Suk, who was a great patriot.

The conductor Karel Ančerl emigrated almost immediately. He had lost his first wife and his son in Auschwitz and couldn't bear to risk his new family also, especially when there were signs of anti-Semitism again, right from the start. I remember meeting a conductor acquaintance who was on the Central Committee of the Communist Party, and he was shocked to see me after the occupation. 'What are you still doing here, Zuzana?' he asked. 'As a Jew, it is too dangerous to stay!'

Karel Ančerl was really afraid of going through all of that again. We had a summerhouse not far from each other in south Bohemia so we went to see him and he told us what he was thinking, and we talked it over and over. Soon afterwards he took his new wife and two sons to Canada, where he became the chief conductor of the Toronto Symphony and from where he corresponded with us secretly. He came back only once during 1969, for the annual Prague Spring Music Festival, when it was still possible for him to return. The Czech Philharmonic gave him a very warm welcome, but still he didn't stay.

We decided to remain in the end, even though the atmosphere became so oppressive and we longed for our freedom. Prominent people were still being imprisoned or expelled. All of us were being watched. Our telephones were listened to. Our conversations were monitored. The authorities knew whom we were friendly with, and whether we were conforming to the new laws that increasingly restricted us.

Viktor sunk into the deepest depression but he was so good at expressing himself, he could have been a writer. He never stopped composing, and was at his most prolific during this time, writing music for many different instruments. He especially expressed his feelings in a few of his sonatas and in his poignant Symphony No. 3, Op. 33, written in 1970 to reflect the times. That was not long before he left Prague Radio to devote himself entirely to his music.

Once again, hope tricked us because we still had some hope. Those of us who remembered the First Republic hoped against hope that it would come again.

Instead, we were in a new era – not Stalinist – but just as cruel. It was another, much more sophisticated way of torture. Loved ones were physically held hostage or used as an emotional bargaining chip in all sorts of unkind ways. The message was: do this or your children will not be allowed to study, your husband or wife will lose their position as a teacher, a doctor, or at the university, and your mother or father won't get the hospital treatment they need. They were always threatening your nearest and dearest.

When you were in a restaurant – which were now categorised from first to fourth class – you couldn't talk openly about anything. There were hidden listening devices everywhere. If a group of more than three students met in the corridor of the academy or gathered together on a tram, there was always somebody who broke up the meeting in case it was subversive. People were encouraged and expected to spy on each other and report back. Citizens were harassed and often mercilessly persecuted for the slightest misdemeanour. Scores of writers and musicians were dispossessed. Hardly any new books were published during this time.

All of us lived under constant threat during this 'normalisation' process. Unless you were paid in foreign currency like me then you could only reach a certain ceiling in your career. If you were not in the Communist Party then you were never allowed to reach a position above a certain level of importance. Your career path was blocked. Viktor had a good friend, Karel Matoušek, who was interested in local politics but not allowed to develop that gift during the communist regime. He could have been mayor or maybe a senator and had a wonderful political career. After the revolution he was appointed mayor of his town immediately and then re-elected three times. It was the same with Ivana, a teacher we knew, who taught at the local grammar school. She did wonderfully but I think she could have taught older children at the gymnasium, not just small children. Just as Viktor wasn't allowed to be a director of the radio station and I wasn't allowed to teach the harpsichord, all of us lost not only the best years we could have used for our career, but also the best society could have got from us.

This kind of oppression went on for years, along with the threat of war, which was imminent at that time. There was a joke that went around Prague after the occupation that perfectly summed up the situation: '*Don't bang your head against the wall, you might loosen a stone and kill the prisoner in the next cell.*' The message was that every action had a reaction and if you did something unlawful it would adversely affect those closest to you.

The sense of oppression struck me most whenever I was allowed out of the country – and I still was, because the authorities were more eager than ever for the foreign currency I could bring. They sent me to literally hundreds of competitions as a juror and to many concerts, hungry for my earnings. Only this time, I had to fill in a long questionnaire each time about where I went, who I met, and who I corresponded with. In the late 1960s, I was invited to the Royal Academy in London to give a lecture about Bach's cantatas, and immediately afterwards some of the students approached me and invited me for a glass of wine. I was almost in tears, knowing that our students would never be able to gather like that or to invite a foreign lecturer to discuss ideas.

On another occasion, I was summoned to the secretary of the Prague faculty, a man who was the chief communist there, who asked me to pass on a message to a professor I was friends with. 'Would you please tell him that we know that he is telling political jokes,' the secretary said ominously. 'Tell him to stop.'

Life went on, as it always somehow did, and Viktor and I continued to work and teach and play music. In August 1969, I hosted an international interpretation course in baroque music at the academy with Professor Jiří Reinberger. The first year featured harps and organs and was attended by musicians from nine countries so the following year we opened it up to clarinets and the bassoon.

One day at the academy soon afterwards I met Karel Sádlo or 'KPS', my former professor of chamber music, who told me I was going to receive a state prize as an 'Artist of Merit' for my musical contribution to the country. Viktor had already received his that same year. Professor Sádlo had a strange smile playing around his lips when he asked me what music I should like played at the ceremony.

It struck me then and I told him, 'You know, I would prefer not to get any prize at the moment, if that is all right.' He immediately understood but a week later I met a famous singer – maybe by chance, maybe not by chance. This soprano was a member of the new 'normalisation committee' and she looked at me threateningly and said, 'I hear that you refused the state prize. Why did you do such a thing? One doesn't refuse a state prize!'

Not long after that I was in bed with flu when someone rang the bell and delivered an official-looking letter. It instructed me to be at Prague Castle the following morning at 11 a.m. to receive my prize. There was no warning and I wasn't told anything else or given the option to refuse. Normally when someone receives this prize, the press take photographs of them and a public announcement is made. This time there was nothing and I wasn't even able to say no because the ceremony was the following day. It was curious.

I was so ashamed that I had to accept an award at a time when the government was denouncing everybody and everything with such terrible reports in the daily press. I thought of my father being so proud and courageous and wondered what he would think of me going to the castle like that, but I had no choice. I didn't want to lose my music.

I had fought so long for it that I just had to go through this indignity.

One of the reasons they forced me to accept this award and others like it later on was because it was good propaganda in the West to say that the 'world-famous harpsichordist' Zuzana Růžičková had accepted them from the state. If I hadn't, they would probably have stopped me from travelling and even playing. I'm sure some people may have viewed my appearances at these ceremonies and on television as some sort of collusion with the communists, but it was far from that. Instead, I continued to travel and play and show the world that Czechoslovakia was a country full of great culture and music and talent.

The communists did not have the final word.

Depressingly, it seemed unlikely that anything would change. Brezhnev was firmly in charge of the Soviet Union and all the satellite states and would be for another fourteen years. Dubček was gone. He thought Brezhnev and his government would understand that what he was attempting in Czechoslovakia was progress. Instead, he inadvertently put us back years. The period immediately after the occupation was one of greyness, of no joy, of nothing being permitted. We were so downhearted.

It wouldn't be until 1985 and the arrival of Mikhail Gorbachev in the Kremlin that somebody would finally understand what Dubček had tried to do. Until then, we were still the slaves of dictators and tyrants – just as we had been since 1939. There was a terrible symmetry to it all. Only, like all slaves – even those terrified of the regime – we still dreamed of freedom, and we sometimes behaved in cheeky ways.

As Viktor told me, 'You can't be a slave forever.'

In the years that followed the Soviet invasion, Viktor and I received many letters from the West applauding us for staying. 'Your people need you,' our friends wrote. 'You don't know how important your music will become to them.'

There were only two television stations at that time, one which broadcast communist propaganda all day and the other which broadcast mostly classical music, so anybody not sympathetic to the party or who'd simply had enough of the rhetoric switched to the music channel.

I had already appeared on Czech television a few times but now that I was gaining a reputation for being an international musician, I was invited on much more often. I was even offered a series to discuss the importance of Bach, which involved researching his life and inviting people from all classes who felt passionately about his music to appear on the programme. I loved it because these ordinary people would tell me when they first heard Bach as they passed a church or a concert hall and how it changed their lives. One man said, 'I felt like I heard a voice from above that told me Bach should always be played in church.'

With my new prestige, I began to be paid in tokens known as Tuzex. These could be spent in special Tuzex shops where one could buy clothes, alcohol and cigarettes not readily available elsewhere. We did use them but mainly we saved our money to try to buy a car. It took many years.

For a short while there was a tendency to not let me out of the country but once or twice I got permission to travel, most often with Josef Suk, and neither of us knew why we were sometimes denied a visa and sometimes weren't. After a time I met a friend who was a prominent communist and he said, 'Luckily, you have your problem solved.'

'What problem?' I asked.

He was surprised and said, 'You don't know? There was a meeting of the Central Committee and someone suggested that you shouldn't go out of the country any more because you are not party members, the capitalists finance your performances, and all of your fame is the artificial product of Western propaganda. They suggested that the committee promote another duo instead, a violinist and pianist. Then someone asked, "Is it worth the scandal?" and everyone agreed that it was not.'

The committee knew that too many questions would be asked in the West if we were suddenly prevented from travelling. Plus, they needed our money and prestige, so they allowed us to continue to travel but felt that they had to 'punish' us for our subversive connections with the West somehow. After some thought, they decreed that we could not play in spa resorts. That was the only punishment they could think of.

The so-called 'normalisations' devolved slowly and the new director of Pragokoncert managed the classical music department quite well, accepting invitations on my behalf. I was still giving master classes in Zurich to some famous musicians, so from there I would be able to travel elsewhere in the West, such as to the Schwetzingen summer festival in Germany in 1971, where I performed with Hungarian cellist János Starker. That was a light-hearted trip for me because János was a great joker and I remember after the festival I changed for supper only to discover that I still had on my gold concert shoes – with a summer dress. I had left my casual shoes in the locked castle. The following day I was back giving my master class when János suddenly appeared at the door, my shoes in hand, and said with a wink, 'Zuzana, you left these behind last night.'

Of course everyone laughed.

The director of Pragokoncert was my puppet master and it was he who would call me and say, 'You are going to Armenia for three weeks from this date to that date.' Usually, I had no choice in the matter and there were still lots of places that I didn't want to go to. In 1970 when I was told I was going to Turkey, Viktor took the unusual step of intervening.

'There is a cholera epidemic in Turkey,' he told me. 'I will call the agency and tell them that you can't go.' He did just that and their response was not quite what he expected.

'Very well,' they told him. 'In that case she is going to Iran.'

I arrived in Tehran when the Shah was still in power before Ayatollah Khomeini. The city was beautiful – a little like Paris, with elegantly dressed women and fine cars. The Czech embassy presented me with a huge bouquet of flowers and I was treated very nicely. I was sorry never to go back.

The academy in Prague offered me an associate professorship, but with no field of study because the harpsichord was still not taught there as a separate discipline. So, when the Academy of Music in Bratislava offered me a teaching post there I took that instead, travelling on the overnight train and giving a day of lessons every few weeks. I did that for five years until my assistant took over, but the Slovaks kindly told me, 'There is always a place for you in Bratislava.'

I was eventually offered a residency at the Ansbach Bachwoche, or Bach Week, a relatively new festival directed then by the harpsichordist and conductor Karl Richter, where I ended up playing everything from the Goldberg Variations and the Brandenburg Concertos to *The Well-Tempered Clavier* and Invention No. 1 in C Major. That led to invitations from lots of different countries, and to Bach and other festivals in Leipzig, Stuttgart, Heidelberg,

Frankfurt, Bath and Oregon, as well as the Soviet Union, all of which paid quite well.

Although eighty per cent of the foreign currency I was paid was confiscated by the state, they couldn't rob me of the pleasure of performing. I was given some Czech money for my work and that was enough. Viktor, too, started earning satisfactory royalties for his compositions. We were not supposed to be well off – and the authorities knew every detail of our financial affairs – but Josef Suk and I were still probably the best-paid artists in classical Czech music. Our economic situation improved and life was easier then. Best of all, I was finally able to buy myself a harpsichord, so we sold the grand piano and bought an Ammer I found in East Germany instead, which meant that I could play it at home to my heart's content. This was the harpsichord I played at home, took on tour with me, and became most closely identified with until the 1980s, when I bought an instrument by German builder Georg Zahl.

One day I was called to the Ministry of Culture and told that a female Russian professor was coming to 'listen' to my teaching for six months. I still wasn't allowed to teach Czech students or any influential people from socialist countries, but I had a colleague who was teaching organ in the Soviet Union and he sent his Russian students to me to study the harpsichord. The professor came and sat in on my lessons and took notes. A pretty blonde translator with wonderful braided hair accompanied her. I called her 'Baboushka'.

Two hours into my lesson I was carefully explaining what I was doing and the professor said quietly in English, 'You needn't be grand. She just wants an easy life. That isn't even her hair – it's a wig because she wants to look more Russian.' We became friendly and kept in touch and when I was next in Minsk she took me to some museums and to illegal concerts. We had to wait until after my translator went to sleep and then she'd ring me and I'd sneak out. She was nice and had a daughter who was also called Zuzana but who later died in the 1986 Chernobyl nuclear disaster.

And so my travels and my performances continued, although I rarely knew what went on behind the scenes. I had a friend in Pragokoncert who was in the foreign office but also a cellist and, fortunately, there was solidarity even from people in high places, or at least those who knew me. He called me to his office one day in the 1970s and said, 'Look at what I have here.' He showed me a letter from the Czech embassy in West Germany complaining that I was there too often and had too many concerts. The letter requested that my friend see to it that I didn't go there again. Laughing, he tore it up in front of me and swept the pieces into the bin.

Viktor was also allowed to work and, occasionally, to travel. In the 1960s he was nominated for the jury of a composer competition in Paris and asked to choose some of the best music from our country.

We were sitting at our kitchen table surrounded by sheet music and his notes when he told me he had selected three compositions for the competition. One of them was written by the colleague who'd denounced him years earlier, and lost him his teaching job at the academy.

'Do you really mean this?' I asked, stunned.

'Yes, of course,' he replied. 'It is good music.'

The colleague didn't win the competition but he did win a prize. I don't think he ever knew that it was Viktor who had nominated him.

Aside from his remarkable compositions during the '60s and '70s, Viktor formed an excellent children's choir. Perhaps his greatest achievement, the Concertino Praga sprang out of a lunchtime meeting with colleagues at Czech Radio in 1966. He didn't like the noise in the staff canteen and suggested that everyone on his staff should eat their lunch in the office instead.

'But who will wash up?' someone asked.

'I will,' he replied. 'I'm the dishwasher at home anyway.'

The whole office loved him and one of his biographers later described him as the glue that bound them all together. Different ideas came up over lunch and were discussed, and one of them was his suggestion that the radio station host an international music competition for children.

'But how will we get the children here?' someone asked. Viktor said that he would think about it. Later that night he came up with the idea of enlisting international radio stations to listen to submitted tapes, judge them, and send only their winner to Prague. It was a brilliant and unique idea. There were different categories for brass, wind, cello, violin, a chamber group, and piano. Up to fifty winners arrived in Prague every year where they were given a concert with an orchestra and received a CD of their performance.

I hated sitting on juries but I loved this one because when you listened you didn't know if the musician was a boy or a girl, how old, or from where. You might hear a wonderful violinist and imagine a boy from Russia but it would turn out to be a little girl from Belgium. It was amazing because we suddenly discovered unknown fourteen-year-olds playing like masters. Music is so much more important than we realise and whenever we were able to discover these incredibly talented young musicians it was often life changing for them – and for us.

There was one beautiful story that emerged from the competition that I never forgot. It was after the winners came to perform and that year the presenter Lukáš Hurník asked them all a question, which was, 'What would you do if your government banned classical music?'

Two girls from the West were asked and gave different answers. One, from Berlin, said her father had a factory, so she would go to work there. The other said she liked taking photographs. So each of them said they would choose a different career. When the Czech quartet was asked the same question, they replied, 'We would do something to make the government fall.' They were our winners that year.

Concertino Praga continues to this day and is recognised as one of the world's major music competitions for under-eighteens. Along with his music, it is one of Viktor's greatest legacies.

If I feared that my travelling would be curtailed by the arrival of the Soviets, then I was mistaken. In fact, in 1968 I went to Japan for the first time at the invitation of Mr Yoshita, an interesting man. He was the son of a wealthy family and music was his hobby. He only invited people that he liked – a few famous singers and me playing harpsichord.

In 1970 I was reunited with Rafael Kubelík, the Czech conductor who had refused to play with me in Munich fourteen years earlier, leaving me to struggle on alone. I gave a recital of Purcell's complete solo harpsichord works in the Chamber Hall of the famed Bunka Kaikan concert hall in Tokyo, played on a condor-quilled instrument crafted by Michael Thomas. Then Kubelík and his Bavarian Radio Symphony, performed *Má Vlast* ('My Country') by Bedřich Smetana. After the concerts, some musicians I knew from the visiting orchestra came to see me. 'The chief wants you to go and see him after your concert,' they said.

'I won't have time,' I told them. I also knew that it was forbidden for me to meet privately with someone from the West.

'We have to bring you or he'll be furious with us,' they pleaded, so I went along solely to save them from getting into trouble. I went to his room and found him sitting in a bathrobe. He knew all about me and he apologised for what had happened in Munich. 'If I had heard you play I would never have done it,' he said, graciously.

Japan became one of the countries I came to know best because my promoter always insisted that I stay two days longer than my schedule allowed, lying to the authorities and claiming I had another concert when I didn't. Instead he took me all over the place to see the cherry blossoms in bloom and other memorable sights. He was so very kind.

I acquired a lot of Japanese admirers as well as students and completed many recordings there for the Nippon record company, including an album of famous encores and my favourite, which is ascribed to Purcell but may have been written by a man named Croft who nobody knows much about. The Japanese temperament seemed quite suited to the dedication being a musician requires. It is not enough to be gifted, or diligent. You have to be a little bit crazy. You have to have the feeling that you cannot live without music. Then you have to sacrifice so many things – no weekends and no real holidays. You have to practise for hours and you have to enjoy it more than holidays, more than weekends, and more than relationships sometimes. The diligence and discipline is secondary.

You have to love it and you have to love how you can express yourself through music.

I so enjoyed working with young people. I looked forward to seeing the development of their relationship with old music. Those who wanted to study the harpsichord seemed to not just be seeking light, relaxing mental stimulation, they were looking for the demanding intellectual cooperation required by Johann Sebastian. I used to ask my Japanese students, 'Why do you like European music so much?' and they said that the way of living in Japan was so strict that they were not supposed to express their feelings.

'When we discovered European music it gave us a way to express ourselves in a rare manner – there is such freedom in it. Psychological freedom.'

That I understood. Bach had penetrated every facet of my life and given me spiritual freedom at times when I had nothing else.

A few of my students formed a fan club and wanted to do something for me, so they threw me a party and invited some sponsors and one of them asked me to perform with the Beatles in a light and colour show, but I declined. My fans were flabbergasted. They said, 'But you could earn thousands!' I told them I didn't care. 'But you are a free person here,' they said.

'I am far from free and I am not to be bought,' I replied.

It was a novelty for me to have fans that were so interested in me, and my music. I was once playing at the home of some extremely rich people who arranged a concert where each ticket cost the equivalent of £500. One of the sponsors told me that there was a young man at the door begging to come in but he didn't have the money for a ticket. I said, 'Please let him in.'

I met him afterwards and he was so excited. He told me, 'I rang my college friends and told them, 'Guess who I am seeing play today? Zuzana Růžičková!'

They were astonished and asked him, 'Does she really exist?' They had all my recordings but no one had ever seen me play.

Viktor continued to not only support me, but was also always my greatest critic. I used to say to him, 'Please don't tell me how

I played right after the concert. Wait until the morning.' This is because after a concert, I am always a little bit unhappy. First, I'm never sure that I had the right idea, and then there's a bit of regret that it's over. That's why I don't like to be alone after a performance and need the company of friends.

I would then need to stay awake the night after my performance so that I could analyse all my failures and mistakes. In the morning, Viktor would usually then tell me what I already knew. Sometimes he'd surprise me, though. I might be quite satisfied that I'd made no mistakes and he would say, 'Yes, but you had no spirit!' On other occasions, my performance would be full of mistakes and he'd tell me it had great spirit and was excellent. I needed someone objective.

For a long time Viktor didn't write for the harpsichord. He had to play it quite a lot and to listen to it, plus he never had time. There is a Czech proverb that a shoemaker's wife goes without shoes, and that was how I felt. I used to tell him, 'I will be the last one for whom you will write.' Then he started to write for harpsichord and his first piece for my instrument was his Concerto for Harpsichord and Strings, Op. 24, written in 1974, on which he gave the harpsichord a serious virtuoso part. He also wrote the Violin Sonata for Josef and I, which we had played in Vienna, but that was only fifteen minutes long. Viktor always said he liked to write for a special interpreter. He knew me, he knew Suk, so that was easy for him.

Then one day he was working on a new piece and he asked me, 'How difficult can I be?' and I said, 'Write whatever you want.' So he completed his Six Two-Part Canonic Inventions, Op. 20, a masterpiece of harmony and counterpoint inspired by Bach and Scarlatti. They are extremely difficult to play because one hand plays the theme and then afterwards the left hand plays the theme, and they both have to be the same, just a little bit after. It is a funny piece, with one hand mocking the other, but you have to work very hard every day to get it right, and when I was on tour I couldn't do that, so I asked him for the *Aquarelles,* Op. 53, which he composed especially for me in 1979, and which was much easier to play.

The *Aquarelles* was a cerebral piece with a sarcastic commentary underneath the melody that said – now you are in love and you are singing, but the melody wanes and death still waits for you. It is still there. Then in the end, the harmony is victorious and wins the game. It ends in a beautiful harmonic chord. It was composed of three parts for the harpsichord, about which Viktor wrote: 'I love this instrument for the beauty of its sound, for its quiet monumentality and last, but not least, for the demands it makes on the composer.' The premiere was at the Circle of Friends of Music in Duchcov in the Ore Mountains in May 1980.

There is another funny story about Viktor and the harpsichord, which happened when I went to Switzerland and played Martinů with the Swiss Chamber Orchestra during some of the worst days of the regime. Afterwards, one of them asked me, 'You are from Prague so do you by chance know a composer called Viktor Kalabis? We played his chamber music for strings and we so much like to play it. Do you know him?' I told them that yes, I knew him very well. 'He's my husband.'

We laughed and then they asked, 'Couldn't you make him write a harpsichord concerto for us?' So I went home and told Viktor and he was so happy, he immediately sat down and started to write this concerto. It was very beautiful, but I told him that at the end I wanted something really brilliant so that the audience left happy. As Viktor neared the end, though, it became sadder and more depressed. He ended it with a violin and harpsichord playing alone without orchestra and just fading away. I told him, 'But Viktor, you made me die!' He apologised but said he was depressed about the political situation and just felt that he could not end it on an optimistic note in these terrible times. He was always so truthful in his music. He couldn't pretend. Years later he offered to change the end but by then we already loved it so much, and the audience loved it, so it stayed. He often conducted this piece himself. He was a good conductor but he refused to conduct anything other than his own pieces.

This was an extremely productive time for Viktor because not long afterwards he was invited to write music for my colleague and friend the German conductor and organist Helmuth Rilling, whose Bach-Collegium Stuttgart company was playing in Prague. The Song of Solomon inspired his subsequent *Canticum Canticorum* cantata for alto, tenor, chorus and chamber orchestra.

What Viktor understood perfectly was that the harpsichord is a monumental machine with many colours and resonances. Its renaissance in the twentieth century was unique and had never happened to any other instrument before. With his help, and the help of other composers such as Jan Rychlík and Luboš Fišer, who also composed for me, I hoped to return it to society as a mainstream instrument.

More than that, though, I couldn't help but think once more, *What would Bach do?* His music had never fallen out of favour but I still wanted to bring it, and the means he used to create it, back to life by playing the instrument he so loved.

12

Bergen-Belsen, 1945

After leaving the ruins of Hamburg far behind us on the train, we arrived at a remote railway station and were marched six kilometres to the concentration camp of Bergen-Belsen, situated on a barren heath one hour north of Hanover.

It quickly became apparent to us that 'Belsen', as it became known, was the place where we were meant to die. There was little or no organisation. We hadn't been given any food on the train and were so terribly hungry that as we were marched through fields full of frozen sugar beet many of us risked our lives to duck quickly down and grab a beet or two. When we came to the camp on the heathland, known as Lüneburger Heide, we passed piles of dead bodies lying around the camp and saw funeral pyres burning. Nobody even registered our arrival and the guards crowded us into purpose-built wooden blocks, between 500 and 700 women in each building, all standing around or lying in bunks on straw mats. There was so little space that it was not even possible to lie down on your own. If we wanted to sleep we had to lie like sardines with our head in another's lap, and if we wanted to get up to use the toilet all the women started swearing because of the upheaval. There was still nothing to eat – not even the horrible soup that we would have gladly eaten. And when a little soup did eventually come several hours after our arrival, those who got to it first finished it all so we received nothing.

In the women's camp there was no work to do, so the days seemed extremely long. Until the soup kettles arrived – full of a disgusting liquid made from the kind of beets they feed to cattle – all we had to eat or drink was water drawn from a single pump. A bad epidemic of spotted typhus was killing people all around us. Those afflicted were covered in spots and had ugly swellings in their armpits and groins. Exhausted, starving, and mentally as low as we had ever been, neither Mummy nor I expected to survive more than a few days in that place. I was so worried when she became ill with a fever that I fed her the last of the raw beets we'd stolen from the field, little piece by little piece. Once they were gone, there was nothing. I realised then that I had to do something to get food or my mother would die before my eyes.

Apart from their presence at *Appell* and a few other tasks, there were few German guards around as Allied planes wheeled overhead and the sound of the guns grew ever closer. The 900 or so SS guards lived in a separate army camp and tried to avoid contact with any typhus-infected prisoners, but a small group arrived one day and announced that any of us who were prepared to handle the dead and carry them to the pyres would be allocated some extra soup.

My mother was far too weak to do anything but I immediately volunteered.

I can't fully describe the horror of that task. We had to drag the corpses by their arms and legs and pile them up in the forest at the fringes of the camp to be burned. A human being wasn't human anymore. A person ceased to be an individual. There was no time for principles or ideologies. The bodies were rotten and full of disease and the woods were full of rats. It was grim, heavy work, touching those cadavers every day. At the age of eighteen, I became uncomfortably familiar with death.

Considering how weak I was I'm amazed that I even managed it, but I did that foul work in the hope that I would receive one or maybe two extra soups for me and my mother. Every day I brought some back, fed her first, then ate a little myself.

Sometimes I could do the work and sometimes I couldn't. It was heartbreaking but whenever we became too hungry I would force myself to do it again, until the guards stopped even that 'privilege'.

We all did things to survive.

As in Auschwitz, watchtowers with searchlights and barbed wire fences surrounded Belsen. Unlike Auschwitz, the fence wasn't electrified. Beyond the wire were hectares of tempting beet fields, so when we were nearly dying of hunger I decided that I had to try to get some.

It was the craziest idea. I can't now believe that I did it. Yet I planned the entire operation by going to the fence a few days before to watch where and when the guards patrolled, trying to decide where best to dig my way into the field unseen.

I don't consider myself to be a brave person but fear can make you brave.

Very early one morning, at about 3 a.m., when it was still dark, I slipped out of the block and went to the fence. With my bare hands – my once-precious piano hands – I started to scrape away at the earth. My mother was terribly anxious for me. She was against the whole idea but when she saw how determined I was, she stood guard by the block wall keeping watch, trembling all the while.

The ground was hard with frost on the top but wetter and a bit softer underneath. My hands and fingernails were soon caked with mud. I had to lie flat and stay still each time the beam of the searchlight swung around towards me, or when the guard was on my side of the watchtower. Each time he began to march back in my direction, Mummy would give me a sign or desperately call, 'The guard's coming! Hurry or he'll shoot you! Come back, Zuzana, please!'

It took me at least two hours to create a gap big enough to wriggle the top half of my body through, and by the time I did it was almost first light. Right at the end, the guard spotted me and started shouting, but I still managed to pluck two large beets from the earth and run back to the block with them without being shot.

Unfortunately for me, a group of gypsy women had been watching my progress from the doorway and the minute I returned, they crowded around me, pushing and shoving, before snatching one of my beets. I kept hold of the other and Mummy and I fed on it for the next few days, nibbling at it like mice. It was half-rotten but it tasted good to us and undoubtedly saved our lives. Deciding to keep the rest for when we were really desperate, we hid it under our straw mat. After that my mother had to remain in our bunk at all times to guard our beet – literally lying on it so that no one would steal it. She guarded it with her life.

Sadly, that beet only kept us going for a week and then it was gone. My mother and I knew it would be too risky to try for another and were frantic for something else to eat. Mummy still had a high fever and it was terribly cold so I lay against her miserably, trying to keep warm.

Bergen-Belsen is not an easy place to remember. Even though we were with women we had known since Terezín, there was no room for support, humour, or friendship. We were all just fighting for survival.

The only people who were kind to us were a group of Czech prisoners recently arrived from Buchenwald. They were healthier than we were, as they hadn't been forced to endure Terezín, Auschwitz or slave labour as we had, so they undertook many of the physical tasks that we couldn't, such as carrying the soup kettles, removing bodies or fetching water. Towards the end of March, one of them somehow produced a set of tarot cards after they heard about our 'prophet' Klara – who had been transported to Belsen with us – and we all begged her to read them and foretell our future. At first she was too frightened and claimed she'd sworn never to use the cards again, but things became so bad that, after some more persuasion, she reluctantly laid them out before her.

'When will the end come, Klara?' we asked. We used the Hebrew word '*Sof*' for 'end'.

Surprised, she looked up from the cards and said, 'On 15 April the Germans will leave.'

Of course we didn't quite believe it, but a few of us half did.

I hurried to tell Mummy the good news. 'The fifteenth of April is only a few weeks away,' I said. 'We just have to stay alive until then.' Weak and still feverish, she looked at me as if I was mad.

Over the next few days my mother came as close to death as I had ever seen her. I was too weak to carry any more bodies, and there were so many by then that people were just piling them outside the blocks. With no extra food, we all lay together, semi-conscious, trying not to think about food and losing track of time. There were no toilets so we just had to go where we could.

On an evening in mid-April, the SS came back into the camp to enlist any who could still walk. Presumably as part of their plans to flee, they had wrapped their uniforms and personal items into bundles and needed prisoners to carry them to the railway station on their heads. I didn't think I was strong enough but in the hope of anything extra to eat, I volunteered to join the detail. As usual, we were marched in close formation in groups of five, heads down, focusing only on the person in front of us. Whenever the SS said '*Marschieren!*' we marched. It was how we'd been moved everywhere since Terezín so, after more than three years, I'd grown accustomed to the sensation of never looking up to see where I was going.

It was almost dark by the time we came back from the station, and I was in a kind of fugue state watching the legs of the woman in front of me. I was the last in line and I can't recall if I heard a vehicle approaching, but what I presume was an SS car suddenly drove up very fast and struck my leg as it passed. I didn't feel anything and I dared not break my stride but when I got back to the block and lay down next to Mummy, someone in the bunk below ours began to cry out that I had wet myself. All the women around me were cussing, but I hadn't lost control of my bladder, I was dripping blood from my leg. In my calf there was a gash several centimetres long that would give me a lifelong scar. Somebody handed me a dirty cloth to press on my wound but by the following morning my leg was badly swollen and I could barely stand.

There was a prisoner-doctor in the camp and some friends asked him to examine my leg, but he was allowed to treat just one or two people a day, and then only those who might survive. He took one look at me, a *Muselmann*, and refused to help. *Appell* began at six o'clock every morning and always took an age to complete and I was afraid I wouldn't be able to stand all that time. Some of the women helped me up and half-carried me outside. We waited and waited as an hour passed and then another but the Germans never came. We waited some more, listening to the guns in the distance, but still no one arrived to count us and take their daily tally of the dead.

People started to get excited then and someone cried, 'What date is it?'

The stronger prisoners from Buchenwald left our area and went looking for the guards. When they came back they told us that the watchtowers were empty and it looked as if all the Nazis had left our part of the camp. Everyone went mad then, crying and laughing, singing and dancing. Some organised raids to search for food but my mother and I just shuffled back inside, too weak and in pain to do anything.

Lying together then, we could hardly believe that we might be free at last. We experienced one of those rare moments of unadulterated joy – the kind you can only know in the darkest of times. We were happier still when a friend came and told us that the Buchenwald Czechs were raiding the German stores and would bring us some food soon. Then came the bad news – they had left nothing to eat and had disconnected the water supply. All that remained was a little flour, so the prisoners tried to make some bread with some standing water, but it was not enough. There were no beets left in the field and nothing at all to eat or drink. We had been abandoned.

Word came then that a group of young Hungarian soldiers with white armbands had arrived in the camp, claiming they were 'neutral' and had been instructed to take over. We assumed the Nazis had put them in charge. They were immediately mobbed by some of the stronger prisoners and we heard that they had started blindly shooting into the blocks in an effort to save themselves and not be lynched. It seemed then that they were not neutral at all but may have been sent to finish us off. We feared it would only be a matter of time before they'd appear at our door with guns.

Everyone hid in their blocks, listening and waiting for the end. The Allied armies were no longer so close and the sound of their guns was moving further away, which was the most terrible realisation of all. Nobody was coming to save us. My mother lost all faith then. She already had the typhus swellings and although I kept promising her that the British or Americans would come soon, she just kept saying, 'No, no, the Germans will come back. They'll be back.' She was very near to her time but I begged her to hold on for just a little longer.

The last three days were the most desperate of all because we'd had hope and then we lost it again. I truly believed that my mother would die before we were liberated, so to be almost liberated felt unbearable. I thought then that I would almost certainly die too and I don't think I cared.

A day or so later we suddenly heard the rumble of tanks and the noise of trucks and, to begin with, we feared the worst. Mummy was semi-conscious and kept murmuring, 'It's the Germans! It's the Germans!'

I got quite angry with her then and scolded, 'Why do you have to be such a pessimist? It could be the English or the Americans.'

When people ran out to confront the trucks they couldn't believe their eyes.

They were full of British soldiers.

They had come to liberate us at last.

The date was 15 April 1945, exactly as Klara had predicted.

Kissing my delirious mother with happiness, I didn't have the strength to celebrate but somehow found the energy to get up and limp out of the block. The sight of those clean, healthy Brits in uniform was like some sort of vision.

It was a wonderful sunny day and I really felt as if I was hallucinating.

I learned later from an RAF pilot and senior army officers how the British came into Belsen. The Germans in charge of the camp knew that the war was ending and tried to negotiate with the British. They told them of the typhus epidemic and suggested the Allied armies avoid the camp or go around so as not to spread disease to their men or the surrounding area. In return, the Nazis agreed that a neutral force be sent in to care for the remaining prisoners.

When the British heard that some prisoners had been shot, and examined aerial photographs taken by a reconnaissance plane that showed piles of dead bodies lying around the camp, senior officers decided to send a unit into Bergen-Belsen to find out what was going on. If they hadn't, we would have died there.

Everyone crowded around our stunned liberators, weeping and laughing and begging for food. The terrible thing was that, quite understandably, the soldiers gave us everything they had – all their rations. This was deadly. I was thrown a tin of fatty luncheon meat, which I devoured immediately and somehow survived. Sadly, many others didn't and an untold number died in that way because, having had nothing to eat for so long, their digestive systems absolutely couldn't take it. Food was fatal. After eating the luncheon meat I was terribly sick, which probably saved me.

Summoning the English my father had taught me, I begged the soldiers for their help. Hearing someone speak their language, they immediately took me in one of their vehicles to the senior officers to tell them what had gone on in the camp. I told them as much as I knew in my remote corner of the camp. Then I asked them to send a doctor to my mother.

'Please help us,' I pleaded. 'She is dying.'

A medical officer asked me what was wrong with her and I told him she had typhus. He wrote me a prescription and told me that a mobile dispensary had been set up a kilometre further inside the camp and he pointed the way. I was amazed that they could have organised something like that so quickly. It was so wonderful how the British handled the crisis.

I started to make my way there but I, too, had a fever and ulcers on my skin, and I was still very weak. Exhausted after a few hundred yards, I decided to take a rest in the shade of a birch tree, so I sat on the ground and quickly lost consciousness. When I came to, several hours had passed. No one had taken any notice of me. I was just another sick prisoner in a camp of between 50–60,000, with some 10,000 bodies lying around. Pulling myself to my feet, I made my way to the dispensary, got the prescription filled, and hurried back to administer it to my mother.

Entering our block, I was horrified to find our bunk empty. 'Where is she? Where is my mother?' I cried, becoming quite hysterical. The other girls told me that a medical truck had taken her and others away. Thinking that she must be either dead or dying and distraught that I wouldn't be with her at the end, I passed out.

When I woke up, I was in a bed with clean sheets and a proper mattress – luxuries I hadn't known since Plzeň. For a moment or two, I thought I was in heaven. I had no idea where I was or how long I had been unconscious. I was too sick with typhus to do anything but marvel at the way everything was being handled. My filthy body had been washed and I was in some sort of crisp white gown. All I could hope was that my mother was somewhere nearby being taken care of just as beautifully.

The British were so wonderful – what organisation! How they handled that camp with so many dead and so many thousands infected was incredible. I will never forget it and will always admire them for it. They were a fighting army and the war hadn't ended so they still had to fight on, but they wouldn't abandon us. They only had a limited number of medical staff so everybody helped, including soldiers who volunteered as male nurses once they saw the scale of the task. Quickly and efficiently, the army took over the nearby German military barracks, as well as schools, and every large building in the locality.

In the army camp just two kilometres from where we had been starving to death, they found warehouses full of food including Red Cross parcels that had never been handed out, a fully equipped hospital, and a dairy that had provided supplies of milk and cheese to the SS. British orderlies carried as many of the sick away from the blocks as they could and turned the requisitioned army buildings into a sprawling 15,000-bed British general hospital, which they sprayed with a newly invented insecticide called DDT.

The British Army Medical Corps solved the problem of staff shortages by inviting final-year medical students from the UK and liberated countries to volunteer. They were promised that if they did, they wouldn't have to take their final exams. Hundreds of young men and women arrived from Britain, Belgium, Holland, and France, and it was a very courageous thing for them to do because they had no idea what they would be facing and we were all infected with typhus, dysentery and other nasty diseases.

After ten days in their care the doctors assured me that I had passed the worst stage of my typhus. Once my fever dropped and the ulcers disappeared they stood around my bed telling me to 'hurry up and get better' as they needed my help. One of their biggest problems was communicating with patients and they were in desperate need of interpreters who could tell them where people had pain and gather their medical histories. They knew I spoke English, German, and Czech and could understand Polish and Russian.

'Will you help us translate?' they asked.

Of course, I said yes. I was so grateful to them for saving me and wanted to do anything I could to help, but my primary concern was to find my mother amongst the thousands in their care. I hoped that working with the doctors and visiting the many hospital buildings with them would give me a better chance.

Everyone was terribly kind to me, especially the soldier-nurses who cleaned the attic of the main administration block and made a little room up there for me with my own bed. I had no clothing of my own so they plundered the home of a local German family and selected some garments they thought I might like. I did – they were lovely – but the dress they brought me was a black evening gown with a deep décolletage. I weighed approximately twenty-seven kilos – just over four stone – so it hung off me and had to be tied with a belt.

The British wanted me to start to enjoy life again, so they took me to a makeshift cinema they'd set up in a huge tent. The first and last time I had been to the cinema was with my mother in Plzeň in 1939 to see *Snow White and the Seven Dwarfs*. The thought of that happy afternoon, with Tata waiting at home to hear all about it, almost broke me. Then in the tent they played 'God Save the King', the British national anthem, and I was in tears. I will never forget all those men and women standing to attention to salute their figurehead silently. The film showing that night was *The Last Gangster*, a thriller starring James Stewart and Edward G. Robinson and as I sat in open wonder staring at the screen, not even really aware of the plot, I knew how lucky I had been.

I was alive.

I'd survived.

Life went on.

After the film they took me to the officer's mess and gave me my first proper meal in years. At a table with a linen tablecloth I was served food on a proper plate with proper cutlery – I think it was mutton and vegetables. It was wonderful to be able to eat like a normal person again. They gave me some whisky to drink in a proper glass, and my first cigarette – starting a lifelong addiction. After that I was offered cigarettes all the time because the medical opinion back then was that smoking might prevent infection and protect against TB.

It was a crazy thing for me to have eaten all that rich food at dinner because when I returned to my quarters later that night I was terribly ill. I truly thought I might die up in my attic room alone, but at least I'd eaten a proper meal and was wearing proper clothes. Not even being so ill could spoil that wonderful evening for me.

I was so happy that I remember saying to myself, 'All right, let me die, but I am free.'

I searched for my mother for weeks but when she was nowhere to be found I became frantic. There were so many requisitioned buildings to search, as well as tent encampments and even some of the least infected blocks at the concentration camp that had been transformed.

My new boss was a British Army major named Spicer and he did all he could to help me find her, but the longer we searched without result the more likely it seemed that she had died.

Those who'd perished after liberation had been buried in ten or more mass graves at Belsen along with the thousands already dead. Among them was the teenager Anne Frank, whose secret diary would later become one of the defining books of the Holocaust. Years later I met her father Otto, who asked if I had ever met her there, but I have no recollection of doing so.

As a handful of survivors and soldiers watched, the worst of the lice-infested blocks were finally set ablaze and burned to the ground. The survivors were gradually evacuated and, once they were strong enough, began to trickle back to their homes. If Mummy wasn't in one of the remaining beds, then I could only fear the worst.

Major Spicer paired me up to work alongside Clement Morgan, one of the young student doctors who'd volunteered to help survivors, and he became a good friend. He was so kind to me and knew how upset I was about my mother. He also knew that my translation work gave me a sense of purpose and kept me sane. I really wanted to work and I was eager to help. It was liberating in a way. In my heart I believed my mother to be dead but talking to other patients as sick as she had been gave me a little hope and I still prayed to encounter someone who might at least be able to tell me what had happened to her.

There was also a British orderly I was friendly with – I think he was a little bit in love with me – and when he went on leave back to London I asked him to take a message to our relatives there, including Walter Vogl, my mother's cousin. The family immediately got in touch and sent me a letter, photographs and a red carnation. I was grateful to have someone left in the world, although I still hoped to be reunited with my Uncle Karel, Aunt Kamila, and my cousin Dagmar, who I had last seen in Terezín two years previously.

I was also friendly with a Dutch cardiologist called André Van Loo, and two British nurses, Sister Mary Wilson, and Nurse Mills (known by everyone as 'Grenade Mills' after the Mills grenade), who were wonderful to me. Nurse Mills taught me how to give shots and to make beds with 'hospital corners'. I did some office work and I even took night watches on the wards, effectively becoming an assistant nurse although I wasn't qualified and didn't wear a uniform. I was fascinated by the absolute discipline of the British. If there was a crisis, a nurse could talk to a sister but not to a doctor because of the hierarchy. As one of their few translators I could go straight to a doctor and bypass all that.

One day one of the male nurses I knew well told me that there was a seriously ill female patient with the same surname as me who was constantly crying for 'Zuzana'. Thinking it had to be Mummy, I rushed to see her and was shocked to find Dagmar, who was dying. Even though she was terribly unwell she recognised me immediately, and her face lit up. She was able to tell me what happened to her and how she, her parents, and brother Miloš, had all been sent to Auschwitz on one of the later transports from Terezín. When they arrived at the railway ramp, my Aunt Kamila and little Milošek, aged nine, were sent straight to the gas chambers. Dagmar and her father survived, although he was sent away to a subcamp to work.

Dagmar remained alone in Auschwitz for some time before being sent to Bergen-Belsen, where she had been for months. The tuberculosis she had undoubtedly picked up as a child – but which her mother chose to ignore – came back, and she was so weak from hunger and neglect that she couldn't fight it. My doctor friends warned me that she wouldn't survive, so I spent her final three days at her side, reminding her of our happy days in Dobříš when we had played in the castle grounds and enjoyed Sabbath with our grandparents. I promised her that we would both return to Plzeň and be reunited with her father, who would take care of us forever.

Dearest Dagmar, my sweet, kind cousin and 'sister' who had wanted to spend her life working with animals, died in my arms. She was eighteen years old.

It still makes me weep to think of her.

Losing Dagmar made me physically ill; so ill that I don't recall any funeral for her or even know what happened to her body.

I presume it was put into a mass grave with the rest who were buried in a small cemetery within the army camp.

Feeling sick at heart and horribly feverish, I took to my bed. I didn't believe that I had ever been cured of the typhus. I stayed in the attic where it was quiet and I wouldn't be disturbed, but that was almost the death of me. I woke a day or so later with a high fever and unable to move, so I just lay there in a delirium hoping that somebody would find me. My friends downstairs thought I must have taken some bereavement leave after Dagmar's death, so nobody came looking for me until the fourth day when a nurse thought to check and found me in a dreadful state. I was immediately carried downstairs and put on a ward, but by then I was dangerously ill.

Clement Morgan was going on leave to visit his fiancée in England and when he left I was unconscious on the ward with little prospect of surviving. He had correctly diagnosed malaria and nobody believed him, as it was little known in northern Europe. Years later, doctors told me he was right. Whatever I was suffering from, he was without hope for me and said his goodbyes, convinced that I would die. I don't remember much about it, but I must have had an enormous will to live because the moment I woke up I absolutely knew that I would make it, and that I had to eat something. The doctors had put me on their prescribed 'Diet No. 1', which comprised milk with sugar, but I instinctively knew I was suffering from starvation so I changed my medical notes to 'Diet No. 4' with solid food including meat, which really helped me. Whatever I ate, I immediately threw up but something must have remained to make me stronger and I recovered quite quickly.

By the time Clement Morgan returned, I was still weak but sitting at my desk in Major Spicer's office. On his first day back, he opened the door and started to come into the room. I was so pleased to see him that I looked up and smiled. Stopping dead, he stared at me blankly before turning around and walking straight out without a word. I was shocked. I had expected him to embrace me and was worried I may have done something to offend him. When he eventually returned, having found some of the nurses who assured him that I was alive, he burst in and hugged me most warmly.

'I never thought you would survive, so when I saw you I thought you were a ghost!' he cried.

I was quickly set to work translating again, visiting Polish, Czech, and Russian patients of all ages and genders. Seeing some of them still painfully thin, I advised the doctors to try them with proper food, not just milk and sugar, as I was sure that was what they needed. In most cases, it helped.

Moving from bed to bed I worked automatically, trying not to think about the next day or the day after that. I was still extremely thin and feeble. I had no idea what would happen to me or how I would live once all this was over. I only hoped that my uncle had survived or that someone else might take me in. Thankfully, there were plenty of distractions – including the kindness of the staff as well as social events and dances, all of which helped make me feel normal again.

At one of those dances Dr Van Loo and I won the first prize for best waltz. I was pleased to win and grateful for the dance lessons I'd been given in Plzeň when we shared a flat with the kind German Jews – until I realised that they were probably all dead too.

Part of my work took me to the gypsy camp, which was beyond the main hospital in a tented encampment. There was a child there that I needed to see and one day I walked in on a Czech family wedding, which was such a happy event. The gypsies were nice to me and invited me to stay and eat something with them. An old crone asked me if I would like her to read my palm.

'Why not?' I replied.

She took my hand, studied the lines closely, and looked up with a smile. 'You will be rich and you will be famous,' she said. 'You will marry a man who will love you, and you will love him, but you will lose him before you die.' I believed her completely.

On my way back to the army camp I crossed 'Freedom Square' and what was locally referred to as 'Speaker's Corner', where people could stand on a podium and say what they liked. As I walked past, I glanced at a man addressing a crowd with both his arms in the air. He waved his arms one way and said, 'This way is the Nazis.'

Then he waved them in the opposite direction and said, 'This way are the communists.'

Catching my eye, he stared at me and shouted, 'Take care!'

Early one morning Major Spicer asked me to accompany him to a medical outbuilding I wasn't even aware of. It was a huge pavilion called the Rotunde, or Roundhouse, and it was crammed full of some of the most severe cases.

His expression grave, he told me, 'I think I have found your mother, Zuzana. She is very unwell and I'm afraid there is little hope of recovery.' When I burst into tears, he hugged me and immediately offered to adopt me and take me back to England to live with him and his wife.

Thanking him, I dried my tears and wandered inside, scanning the scores of beds before my eyes finally fell on the painfully thin figure of Leopoldina Růžičková. Rushing to Mummy's side, I found her unconscious and emaciated, her skin covered in ulcers. There was little medicine available for those treating her, and penicillin was a revolutionary new drug only available to the military. All anyone could do was watch and wait. My mother had been looked after beautifully by a Hungarian orderly named Lajoš, who took care of her as if she was his own mother. I learned from him that she'd been in the Rotunde all the time I'd been searching for her.

After that, I visited her every day and, although she regained consciousness, she did not get better. She was shockingly listless and either didn't want to recover or she didn't have the strength. She was also unable or unwilling to communicate. I think she couldn't face the thought of going home without my father and I realised that my brave mum was afraid of only one thing and that was to return to Plzeň and find that there would be nobody left from our family. She kept saying, 'I will never go home … I will never get better … I will stay here.' The situation looked hopeless.

There was nothing I could do for a while, even if I had wanted to. All those with typhus and other diseases had to remain in quarantine for three months until July. My friends and most of the patients talked of nothing else but where they should go and what they should do when quarantine ended. Many didn't want to return to places where they knew they had enemies who'd denounced them, or where none of their families would be waiting. For thousands the concept of 'home' no longer existed, as bombing had obliterated all they knew. Some were so shell-shocked that they refused to leave the care of the British, and many considered remaining in what would become one of the largest DP or Displaced Persons Camps, where the Allies would continue to care for them. Others were waiting for visas to Palestine, America, Canada, Sweden or England – if they could get in – but many doors were closed or closing, which led to angry demonstrations. The Russian prisoners were warning that the parts of Europe liberated by the Soviets would become communist, which also impacted on decisions.

I knew my aunt in New York would take us in and I was grateful for Major Spicer's kind offer to adopt me in England. There were other offers from medical staff, too, but it was suddenly clear to me that I wanted to go back home to my own country. Just as Fredy Hirsch had said, the whole Zionist idea was, I'd discovered, theoretical. There was no place else I wanted to live.

There was a radio in Major Spicer's office that was almost permanently on. Every day it broadcast the latest news and messages from families looking for loved ones. On a glorious summer's day that June, I was sitting at my desk with the sunshine beaming in through the window when I suddenly heard my name. The radio announcer was broadcasting a request for any information about the Růžička family from Plzeň and their daughter Zuzana. The enquiry came from Madame, my beloved piano teacher, who was searching for me.

Jumping up, I listened carefully and wrote down the details of who to contact to let her know that we were still alive. My eyes filling with tears, I was so pleased and relieved to hear from Madame that I wanted to get back to Plzeň as soon as possible. I knew in that moment that unless I was able to get Mummy out of the hospital soon, we might never leave and she would never recover.

It was time to take her home.

13
Plzeň, 1945

Taking my mother away from Bergen-Belsen was never going to be easy. She was still very ill and stubbornly refusing to leave, so I knew that if I was going to save her I would have to do something extraordinary.

As soon as quarantine was lifted in the various sections of the camp – depending on the health of individuals – anyone who was well enough to leave started looking for ways to get to their destination of choice, but it wasn't as simple as we'd hoped. There was a Europe-wide shortage of fuel, and only a few trains available to survivors – the rest had been requisitioned by the military – and there were so many thousands of people wishing to go to so many different places that the organisation of the evacuation was chaotic.

A few private vehicles arrived from Czechoslovakia to collect survivors, but these were always full, with no room for extra passengers, in spite of my pleas. Then another car drove into the camp, but its driver couldn't find those he had come to collect, so I asked him if he would take my mother and me to Plzeň instead.

'Fine,' he replied, shrugging. 'But you'll need to find me some petrol first.'

One of my doctor friends told me I could try applying for fuel at the British headquarters and gave me papers that allowed me access. By this time I wore a kind of apron and looked more like a nurse, so when I walked into the inner sanctum of this building on a hill and asked to speak to someone, I received a warm response. I spoke to three different officers – who all seemed enormously tall to me – and the last offered to summon me a general. When this senior officer arrived I told him that I needed some petrol but I forgot to say what for. He disappeared and returned with a small flask, thinking I needed a little for cleaning insect-infested clothing, as was common in the camp. I thanked him but said, 'Sorry, that's no use to me. I need enough for a 600-kilometre drive to Plzeň.'

The general laughed, shook his head, and told me that was out of the question.

Back in the camp I learned that there were so many Czechs wanting to get home that the authorities were trying to arrange a special train for us. It would take weeks, and wasn't likely to be available until at least the middle of August, but that would give me enough time to prepare the next part of my plan.

The doctors kept insisting that Mummy couldn't possibly leave yet as she wouldn't survive the journey. That wasn't going to stop me. When we are young we have such courage and intuition, and I just had this feeling that she was resisting getting better for the sole reason that she couldn't face the thought of going home. I have always been led by my intuition in music and the same applied in life. Now, I wouldn't have the courage but I basically planned to kidnap her, which was another crazy idea. My friends were worried that I might be caught, but I didn't care. I just knew that I had to get her home.

My friend, Dr Van Loo, agreed with me and wrote out some false papers that would allow me to take her out of the ward for some tests. Some of my friends found a dress for Mummy to wear and, with everything ready, I said goodbye to everyone I could trust to keep my secret and jumped to action. Very early on a morning in late August 1945, on the day the train was due to leave for Prague, I hurried to the Rotunde, handed the fake documents to the night nurse who knew me well, and told her I was taking my mother to be X-rayed.

I then quickly dressed Mummy, who was extremely resistant to being manhandled or moved. She kept asking, 'What are you doing? Why are you dressing me? You know the doctor said I wouldn't survive being moved. I won't make it, Zuzana!'

I was quite cruel to her then because I knew this was the only way. I told her, 'Mummy, I don't want to stay here any more. I want to go back to Plzeň and I'm not going back without you, so you *have* to come with me.'

I think that was probably the very thing that made her try. She felt she had to make this last sacrifice for me, even though she complained the whole time that I was taking her to certain death.

Somehow, even though she was hardly able to stand, I managed to smuggle her out at a time when there was no watch on duty, and help her onto the train. We found our place in a cattle wagon – carriage number 13. My mother, who was superstitious, cried, 'You see! Number 13! This will be my deathbed. I won't live to see Plzeň.'

The 600-kilometre journey took three days and was extremely difficult as the tracks were bomb-damaged and there was no regular schedule. Other trains had a far higher priority than ours, so we often had to wait in sidings until they passed. The British had given us packed lunches, but it wasn't enough with all the delays, so – once again – we were very hungry. Each time the train stopped, passengers would slide open the doors, jump off and steal fruit and vegetables from the allotment gardens of the little houses that lined the tracks as we passed cities such as Magdeburg, Leipzig, and Dresden.

It was a strange thing, my compulsion to be decent – instilled in me by Fredy Hirsch. In many ways, it handicapped me. The other girls never had second thoughts about pillaging in the circumstances but I could never bring myself to steal from a stranger. Instead, I begged from my friends who had more than enough and were glad to give us some.

Most of the journey my mother lay listlessly next to me saying, 'This is my last day. I will never reach home.' That was until the train reached Bohemia and we started to notice Czechs waiting at every station. We were late arrivals compared to those who'd come home from the camps in the months before us and were no longer quite the sensation, but still people watched and waited as the train stopped and started to let people off. They were waving and crying, looking for loved ones and gaping at the sight of us, all skin and bone and wearing mismatched clothes.

I was still not in good health myself and hadn't increased my weight much from the twenty-seven kilos I'd weighed upon liberation, so I was a spectacle each time I got off the train to see if there was any food to be had. People kindly gave me a few things to eat and officials assured me that when we reached Plzeň the staff at the repatriation office would give us a free meal and tell us where we could stay.

The train rolled on and I kept telling Mummy, 'Look out of the window! Here's that village your friend comes from and next is the town of Litoměřice.' We reached the village of Nová Hut where we had sometimes gone for family holidays and I said, 'Look, Mummy! Nová Hut! Remember how Tata loved it here?'

That was the moment she started to come round. It was if a switch flicked on in her mind. She rose shakily to her feet, looked out of the little window and – incredibly – spotted some people who remembered her from the shop, where she was relatively famous. When they saw her they called, 'Mrs Růžičková! Oh, Mrs Růžičková! Is it you? You've survived!' That was the crucial point when my mother revived and started to take an interest. She melted and started to wave back at them, suddenly appreciating that she was back in a country where people knew and loved her.

We were the only ones getting off at Plzeň, so when the train stopped the two of us disembarked alone. It was a lovely warm day, so I told Mummy, 'Sit on this bench in the sun and rest. I'll go and find the repatriation office. I'll bring you back some food.'

It wasn't far to walk although I was still very weak and dizzy, but I found the office quite quickly and was handed identity cards and other documents that entitled us to spend that night in a municipal dormitory if we had nowhere else to go. The authorities promised that the next day they'd try to find us our own flat. Ours had been taken over by Czechs years earlier and the authorities were giving survivors from the camps the apartments of Germans who'd been forcibly repatriated after the war. A woman told me it was unfortunate that we'd arrived so late, because most of the best places had already been taken.

The officials then asked me if I wanted to eat something. Suddenly hungry, I found the dining room, which was serving lunch. The menu offered *svíčková* and *knedliky* – sirloin beef in a cream sauce with dumplings – my first Czech dumplings in years. I was served four but only ate two, putting the others in a napkin for my mother. Because I got everything done so quickly, I couldn't resist the temptation of going to visit Madame, who lived nearby.

When she opened the door and saw me standing there, she gasped and burst into tears. So did I. We embraced warmly but could hardly speak. It was such a joyous moment. Drying our eyes, we walked arm in arm to the piano room where I had taken my first and last lessons, and I began to tell her what I could. Suddenly, she began to cry again. Taking my hands in hers, she wept and wept. I looked down at my fingers – all gnarled and ruined by digging out pipelines and hauling bricks – and felt ashamed.

Madame was such a thoughtful woman and, trying to be kind, she dried her tears and told me, 'The main thing is that you are back. And of course there are other careers than music, Zuzanka. You have wonderful mind for languages. Go talk to the Americans. They need translators. Then later you can go to university and graduate.'

Feeling suddenly flushed, I told her, 'I have to go now and find my mother. She is waiting for me at the railway station.'

I hurried down the street, so upset and worried about Madame's reaction to my hands that I almost bumped straight into my mother. Incredibly, she'd felt well enough to walk to the repatriation office and eat some dumplings (saving two for me). It was a miracle.

Mummy and I didn't think for one minute that we would have to sleep in the public dormitory that night, as we had so many friends in the city and couldn't wait to be reunited with them. We went first to see my cousin Sonja, the seventeen-year-old daughter of my dear Aunt Jiřina. She was from a mixed marriage so we expected her to have survived. She had, but when she opened the door and saw us, this young girl behaved in such a curious and unexpected way. Instead of welcoming us with open arms, she seemed agitated and told us, 'I am terribly sorry but I have to leave. I have an appointment. Could you come back at 6 o'clock?'

We looked at each other in shock and immediately wondered why she didn't just offer us the keys to her home, but she didn't. We had the feeling of being revenants; those who'd already been wept over, buried, and suddenly emerged from the grave.

Feeling so awkward, we left and went instead to see the chief saleswoman in the family shop. This lady had almost been a member of our family and we had given her quite a lot of our things to keep – fine rugs and porcelain, gold, plates and silver candles. We rang the bell and hoped for an outburst of joy once she saw us, but she was also embarrassed and said, 'I really can't invite you inside – my cleaning is not done. Perhaps you would care to sit in the kitchen?' We virtually ran away.

At someone else's door they said we couldn't come in because there was sickness in the house. Not one of them invited us into their homes. Nobody offered us any coffee or food. No one asked about my father or the rest of the family.

We realised then that none of these people had ever believed that we would come back. We suspected that they had either sold our things or had them on open display, intending to keep them for themselves. They didn't understand that we weren't there looking to reclaim our belongings, which were almost meaningless to us by then. We were looking for some food, some shelter and a kind word. When we saw we were embarrassing them all, we left and didn't dare visit anyone else.

Walking away in a daze, we bumped into a former servant of ours on the street, who also hurried away. Astonishingly, she was wearing one of Mummy's dresses, entrusted to her for safekeeping.

We knew then that this was how it was. There was far more horror in people's faces than joy. To them, we were dead and buried. We were ghosts, and ghosts are not supposed to haunt people from the grave.

My mother and I sat down on a park bench and looked at each other sadly. It was already evening; we were tired and hungry and didn't know what to do. After some time, the park keeper approached us to ask us about our fate. We were still wearing those terrible clothes, so he would almost certainly have known that we were repatriates. He talked kindly to us and we told him what we could bear to. Telling us to wait, he went away and came back with his wife, who carried a jug of milk and a big plate of *koláče* – the sweet Czech pastries that had been such a part of my childhood. We were incredibly moved by the kindness of those two strangers who did more for us on that first day than anyone we knew.

Feeling a little better, we decided to go back to Sonja's building at 6 p.m. as requested, but she was not even there. Exhausted, we sat on the stairs. We waited and waited but she never came. By nightfall, there was still no sign of her. For us that was a very bitter experience. Rising wearily to our feet, we had no choice but to go back into town and check into the municipal dormitory with our official coupon for the homeless. Mummy and I spent our first night back in our hometown lying together on a single bed in a home for the destitute, crying and crying.

After three years of forced separation, this was not at all how we had imagined our first night in Plzeň to be.

The incredible thing was that the following morning, my mother was well again and back in charge. When we left Belsen, I was the parent and she had been the child. In Plzeň, she suddenly recovered her strength and took over again.

The next morning we went back to the repatriation office, where she insisted they help us. They gave us some money to buy food and clothes, although everything was still rationed and there wasn't much choice. Eventually, they provided us with a flat where we were expected to remain until we could find something else. We spent just one night there, however, surrounded by the belongings of German Nazis with pictures of Hitler on the walls, and we could hardly sleep. It was so claustrophobic and the place had such a bad atmosphere. When we awoke in the morning we took one look at each other and said, 'We can't stay here.'

Mummy went back to the authorities and – with the help of my father's friends from Sokol, who she was able to reconnect with – we were given a modern flat, where my mother would live until the uprising in Plzeň eight years later. She arranged all the restitution documents, including a death certificate for my father, and we were allowed to apply for furniture from the so-called 'national fund' of things taken from banished Germans. In this way, we acquired a table and some chairs, two beds and a wardrobe. I also applied for a piano, and was pleased to be given a Bösendorfer baby grand. Once I could start practising piano again, my interrupted life felt as if it had resumed. The very next day we went looking for work, and were prepared to consider anything to earn some money of our own. Most importantly of all, though, we both had to get used to the idea of being free.

Trying to get back into normality was immensely difficult. I had a terrible feeling of depression but I couldn't show it because I was supposed to be getting on with my life. There were so many strange liberties to re-accustom ourselves to, chiefly the sense that we could go anywhere we liked, even the toilet, without asking permission. There had been no doors in our world for years and no privacy, so to be able to walk into a room, close the door and have it to ourselves felt like something remarkable.

Sleeping in a proper bed with sheets and pillows was another great luxury, as was the concept that we could eat whenever we liked. One of the most peculiar sensations, though, was walking around on our own and not in groups of five, head down, constantly watching the feet in front of us. To begin with, I couldn't do it unless I held on to someone else or a wall. The unfamiliar motion made me nauseous and dizzy.

When we learned that less than 300 of Plzeň's 3,000 or more Jews had returned home after the war, we knew we were lucky to have survived, but that didn't mean our lives were significantly better. In fact, they were so much harder than before the war. We had no family. We had no work. We had no money. There was little meat and few vegetables.

The only highlight came when I was sent to a voluntary rehabilitation camp in Ostravice in the Beskydy Mountains for two weeks. It was a spa resort requisitioned for children and adolescents who'd survived the war. We were given wonderful food and treated for exhaustion and other health issues. That is where I met the writer Arnošt Lustig, who was in the same group as me, and I had many intense debates with him about the war and about Russians and their politics. Lustig was ecstatic, almost a fanatic at that time, and completely believed in communism, as did many others. I wasn't so sure.

It was in that rehabilitation camp that the first photograph was taken of me in years. At eighteen years old, I looked more like a woman in her thirties. When I returned to Plzeň after a fortnight away, I was shocked to realise that my mother looked more like she was in her sixties than her forties.

Through our Sokol friends, the mayor of the city went to great lengths to help us speed things along so that my mother could apply to get her shop back – although we could never have suspected that it would be taken from her again a few years later. We first needed affidavits confirming the deaths of my father and grandfather, detailing precisely where and how they had died. We still prayed that Uncle Karel might come back to us, which would have been such a blessing as Mummy would have had a business partner and I'd have had a father figure in my life again.

It was some time later that we learned of Karel's fate. He had survived Terezín and Auschwitz, then a subcamp, and finally a death march. When he was put into a cattle wagon in the final days of the war, probably to take him and his fellow prisoners to Mauthausen concentration camp in Austria, he somehow managed to escape from the train in Czechoslovakia. He made his way to the town of Sadská, east of Prague, where the Czechs immediately realised he was an escaped prisoner and hid him in the local prison for safety. Sadly, someone in the town informed on him, and on 4 May 1945, four days before our country was finally liberated by the Soviets and the Americans, the Nazis went to the prison and shot Karel dead.

To begin with my mother was distraught and angry. She was all set to go to Sadská and find out who had betrayed him to the Nazis so that they might be punished. Then she remembered what my father had said to her on his deathbed – 'Revenge belongs to God' – so she reluctantly decided against it.

The rest of our family had also been wiped out, including all of my aunts and uncles, and more than ten cousins. Vlasta, the singer with the beautiful voice, had been murdered in 1942 along with her husband Arnošt and her two children Jiří and Věra. My Aunt Zdenka had died the same year, and my Aunt Jiřina in Auschwitz.

My mother's family from Dobříš had perished too, so, aside from those relatives in America and England, we had no one apart from my cousin Sonja, who did help us in the end. Later on we came to think that her behaviour when we'd first arrived on her doorstep was understandable. She was only a child herself and she must have heard us confirm that her mother Jiřina had died and thought, 'Why did they survive and not my mother?' We did eventually get back some of the family things from friends, including some pieces of jewellery and the photo albums – which we cherished above all else.

It was also largely thanks to Sonja that we didn't starve in the first few months after the war. We were hungry all the time and just ate and ate. Everyone who survived did. Food became a compulsion. Sonja had a lot of potatoes stored in her cellar from the previous year and she told us we were free to help ourselves, so we did. It was like an obsession. Still a teenager, I was physically malnourished yet thickening round the middle from eating so many potatoes and became quite a chubby girl. My weight went up to sixty-five kilos, a weight I had never been before or since – and my mother was the same.

We had arrived in Plzeň with our requisitioned German clothes on our backs and nothing else. We'd left all of our fine pre-war clothes in the care of friends but the clothes were lost to us, and there was little else to choose from the repatriation centre. I had just one skirt and one blouse that I had to wear every day.

My mother had a lot of Gentile friends who were still around and kind to her but I had lost almost all of my contemporaries in Plzeň, which made me feel extremely lonely. Hanuš, my boyfriend in Terezín, had read the postcard I'd sent from Auschwitz with the Hebrew word for dead on it and naturally assumed I'd been murdered. It was a while before I discovered that he had survived and made a new life for himself in Brno, with a young woman he would later marry. The girlfriends I had been with throughout the war – Dana and Zuzana especially – meant so much to me, but they didn't come from Plzeň and had each gone back to their former homes in other parts of the country. It would be some years before we were able to reconnect.

When Mummy eventually got her shop back she immediately set about re-employing her old staff and re-establishing Hračky Růžička's reputation in the town. Her one stipulation was that no one who'd stolen from her would be given a job. It was very hard-going to begin with. There was a shortage of everything – nothing to sell and no one with any money to buy, and yet with the support of her neighbours and a few loyal customers she put the shop back on its feet within half a year. She took a loan from the Živnostenská bank, and the director used to drop in and check on her regularly until he became a friend.

In one part of the shop Mummy sold toys and in the other she sold paper and linens and all manner of necessary goods – just as my father had taught her. Her energy amazed me, especially when I recalled how sick she'd been and how much she had suffered. She came up with the idea of hiring poor peasants from the villages in the border regions to carve wooden toys – wonderful handmade items that she sold in the shop and the children loved. She also wrote to her sister Elsa in New York and asked what was popular among American children. Elsa sent her a big bag of rubber balloons, which were really something new and all the children from Plzeň crowded into the shop to buy them. Mummy was in her element.

The only work I could get was as a translator for the US Army under General Patton, who had liberated our part of Czechoslovakia. They weren't allowed to go further because the

Soviets had liberated the rest and would eventually claim the whole country as their spoils. The Americans hired me to translate the local press for their intelligence department and paid me a small wage. The officers were very kind, but I didn't socialise much at first as I had no confidence and didn't yet feel part of normal society.

When some of the GIs invited me to a dance, I turned them down because I felt too unattractive and had nothing to wear. Mummy insisted I accept and she made me a short-sleeved dress out of some old blackout material, with two bands of blue satin and a blue satin sash. She even found some satin gloves, a string of pearls, and a spray of flowers for my hair. Even though I was self-conscious about how much weight I'd gained, I felt like a princess that night and she arranged for me to have my photograph taken as a memento.

I was having a lovely time at the dance until an officer I was waltzing with suddenly spotted the number on my forearm.

'What does this mean?' he asked.

'It means I was in Auschwitz,' I replied.

He stopped dancing and laughed. 'Do you expect me to believe that fairy tale?'

I slapped him really hard across the face and ran from the room. It was the first and last time I ever hit anyone.

From that day on – and despite an official apology – I refused all further invitations and focused only on my translation work and my piano. I spent hours and hours at my Bösendorfer. It was all I had time for. I went back to see Madame and asked for some lessons but she wouldn't give them to me. 'If you really want to study music then you have to pass all your examinations in an official music school first,' she told me. She had another star pupil by then and was focusing her attention on her. I have to admit I was terribly jealous.

She did recommend me to Professor Bohdan Gselhofer, the director of the Bedřich Smetana Municipal Music School in Plzeň, however, and she persuaded him to teach me so that I could finish my studies. He agreed only as a favour to her because he was already famous, conducting a choir and winning prizes. To take on somebody at eighteen who hadn't practised for four and a half years was a huge undertaking.

In September 1945, four months short of my nineteenth birthday, I took my place with young children in the third grade and went back to basics. I had to relearn the complete series of Carl Czerny's *Art of Finger Dexterity* just as I had done as a nine-year-old with Madame, working my way through the études like a novice. Because of my ruined hands, I could no longer play with the ease I'd once known and whenever I tried, my fingers shook afterwards as if with a nervous tremor. Professor Gselhofer quickly agreed with Madame that I should give up music, but I refused to be dissuaded.

I knew Bach would be too difficult to play and I didn't even want to attempt it until I was good enough. At home, I began instead with Mozart's Piano Sonata No. 8 in A Minor, whose 'Third Movement' is one of the most desolate the composer ever wrote. With its underlying mood of tragedy, it was written after the death of his beloved mother. That piece perfectly reflected my mood and playing it so often imprinted it on my brain as the soundtrack to that dark time immediately after the war.

I made fast progress in class and, within three months, the professor changed his mind and agreed to teach me more thoroughly. I was allowed to take the examination for a higher grade, which I passed, and after that I was upgraded every three months. My mother didn't believe that I'd make a living by playing music and everyone else agreed, warning her that she would have to provide for me or that I would end up giving piano lessons in people's apartments. Mummy told them that, as my father would have wanted me to follow my dream and study music, she would help me as much as she could. And she helped me her entire life. By the end of 1946, I was playing in chamber music concerts in Plzeň and even performing solo to quite good reviews.

The studying and practice was very tough, but I was tireless and determined to remain completely focused. I would play and play until my fingers went numb and I could no longer concentrate on the score. In the space of two years I accomplished four years of musical education, in between offering private tuition to local children, going from home to home for a little extra money. As always, my music helped me to not dwell too much on my memories or allow my fears to overwhelm me, although they often did.

One day I was walking in the park when I passed a bandstand where the musicians began to play the 'Marinarella'. As my knees almost buckled under me, I was immediately transported back to the despair and hopelessness of Auschwitz and the infernal tune that had cruelly woken us each morning.

The question I asked myself over and over in Plzeň was: why did the war happen, and could it happen again? In my mind, I was still there in the camps – always there – thinking of those SS and what they did to us. I wondered where they were now and if their families had any idea what they had done. As I walked the streets, I looked into the faces of people passing by and knew that any one of them could have been in the SS. People who came from a good family with a good education could also have succumbed to fear, superstition and mass psychology and turned into beasts. I couldn't help wondering if this man or that woman could have behaved like that.

I began to wonder if anyone was immune. I believe that – with a few exceptions – almost everyone is potentially capable of yielding to the hypnosis of group psychology. It goes right back to Freud and the book that Fredy Hirsch had taken away from me as being too serious in the children's block of Auschwitz. Freud's writings were something I studied a great deal after the war and he made perfect sense to me.

Thanks to Fredy, who taught us that the first requirement for a human being is to be decent, I came to the conclusion that there are two ways of looking at the question of savagery: you can either say that everyone is potentially a criminal, or you can say that everyone is potentially decent. If he or she had lived under different conditions, then maybe they would have been decent. If one of those guards had lived a hundred years earlier in the Weimar Republic and not under Hitler's rule then he might have been a good man and a proud father of the family, keeping up his moral standards towards society.

Of course, the concept of what we might all be capable of is still a scary thought. I know that I must have met former Nazis in my travels, although thankfully I was not always aware of it – such as the time I was invited to the home of Hermann Abs, head of Deutsche Bank, whom I was told afterwards had been one of the most powerful bankers of the Third Reich.

Regardless of what I knew about them as individuals, whenever I met a German after I was liberated I would think: *What did you do during the war?* For me, it was the eternal question.

Thinking back to those days made me decide to try to reconnect with my friend Clement Morgan from Bergen-Belsen. All I knew was that he lived somewhere in England near a place called Newcastle and I can't now remember how I finally found an address for him.

Once I had it, I immediately sent him several letters, which are now held in the archives of the museum at Bergen-Belsen, after his family kindly donated them. In the first communication, I sent him the photo of me in my blackout dress with the caption: 'The girl you see in this picture will ever thank you for her life which you saved, for the faith in humanity which you taught her after four years of Nazi torture, and for the beautiful days spent with you. May you ever be so happy as you deserve it, and as it is the wish of yours truly, Susanne [sic].'

In a longer letter, I wrote:

> Dear Clem,
>
> I wonder if you still remember a certain girl named Susanne, whom you fetched from the white walls of a hospital room and whom you showed the first beautiful aspects of a real human life? I certainly did not forget what you have done for me, and my mother. Perhaps you don't know yourself that you have probably saved our life.
>
> Therefore I feel that it is my duty to let you know that we are both safe and healthy at home in Plzeň, Czechoslovakia

> … I think you would not recognise me I became very tall and much stronger and I am now as normal looking and living as any other girl. I hope that you and your family and your wife are all right and I wish you good luck for your following life.
>
> Best regards, Susanne

He wrote back immediately and I began a correspondence with him that lasted some years, until political circumstances prevented it. He told me that he and his fiancée had split up and that he hoped that I might get a stipend to study at the Royal Academy of Music, as I too hoped at the time, which would mean we could meet in London.

In another letter I wrote: 'I often remember Belsen, especially the first week when you were so kind to me and I felt like a little girl in a fairy tale where the good fairy always helps and cares for everything. I will never thank you enough for that.' Later, I added: 'It seems to me almost that it is only a few days ago as I saw you for the last time in your white doctor-dress. Do you remember when you left for London to visit your fiancée, as I was so badly ill? And how surprised you have been when you found me after your return again, alive and healthy in my office?'

I invited him to spend his next leave with me in Czechoslovakia and warned him to take care when treating TB cases, as I didn't want him to get infected. Our letters after that grew more and more sporadic as we were both working hard and studying for examinations. In one I told him I was working so late into the evening with 'barely time to eat or speak a few words to my mother', and that I was travelling the two hours to Prague by train once a week to have piano lessons with Professor Rauch.

There is only one more letter in the archives from me to Clem. It is undated but must have been many years later, when I was in Zurich and could easily write to the West. I told him of my travels so that he could follow my progress, but I never did get to meet up with him again, sadly. I will always remember him with love and gratitude for saving Mummy and me.

*

In spite of all my hard work and the fact that I was considered one of the best students in the Plzeň music school, I was still uncertain about my ability to become a concert pianist.

Then in 1946 the Smetana Municipal Music School applied to be upgraded to the status of a conservatoire, for which they had to get formal accreditation. To accomplish this, they arranged a concert of their best students and invited Professor Vladimír Polívka, a pianist and composer from the Prague Music Academy, to come and judge, along with three others including an official from the Ministry of Education. I was chosen to perform at the concert and I played Chopin's Variations Brillantes, Op. 12. Afterwards the committee came and asked me whether I would consider applying to the newly formed Academy of Performing Arts in Prague. That was, of course, a dream of mine, but the difficulty was that I had not completed the necessary secondary school education to attend such an establishment, something I was always ashamed of. It even stated on my passport, for all the world to see, that I had only ever completed five years of elementary education, although the best education I ever had was in Terezín – but that didn't count.

Incredibly, they told me that if I took the academy examination and passed, they would apply to the Ministry of Education to dispense with my former studies. I could hardly believe my luck.

My professor went with me to Prague and introduced me to Professor Rauch, whom he asked to coach me for the exam. Rauch was also admired as one of the greatest international pianists of his time with near perfect technique. When he heard me play, though, he was pessimistic from the start. On top of that, after the war a great many well-known concert pianists were also applying to the academy, which had recently been created and given university status, so the competition for places was intense. Professor Rauch turned me down.

I returned to Plzeň broken-hearted and told my mother the news. Though she still doubted that I would ever play professionally, she tried to reassure me that it wasn't the end of the world.

'But I can't live without music!' I told her, aghast.

Seeing how upset I was, my indomitable mother travelled alone to Prague to see Professor Rauch and ask him to reconsider my application, but he was very rude to her. He explained how crucial the four years between fourteen and eighteen were for a musician, and pointed out that my health and my hands were ruined. He added, 'Look here, Zuzana's a pretty girl. One day she'll be able to play the piano for her husband after dinner.'

Mummy came back to Plzeň and told me his verdict, and the two of us sat there thinking about whether I should carry on with my music. She was absolutely wonderful, trying to give me the strength to go on because she saw how important music was for me. I couldn't picture a life without it, so I continued with my studies and she remained encouraging. After much persuasion from her and others, Rauch eventually agreed to see me for lessons once a week.

Nevertheless, Professor Rauch never gave me any credit or showed me any compassion. I once told him that he was a sadist, but he was not that. In fact, he was an absolutely wonderful teacher but I think unsure of himself and severe with his own failings, which made him as severe with his students. He always told us exactly what he thought.

Three separate professors had kindly shown an interest in teaching me when I first arrived at the academy, and the eldest was Albín Ším – the chair of the whole music department – so I naturally chose him. He was kind and gentle and he spoke to me about the poetry of the music. What I really needed, though, was the rigorous training and technique I had missed during the war years, so I did something completely unheard of. I went to the dean and asked him to allow me to switch professors and attend the classes of Professor Rauch instead. He couldn't believe my request.

Rauch was the most feared professor in the academy, even for those much older than me and with successful careers – men who would still pause outside his door before summoning the courage to enter. He was a good teacher precisely because he was so tough, but he was the wrong kind for me emotionally. The master of sarcasm, he told me variously that I was an 'imbecile' and 'completely inept'. Where I needed encouragement and support he gave me none. He kept telling me that a musical career would not be possible. 'You are a nice young woman,' he'd say. 'You should marry. You are intelligent. If you want to take up a career you should study languages. Find another career because you're too old to start and your technical deficiencies are too great.' He never stopped ridiculing me.

Foolishly, I allowed him to get to me – to the point that whenever I left his class I came out feeling that I was the most worthless creature on this earth. Having become quite a fat little girl on a diet of bread and potatoes after the war, in my first year with Professor Rauch I lost thirteen kilograms and I never regained them. I had to work so hard to please him and I was physically and mentally exhausted. As well as my technical deficiencies, he also believed I was inherently unsuited to performing because of my stage fright.

It wasn't only me he picked on; he was like that to all his students. And criticism is something that a young person takes very hard. I remember one day when I was to sit a piano exam and Rauch spotted the necklace I was wearing and challenged me about it. It was a little wooden dachshund that a lady I'd met in a spa resort had given me for luck. 'What's that around your neck, Miss Růžičková?' Rauch asked.

'Something to bring me luck,' I replied, sheepishly.

'If you haven't worked hard enough then luck won't be of any use to you at all!' he scoffed. Thankfully, I passed, but that didn't stop him picking on me.

In my first year at the academy, I emerged from one of his most vicious tutorials feeling lower than I had in years. Rauch was right. I wasn't made for this. I would never be good enough. I'd always thought music would save me, but instead I was beginning to believe it would be my downfall.

To make matters worse, I'd had yet another quarrel with my first boyfriend after the war, a young musicologist and violinist named Rudolf Stehlík I met at the municipal music school. He and I even performed together – we played an improvisation of a piece by the Russian composer and violinist Nikolai Rakov at a pedagogical evening in 1946. Rudolf was a clever, handsome Aryan from working-class stock and we nearly got engaged, except for the fact that he had a jealous streak and caused a scene every time I even went for a drink with fellow students. His emotional highs and lows exhausted and alarmed me and I knew I couldn't spend the rest of my life with such a person.

If I couldn't be a musician and I wouldn't be with Rudolf then I didn't know what was left for me. On that day, after that class, I didn't feel that I could fit into this world. I felt contaminated and sick. I was unable to think or act like a normal human being. I also felt this terrible burden of being alive when all those other people from the camps were dead.

My only salvation was music and I feared I wouldn't be able to bridge this four-year gap in my education and with my hands in such condition. I thought that nobody really understood how I felt, and that it was my fault not theirs. The truth was I was an impecunious student who could only supplement my income by teaching piano to children in their homes. Even if I passed all my exams, I saw a future that involved going back to Plzeň to live with my mother and trying for a teaching job at the music school. I knew that it would be a good living, but I dreaded getting stuck there and never giving concerts. Nor would I have many friends in the city, as so many of my contemporaries had perished and yet I couldn't talk to anyone about losing them.

My new friends in Prague didn't know what had happened to me, or they didn't want to know. Trying to appear normal and fit in with my fellow students was a private torture. I pretended to be the fun one, the girl who was always laughing and telling jokes, so that they would like me and want me to be their friend. I was exhausted by constantly ignoring my past and yet the war informed a huge part of me – the most dreadful years of my life.

Making my way home to my mother's apartment one day – the only place where I had unlimited access to a piano – I caught an earlier train than usual from Prague as I was feeling utterly wretched. I knew the apartment would be empty, as Mummy would still be at work. I had never felt so lonely in in my life.

Like me, ever since liberation my mother had had difficulty sleeping and often took barbiturates to help her. The apothecary was a family friend so she never needed a prescription. Without really knowing what I was doing, I went straight to the chemist from the station and collected some more pills, claiming they were for her, and then I went to her apartment. I took one look at the piano I'd managed to secure from the authorities after the war, and then I lay down and swallowed all of her pills.

My guardian angel must have been watching over me that day because, in what turned out to be yet another miracle, Mummy had developed a terrible headache that afternoon and sent someone from the shop to the chemist. When they returned they told her that I'd collected her pills for her half an hour earlier. Mummy knew she hadn't asked me, and that I shouldn't even be in town yet, so she ran home and found me just in time. The doctor pumped my stomach and I survived.

Once I'd recovered, Mummy insisted that I see a psychiatrist for depression. I was reluctant at first, but the person she found turned out to be the wisest man in the world. He encouraged me to tell him everything I was feeling, so I tearfully explained that I'd lived in constant fear since 1938 and didn't think that life was worth living.

After hours of listening to what I'd been through and how it was affecting me, he said simply, 'I completely understand, Zuzana, and I don't wonder at what you did. I can't help you because, you see, if I were you I would probably have done the same. You are not a psychiatric case.'

His words shocked me and then they gave me an overwhelming sense of relief. I wasn't insane. I was normal. What I had done was understandable. This calm professional didn't prescribe me any medicine. He didn't send me to another analyst. He gave me the best medicine – permission to have done what I did and, most importantly, he gave me the permission to carry on.

I knew then that I was lucky to have survived, and his words helped me appreciate what a gift it was to have food to eat, a roof over my head, and clothes to wear. Not that my recovery happened overnight and there was no definitive point where I felt I had recovered.

Viktor said later that even in the early years of our marriage I was still far from well and toying with the idea of suicide. He was afraid that I might never recover.

Music was essential to me being well, but Viktor was so very, very essential.

Before I met him, though, all I knew was that persisting with my music was necessary for me to keep going physically and to survive emotionally.

For me music was a feeling – a feeling I almost lost – and I had to work very hard to get it back.

Music was my defiance.

My mother was such an amazing woman. She recovered from the war quite quickly and with so much vitality, although of course she never looked at another man again. She couldn't forget my father and it was too painful for her to even talk about him. We bought flowers every year for his birthday, but that was about all she could bear. After we returned home, most of the widows remarried and several men wanted to marry her, especially those who came back from the camps without their wives. But she had the shop and me, and that was all she needed.

Sensing perhaps that I would benefit from speaking to those who had something in common with me, she introduced me to some repatriated survivors my age who had come home looking for relatives who were long dead. Mummy was very kind to them, inviting them to our home and feeding them, so we were able to exchange memories. It was much easier to communicate with them than with other teenagers.

Like many of them, I felt guilt for surviving because so many far worthier than myself had perished. There were such gifted people who died; people who were probably geniuses, and would have been wonderful scientists, artists, musicians, or poets. Why was I here and they weren't? And not just them – there were so many ordinary people with the right to a life and they also died.

I have spent my life trying to pay my debts to those who didn't come back by working hard and trying to make myself worthy of being alive.

This sense of not being worthy pervaded my late teenage years and was one of the reasons I tried to kill myself. It was the kindness of Professor Sádlo and my chamber music group that saved me after my suicide attempt. When he persuaded Rauch to put me on stage, in spite of his doubts, everything changed. I had my first feature-length concert in a hall in Prague and it was a really big success. In a nod to Madame, who was sitting in the audience, I played Bach's Prelude and Fugue No. 1 from *The Well-Tempered Clavier*, Chopin's Etude, Op. 10, some Debussy, some of the once-forbidden Martinů, and Beethoven's Op. 1, because I knew I was a good interpreter of Beethoven.

It went so well that the attitude of Professor Rauch changed towards me immediately. He finally saw that I was able to play and give a good performance. The softer side of him emerged, from which I learned that he had three other passions: fishing, football and cars. I even cycled to his country villa in Šťáhlavy for lessons, and attended a football match with him, for the first and last time as he said my constant questions about the rules of the game were too exhausting. When Rauch was temporarily replaced at the academy by the piano virtuoso Josef Páleníček (who became a great friend), all of us students went on strike until he was reinstated.

It was Rauch who arranged for me to play with two other pianists in the Rudolfinum on the occasion of the two-hundredth anniversary of the death of Bach in 1950. Thanks, in part, to him I began to feel that I possessed a musical life again. I passed my Bachelor of Arts degree, I went on to get my Masters degree in 1951, and was immediately offered the job at the academy teaching piano to a group of composers, including Viktor.

By the mid-1950s, I was playing piano and harpsichord, solo, in chamber quartets and with full orchestras. Sadly, Madame died before I took the decision to focus solely on the one instrument she knew was perfect for me. As well as working closely with Josef Suk and the flautist Václav Žilka, I was lucky enough to perform regularly with the Prague Chamber Orchestra along with many other wonderful and talented musicians.

There were many other performances during that time, but one that was memorable for the wrong reasons occurred in 1954 when the Union of Composers asked me to give a concert of Mongolian music at the Mongolian embassy in Prague. I was glad for every job and the union sent me the score for a piece by Magsaržavyn Dugaržav, the father of Mongolian Art music and an ardent communist. It was a relatively simple pentatonic that probably wasn't even originally written for the piano but for a folk instrument and then reworked. I dressed accordingly and went along thinking that my performance would be a cultural intermezzo after the speech. There was a large table where they sat me between two massive Soviet generals, each of them wearing numerous medals. They started distributing vodka and poured me a glass, and then there was a big speech, followed by toasts – the first of which was to Stalin.

When I merely sipped at my vodka one of the generals looked at me menacingly and said: '*Što ty, ty nelubíš tavaryše Stalina?*' ('What is it? Don't you love comrade Stalin?') I tried to make an excuse but he repeated, '*Ty nelúbíš taváryše Stalina?*' as the other general turned to glare at me too.

I had to reply that I did, and I drank down my vodka. I was not at all accustomed to alcohol at that time; we would only drink a glass of beer at home. My glass was refilled and then came another toast to the Mongolian leader, Comrade Yumjaagiin Tsedenbal: '*Da zdravstvuj tavaryšč Tsedenbal!*' ('To the health of comrade Tsedenbal!'). I thought that maybe I didn't have to love Tsedenbal in the same way as Stalin, so I didn't drink but once again the generals quizzed me, so I had to. More toasts followed and at the moment when I was supposed to start playing, I was barely able to walk to the piano. What I played I don't know, but I'm sure that by then they didn't know either. In the end, they took me home. That was the first time I was inebriated and I don't think I have been drunk since.

The mid-1950s were one of my busiest times as I was establishing myself as a performer, playing in some of Prague's finest venues and with some of our country's most talented soloists such as Ladislav Černý, Karel Šroubek, Ivan Večtomov and Břetislav Novotný. This was the time that I was also touring Czech factories and workplaces to bring them a little culture – in between strongmen and performing dogs. I did approach the state agency about maybe playing the harpsichord at these events, but they just laughed. A career as a harpsichordist at that time was considered a joke. All of this was before the ARD competition in Munich, which of course changed everything.

The dream I had dreamed since I was a little girl had finally come true. It had happened through a combination of luck, perseverance, the encouragement of my mother and my kinder teachers and, yes, the pressure placed on me by Professor Rauch.

Years later, when I became a colleague of his at the academy, I got to know and understand him a lot better. I even used to tease him from time to time. I was married to Viktor by then and I'd tell him, 'You know, Frantisek, your prophecy was absolutely wrong. Viktor doesn't want to listen to me playing piano after dinner at all.'

It became our little joke.

14
Prague, 1989

Change was in the air across Europe in the 1970s and '80s in ways we could never have imagined. Some of it was good and some of it was bad, but the worst of it was the rise in terrorism – much of which was directed against Jews or Jewish organisations, especially in France and Germany.

Synagogues and cemeteries were desecrated and schools firebombed. American tourists were also frequent targets, with Muslim jihadists, frustrated by the impasse in Palestinian–Israeli relations, suspected of being behind many of the attacks.

In the summer of 1981, I was invited back to Paris to judge a harpsichord competition. My friend Christopher Hogwood was on the jury with me, so I was doubly pleased. Viktor was a little nervous, as there had been several terrorist incidents in Paris in recent years, the most recent against a synagogue, but I told him not to worry.

The first day of the competition was very long and, when we finished, Christopher and I went straight back to our hotel, the Intercontinental, overlooking the Tuileries. A message was waiting for me from a musical friend who wanted to have dinner with me. Christopher had already retired to bed and I declined, claiming exhaustion. 'Oh, but at least come and have a coffee with me in the foyer?' she pleaded. 'You are here for such a brief time. I would so hate to miss you.'

Tempted as I was to see my friend, I knew that I needed to rest. Not long after I turned her down, an explosion rocked our hotel. A man had left an attaché case under a desk in the foyer, near the cafe where I would have met my friend. Eighteen people were injured, and when the hotel was evacuated I came down the stairs with the other guests to discover that the cafe was on fire and all but destroyed. Dear Christopher was up on the twelfth floor and had slept through the whole thing. He had to be woken by staff.

I knew Viktor would worry when he heard of the attack, so I was able to call and assure him that I was unhurt. 'My guardian angel always has something to do,' I told him.

Aside from our concerns about the rise of terrorism and anti-Semitism, there was some good news in the 1980s, especially regarding the politics of the Eastern bloc. Even Viktor began to hope that something good might come of it. The new wind first blew in from the Soviet Union with the appearance of Mikhail Gorbachev, the youngest member of the Politburo, and a man who would change the world.

Within two years of becoming secretary general of the Communist Party in 1985, he was shaking hands with US president Ronald Reagan, effectively ending the Cold War. After travelling widely in the West, he announced radical plans to revive the Soviet economy and introduce democratisation through glasnost (openness) and perestroika (restructuring). He admitted that Alexander Dubček and the Prague Spring had inspired many of his policies. Political prisoners were freed, the press was allowed more freedom, and private ownership was permitted for businesses, reducing party control. Addressing the United Nations Assembly, Gorbachev promised to withdraw Soviet troops from Eastern Europe.

Then, in March 1989, he oversaw the first free election in the Soviet Union since 1917. The ripple effect around the world and especially in the satellite states was astonishing – most notably in Poland, where strikes led by the labour union Solidarity eventually sparked the country's first free elections since 1920.

When Gorbachev announced that each country could take its own path to socialism, it was the turn of Hungary – a country I had visited many times and was also sent there to perform soon after the occupation, so I was able to see first hand what the mood was. In a remarkably smooth transition, a new Republic of Hungary was created in October 1989 with a promise of free elections. East Germans started flooding into Prague in their Trabant cars and petitioning the German embassy for help. From there they went to Hungary and on to Austria. There were so many people heading west.

For a while, we had a fleeting glimpse of what it might be like to live in a republic of poets and artists. We were hopeful that we might get some sort of democracy. Our cultural life was already richer thanks to dissident writers such as Václav Havel and others, and many more books were available to us. Havel had been imprisoned multiple times and lived under constant surveillance and harassment from the secret police. There were always petitions for his release. He became a free man when the Berlin Wall was officially opened for the first time since 1961. Like the rest of the world, Viktor and I watched the television news coverage open-mouthed on that momentous day – 9 November 1989 – as Eastern bloc refugees streamed across to freedom through the open gates, or after smashing the symbolic wall to pieces with hammers and chisels.

For several months we had been expecting some economic changes at least, but our economy was relatively healthy and we didn't believe there would be real change until it collapsed. The first thing that really affected us directly was when Viktor, who was on the committee of the Philharmonic, heard that letters were being written by leading musicians, writers, and artists demanding more freedom and a change to the politics of the regime. That was a bomb.

We both went to work as usual and when we came home, Viktor said to me, 'Something is happening. The students are planning a march and demonstration on 17 November.' We both knew that was International Students' Day – so named because it marked the fiftieth anniversary of a bloody student demonstration against Nazi occupation. There had already been demonstrations on 28 October, the anniversary of our country's founding in which thousands had taken to the streets and held up their fingers in a V-sign for victory. We wondered where this would all lead, never imagining the outcome.

The march, which had been officially sanctioned, started relatively small that afternoon and attracted some 15,000 students. When it was over most of them dispersed, although about three thousand remained on the streets chanting, 'Freedom!' and calling for Havel. Instead of going home, they marched towards Wenceslas Square, followed closely by the StB. The riot police were sent in to block their path but the students just sat down and offered flowers and candles to their would-be attackers, telling them, 'Our hands are bare.' It was only when the police moved in with riot sticks, injuring hundreds and arresting even more that the crowd finally scattered. In the days that followed, however, it was clear that the protests were far from over.

Then one night I had a call from one of the professors at the academy who told me that all our students had declared a strike, which they planned to hold in the art deco Café Slavia, opposite the National Theatre. He asked if I would go and help supervise them, which of course I did. Government officials went on television to call for a restoration of order and the prime minister gave his personal guarantee that there would be no violence against citizens, although few believed him. It was still dangerous to be seen to be supporting protestors in any way, but we didn't care and took shifts at the Café Slavia, day and night. There were always two professors to see to the students and make sure that they had enough to eat and drink and were in good condition. The students behaved wonderfully and their action was supported by students at other universities, theatre staff and actors across the country who – instead of performing – went on stage and read a statement calling for a general strike on 27 November.

The movement was gaining momentum.

Then the Philharmonic rang to tell us they were putting on two protest concerts on Radio Prague on 24 and 25 November, and asked all the soloists take part. I immediately agreed to that too, and so did my colleague Josef Suk. There was never any question. We wanted to do all we could to support democratic change. The first recording coincided with another mass demonstration and as soon as we went out we were caught up in the crowds of people flooding into the city, headed for Wenceslas Square where Havel and Dubček were expected to speak to the growing crowds.

I went to the building where Viktor worked on Vinohradská Street and prepared myself for the concert. The first was the Brandenburg Concerto No. 5 for harpsichord, flute and violin in which the harpsichord has a different and important role, as it was really Bach's first harpsichord concerto in which the instrument takes a starring role. The orchestra usually records the whole thing and the harpsichordist stays behind to record the cadenza, which I did.

Viktor was working with his children's choir for a show on the radio station as usual that day. Then he unexpectedly appeared in the doorway of the studio where I was working, looking pale. 'I've had calls from parents asking me to get them home,' he said. 'The militia are on the streets with guns. We must leave at once.'

'But I still have the cadenza to record!' I protested.

I never played the cadenza as quickly as I did that day, and you can hear it on the recording by Vanguard. Reviewers afterwards, especially in the United States, said it was the fastest cadenza ever played but they had no idea why. I had a student from Berlin with me and he was terribly scared and wanted to go to the train station and get out of Prague as quickly as possible. I told him to go and wished him luck. I think it was really touch and go with the militia that night and it could have been the start of a bloodbath.

When I'd finished recording, I was meant to leave immediately for another concert and had a bag with a long black skirt to change into. Viktor didn't want me to go anywhere alone so we got into the lift together. It stopped at the next floor and a young man stepped in carrying a tray of vodka shots with a huge grin on his face.

'What are you celebrating?' I asked, innocently.

'Don't you know?' he cried. 'The government just resigned!'

We couldn't believe it and Viktor hurried me to one of the offices to see if it was true. Sure enough, we watched on television as Havel and his Civic Forum allies announced the shocking news during a press conference they were holding at the Prague theatre where they had set up as their headquarters. We wept and embraced and we were still in shock as we watched them open champagne and toast freedom, crying, 'Long live Czechoslovakia!' Viktor and I decided to go immediately to join the celebrations in Wenceslas Square.

It was the most incredible sensation to be standing in that crowd of some half a million people deafened by the sound of freedom. Viktor kept his arm firmly around me as we were jostled forward with the rest, watching as our fellow Czechs chanted, clapped, waved the Czech flag wildly, and wept for joy. Somewhere up in the distance on a far balcony at the end of the square, Havel and Dubček were soaking up the applause as international TV crews broadcast our so-called 'Velvet Revolution' around the world. Havel took to the podium and urged that the revolution go on until we had democracy. It really was a terribly moving moment.

Viktor and I were euphoric. It was unbelievable to us that all those years of living under two dictatorships and the oppression of a totalitarian regime had come to an end so painlessly, and so quickly.

The last time I had been free was 1939, fifty years earlier. In various ways, I had been enslaved ever since, as had Viktor and the rest of my countrymen our age. It was impossible to imagine how much our lives would change and what that might mean for us both. For now, we just wanted to savour the moment and soak up the remarkable atmosphere.

I was just another face in the crowd but I looked up to the heavens and, with tears in my eyes, I said, 'Father, if you could see this now. This is what you gave your life for. It wasn't for nothing. You can be so proud of your country tonight.'

My one regret was that my mother was no longer alive to witness the revolution with us. She had died six years earlier, at the age of eighty-seven.

Mummy had gradually lost her sight and her hearing in the late 1970s. She suffered from macular degeneration and it made her life increasingly difficult. She was still living with us in our flat, but she could no longer read, write or watch television. She could only listen to the radio sitting right next to it wearing hearing aids. Viktor and I were working as hard as ever and couldn't spend much time with her, so she must have been very lonely on her own. Then she had a slight stroke, which gave her some brain trouble. She recovered quite well, except that she began to fall. I trained myself to wake up as soon as she turned on the light in the next-door room, so that I could help her. I used to prepare her breakfast before we went to work, and then she would go out for lunch, and we would all of us eat together at night. I was so terribly afraid that she would fall down while I was at work or away on tour.

I was as busy as ever and also taught students one day a week from 8 a.m. to 8 p.m., so when I came home I'd be absolutely finished. At the end of one such day I also had a terrible migraine, so I couldn't wait to go to bed. That night I offered her dumplings and strawberries – her favourite – but she told me she'd had them for lunch and wanted to eat something different. As Viktor and I were having fish, I gave her mine and ate the dumplings. I went to bed and slept deeply.

In the morning she turned on her light and got up to make herself some tea and cookies. When I found her in the kitchen later she told me, 'I should have had the dumplings last night because now I feel like something sweet.' I still had a headache, so I didn't sit at the table with her as I normally did and I went back to bed instead. On her way back to her bed half an hour later, she fell and broke her arm. I felt very guilty about that. I should have been with her. She had to go to hospital and the recovery was not easy at her age. The hospital discovered that she had diabetes, which was probably why she fell – due to low blood sugar. After that, she virtually refused to walk, because she was afraid of falling again.

We needed someone to care for her, so I placed an advert in the paper, appealing for someone with a good education. A well-dressed lady answered the advertisement immediately and seemed ideal. She was elegant and cultivated, wonderful with languages, and we arranged for her to start the following week. To my surprise, she never arrived and instead I received a letter from her in the post soon afterwards, in which she wrote, 'I am sorry but I cannot come to work for you after all. I loved you and your mother, but I was sent to spy on you and I don't want to do that.' I was so shocked and couldn't believe how naive I had been in placing the ad.

In the end we found someone local who was not so intellectual, but she was very good and became a part of the family. She took care of Mummy well, but before too long it became apparent that my mother had also developed dementia and could no longer remain with us at home. She needed to go into a hospital for old people. That was a terrible decision to have to make as the places for non-communists in Prague were extremely substandard, and the doctors were often just the children of important party officials so not always the best. I had some contacts in high places and I really humbled myself then and went to a high party official to beg for a bed for my mother in one of the better institutions. My request was – of course – refused.

'Everybody has a mother,' I was told. 'Yours does not qualify to go there.' I did all I could to pull some strings, but even so she ended up in a place with eighteen to a room, and was not taken very good care of.

Mummy hated it at the hospital, but was extremely patient. She hardly spoke to any of the other residents and was no trouble for the nurses. I tried to get her up and walking outside whenever I could, and it was possible every now and again before the dementia worsened. Every time I went there she had such a sweet smile and asked where I had just played. Even in the last days of her life, when she was in an oxygen tent, she would pull off her mask and ask me, 'How was the audience?'

She was in hospital for six months before she died in December 1983. She was buried in a Jewish cemetery not far from our apartment. I discovered that it was possible to erect a memorial there to the people we had lost during the war, so I had one made for the Růžička family and all those from Dobříš, where I placed some memorial stones and candles. Nearby there is also a plaque for all the writers and composers who perished in Terezín.

Mummy endured so much in her lifetime, and never once imagined she would live to be nearly ninety. Like me, the legacies of the war remained with her – physically and emotionally – but, in many ways, for her it was the years after the war that were especially cruel. If only she'd been allowed to keep her shop and remain in the Plzeň that she loved, I think she would have had a much happier and more productive life. Instead, her world suddenly became terribly small, and revolved almost exclusively around Viktor and me in our little flat. She didn't travel and she didn't work. She lost interest in most things and became so very different from the beautiful, vibrant businesswoman that I remember from my childhood.

The one thing she and I were always grateful for was that my father passed away before being sent to Auschwitz – an experience he would never have survived. He was such a proud man, an intellectual, and that place represented the ultimate loss of all human dignity. Having a number branded on your skin and being stripped of everything human – his clothes, his books, everything – would have been too much for him. Many people went insane there and it often happened straight away. Mummy and I were convinced that Tata would not even have lasted a month, so at least he was saved from that.

And she was saved from seeing it.

I know, too, that I would not have survived there but for her. She lived for me and I lived for her. Emotionally, I was broken in Auschwitz, but she comforted me every night. And if she hadn't spoiled me so much as a child and kept me as healthy as possible, I most certainly wouldn't have endured the physical challenges of the war either. Then, she rescued me again after I tried to kill myself, and did everything possible to allow me to concentrate on my music. She attended every concert I ever gave in Prague, always sitting attentively in the front row. She was my greatest admirer.

There's not a day that passes when I do not think of her with gratitude and love.

Our lives changed dramatically after the Velvet Revolution. We all threw ourselves wildly at freedom. We were so fed up with being watched over and we craved freedom. But what is freedom? To many it is an abstract idea.

The borders opened and people crowded across, hungry for a Western lifestyle and consumer goods that were unavailable here. I had seen the problems of the capitalist system and I knew that the West wasn't a paradise. For many of us from the Eastern bloc, the new situation took quite some adjusting to. It was like animals in a zoo that had been kept in a cage and given their food but not their freedom. There were those who didn't know they were in a cage, as they had never known anything else. Others preferred to remain in their cage, being fed and taken care of. They didn't even have any concept of being free or 'unfree', and they didn't want the doors opened.

For those who had wholeheartedly embraced communism, the change was the most shocking of all. Many turned to religion instead, desperate for something else to believe in. Democracy was the one shift they were never prepared for.

The biggest change for Viktor and me was that, suddenly, we were rich beyond words. For the first time, I came to know exactly how much I was being paid to perform, and – this time – I was allowed to keep almost all of it. So, we had money to spend, although we had no idea on what at first. The authorities had already allowed us to buy a little terraced house in Jindřichův Hradec, so that we could work on our music during the summer, and Viktor bought a better car. With the new freedoms of our political situation, I was able to have access to beautifully decorated copies of baroque harpsichords by the Prague maker František Vyhnálek after the style of the maker Ruckers, and after Harras by Ammer.

Viktor and I were also able to travel freely for the first time, visiting festivals and friends in Spain, Switzerland, and Italy, as well as the United States, and were regular visitors to the French home of the Russian pianist Sviatoslav Richter, with whom I had performed many times. I had never lost contact with kind Dr Van Loo from Bergen-Belsen, who lived in Ghent. He had come to see my concerts in Belgium and introduced me to his family there, who remained in touch after his death, so we paid them a visit too.

We bought a few mementos on our travels, but one of the legacies of the camps was that I didn't like to possess anything, and the only things I owned of any value were pieces of jewellery Viktor had bought for me and I lost even these. It happened shortly before the revolution, after I had just returned from taking another master class in Zurich – something I did for almost twenty-five years. On my return to Prague, I discovered that the weather had turned unseasonably warm and, as it was a Friday afternoon, I said to Viktor, 'Let's go to the country straight away. I can deliver the foreign currency and return my passport when I get back on Monday.'

We packed our things and left, but when we returned, our flat had been ransacked and all my jewellery stolen. My unopened fee from the Swiss had also been taken. I reported the burglary to the authorities but had the uncomfortable feeling that they didn't believe me. They also questioned me closely as to why I hadn't handed over my fee immediately upon my return, as instructed.

Then the revolution happened and I forgot all about it. It was only much later when secret government files were opened that I found out how lucky I had been. My file, which was several inches thick, included all the paperwork in place for me to be put on trial for withholding foreign currency. It became clear that the first part of my punishment had been the state-organised burglary and the loss of my personal belongings, which sadly I never got back.

One of the best things that happened to us after the change in our politics was that we had our academic titles restored to us. I was finally entitled to get my professorship, something I'd qualified for years earlier, although I was given no financial compensation for the reduced salary.

The students of my faculty all met then and had a vote and decided to nominate me as their new director, but I immediately turned them down. They were quite upset at first and accused me of caring more about my career than the faculty, but I explained that it was more than that.

'Ask Viktor,' I told them. 'Whenever I see a piece of paper I have to deal with, I turn red. I would be the worst director in the world, and you would be very unhappy with me very quickly.' They had no choice but to agree.

Viktor was finally awarded his doctorate, although he refused to go before the committee making the decision because it comprised several former communists. He said, 'I should judge them, not them judge me!' Regardless of his stance, his doctorate was presented to him thirty-eight years late in a deeply poignant ceremony at the Karolinum, which is a part of Charles University in the Old Town. It was February 1990 when Viktor and a lot of old and famous people who had also been denied their proper titles for the arts and sciences under the communists finally received their awards from the Minister of Culture. I was married to Dr Kalabis at last, not that he ever used the title – except when he needed medical care.

Viktor was offered several senior positions, including head of the Academy of Performing Arts and head of the radio station, but it was all too late. He didn't have the strength for it. Years earlier he had decided to devote himself entirely to creating his own music, instead of having just the two months' unpaid leave he took from the radio station every summer. He was still extremely busy, building what would become a canon of ninety-two numbered works, including five symphonies and a host of scores for harpsichord and strings, almost all of them written on the upright piano he bought for our flat.

In a nod to his lifetime admiration of Czech composer Bohuslav Martinů, whom he considered to be the greatest Czech composer of the twentieth century, in 1993 he had helped set up the Bohuslav Martinů Foundation, founded the Martinů Institute a year later and launched the Martinů Festival. Cleverly, he found Aleš Březina, a very promising young musicologist, then working at the Paul Sachar Foundation in Switzerland, and persuaded him to run it. He was also writing music full time.

In 1989 the Czech Philharmonic played one of the pieces Viktor had written for me – his Harpsichord Concerto, Op. 42 – in Birmingham, England, and it went on to be played to great acclaim across Europe and in Australia. And in 1992, I arranged something rather special for my talented husband in New York after I read an interview in which he had said it would be his greatest wish to have a performance at Carnegie Hall. I will never forget how happy Viktor was that night.

When I was in New York, I went to visit my Aunt Elsa in a nursing home. I was playing and teaching at Vassar College in upstate New York not far from where she lived. The last time I had seen her was in Dobříš when I was a little girl, before she and her husband had emigrated to America. She was ten years older than my mother and, although she lived to 103, she had dementia. I found her sitting in a wheelchair, painfully thin, but still elegant with wonderful skin and beautiful clothes.

Seeing me again triggered something in her dementia, so that she believed she was my mother, Poldi. Clasping my hand, she became emotional and told me, 'Oh Zuzana, I will never forget those dreadful times with you in the camps.' It was touching to see that she had been thinking about it the whole time to such an extent that she had identified so closely with my mother. That was the last time I ever saw her.

Immediately after the revolution I had the honour of being nominated as president of the Prague Spring International Music Competition, which had been started in 1948 by Rafael Kubelík, the anti-communist conductor who had inadvertently forced me to play without an orchestra at the Munich competition in 1956.

Because of recent events in our country, the 1990 festival was feted to be one of the most important ever and I knew I had a very important job to do. Calling in a favour, I immediately contacted Kubelík, then seventy-five years old, at his home in Switzerland and asked him to come to Prague and sit on the jury with Václav Neumann.

'I'm sorry but I can't,' he told me. 'I have such bad arthritis in my back that I shall probably never see Prague again.' But a few months later, after time spent in California, he contacted me again.

'I have had lots of physical therapy and exercise and I am feeling much better. I will be happy to come and preside.'

The first thing he did when he arrived was to arrange a wonderful dinner for Viktor and me at the Palace Hotel, the place where we had spent our wedding night. It was made all the more special because he was accompanied by his wife, the Australian soprano Elsie Morison, whom I'd met and loved long before I knew Kubelík.

The Prague Spring Festival was a huge success. The opening concert in the Art Nouveau Smetana Hall, held on the anniversary of the death of Czech composer Bedřich Smetana, was his set of symphonic poems, *Má Vlast* – something I first learned to play with Madame when I was just a child. The Czech pianist Rudolf Firkušný, who lived in New York, returned to perform a concerto by Bohuslav Martinů. After he heard me play Martinů also, he invited me to the Edinburgh Festival with him the following year. He also saw every concert I played in America and became chairman of the jury of the Prague Spring International Piano Competition.

Václav Havel was in the presidential box for the Prague Spring Festival and every member of the Philharmonic proudly wore the red white and blue badges of his Civic Forum independence movement. The whole room swelled with Czech pride.

Havel was a really great person, whose slogan was 'Truth and Love Will Prevail'. People make jokes about it in modern times and call the fans of Havel 'the truth and love guys', but it was so important to us at the time. I met Havel on several occasions, before and after the revolution, and I liked and respected him enormously. I used to play the matinee concert at the theatre where his plays were being performed, and I also met him in Paris, where some important VIPs from the French embassy and the academy of arts commented to me how impressive he was 'for a peasant'. I corrected them immediately and explained that Havel grew up in Prague as part of a wealthy, intellectual family, and was not a peasant at all. It was Havel who introduced me to the Queen of England when she visited Prague not long after the revolution. I was surprised to discover that she was almost as short as me.

*

Viktor was first diagnosed with kidney cancer the year my mother died. He had surgery and the doctors told me they thought they'd caught it early enough, so I decided not to tell him it was cancer. He was so happy after the surgery that anything else would have been cruel.

I kept that horrible secret from him for almost twenty years and he wasn't told until 2002 when he started to feel unwell and developed prostate cancer. We spoke to the doctors and were debating whether or not he should have surgery when we watched a programme on television about a Czech professor at UCLA in America, who had good results with a new drug. We went to the TV station and got the professor's address, and he sent the drug to us and it worked.

Then, Viktor started to have a series of mini strokes. He had developed diabetes and had more trouble with his eyesight, which had plagued him his whole life. The doctors thought it might be glaucoma, but it turned out to be lesions on the brain. These caused him to faint occasionally and gave him numbness in his extremities. He was also getting confused. Throughout all of this he kept working and stubbornly refused to accept that he was ill. He gave the last of his strength to promoting Martinů and was president of the foundation until he was eighty in 2003, when he finally had to give it up because of his impaired sight.

One day soon afterwards we were sitting having lunch together when he suddenly told me he felt very unwell. I called a doctor friend who said I had to get him to hospital to see a neurologist. That was the beginning of the end.

By the time Viktor was permanently in hospital in 2004, I visited him every day after work and took him soup. I played music to him constantly even though I wasn't always sure that he could hear it, until he'd suddenly say, 'This is being played too fast.' Sometimes he knew who I was, and sometimes he didn't. He was always so witty, and when he was fully present he would chatter away and be his old funny self. Other times he couldn't tell the difference between dreams and reality. It was a great problem and there was no advice about whether or not to tell him the truth.

A dear friend of mine, the cellist Bohuslav Pavlas, came to visit him once and I left them alone while I went to warm Viktor's soup. During my absence, Viktor turned to Bohuslav and said, 'What's going to happen to my Zuzanka when I'm gone?'

'I will take care of her,' Bohuslav assured him.

Viktor slipped into a semi-coma after that and I lived the final stages of his illness with him. I remained at his side and talked to him all the time, describing our village in his cherished Bohemia and the beautiful countryside and all the lovely places we liked to go walking to pick flowers and wild mushrooms. My Viktor died aged eighty-three on 28 September 2006, not long after I had tried to feed him some soup.

The loss of Viktor, and of my music, felt immense. At my age, I would have given up playing anyway. Better for people to say, 'It's a pity she doesn't play anymore', rather than 'It's a pity she still plays', but my music had always given me the strength to go on whenever life seemed impossibly hard.

I am not a person of extraordinary strength. I survived all the camps and the terrible experiences not because of myself, it had nothing to do with me. It was one hundred miracles.

Music was a great blessing, and having lived a life of music was the most wonderful blessing of all. Now when I sit down at the harpsichord or the piano and I am no longer able to play it, I am very sad about that, but then I say to myself, I have had enough. Living without playing music, living without Viktor, is very, very difficult, but I have to say to myself that I have had my fill.

I also have so many happy memories that I have been able to keep Viktor with me in my heart every day and, of course, I will always have his music.

My dream after Viktor died was to have him recognised internationally as the brilliant composer that he was. With the help of friends, family and colleagues, I set up the Viktor Kalabis and Zuzana Růžičková Fund in Prague as well as its sister fund in Washington, DC to promote him and to keep his memory alive.

It was not just a widow's complex; I was really so sure that Viktor's work was important for the literature of the second half of the twentieth century and spent years preparing his manuscripts for publication by Schott Music. Every time his music is published, it gets such good reviews that I am more and more assured of my opinion.

My last public performance had been in 2004, seven years before the death from prostate cancer of Josef Suk, eighty-one, my musical partner of more than thirty-five years. We had stayed loyal to each other all that time and I had to refuse quite a few famous violinists in my lifetime, including Henryk Szeryng, because of my devotion to Suk. I think I was only ever 'unfaithful' to him once when I played with Gidon Kremer, but Suk forgave me.

Even without performing, I was as busy as ever, not least receiving awards – so many awards. I often have to get my medals out to show journalists and interviewers and I sometimes wonder what they all really mean, especially the ones during the years under communism. I remember in 1987, when I was sixty years old, I was invited to the Ministry of Culture to receive some flowers and birthday congratulations. The official in the party there, who was a rather theatrical person, knelt before me when I arrived and said, 'Ms Růžičková, if the title of National Artist could be measured by the foreign currency you earn for Czechoslovakia, then you would be a National Artist today.' Such an honour was impossible for a non-communist then, of course.

But after the revolution it was as if all the awards and accolades were heaped upon me at once. In 1989 I was appointed a National Artist, and in 2002 Supraphon presented me with a Jubilee Platinum Disc for my contribution to the label. The following year I received the Prize for Merit for the State in Arts at Prague Castle, presented by President Václav Klaus himself, and two months later was awarded the title of Knight of the Order of Art and Literature at the residence of the French embassy. In 2005, a Czech author wrote a book about me called *Queen of the Harpsichord* and, in 2011, I won the Charles IV Prize in Aachen for a lifetime of artistic work. The following year I was given my honorary doctorate from the Academy of Performing Arts in Prague, so I became a doctor too. I was also awarded the Czech Culture Prize just as Supraphon released its *Homage to Zuzana* – a CD of some of my best-known recordings to mark my eighty-fifth birthday.

In November 2013, I received the Garnet Star Bohemian Heritage Fund Award at the Rudolfinum for 'the permanent enrichment of the national culture', presented to me by the opera singer Cecilia Bartoli, accompanied by the secretary of the Federation of Jewish Communities and the Mayor of Prague. The citation said that I had: 'lifted the nation through art in the difficult times of our past regime, and allowed access to Bach and other great thinkers. This has allowed us to understand eternal values and spirituality, and has made our lives more dignified.'

One of the awards that pleased me most was to be made a Dame of Czech Culture, something I received in 2017 from the Minister of Culture, Daniel Herman, in the Vinohrady Theatre at the eleventh annual Mene Tekel festival against totalitarianism, evil and violence. The citation read that I was to be rewarded for my 'uncompromising life stances', and for 'constantly adhering to her moral values and for sharing her testimony of human power in the most difficult of life situations. Zuzana Růžičková has significantly supported and shared humanitarian philosophies, as well as the legacies of musical giants.' I was also proud to have been made an honorary director of the New Bach Society in Liepzig.

I was, of course, honoured and flattered by these and so many other awards and prizes, but it amused me a little that I should be so rewarded for doing something I loved.

Although I was no longer recording or performing publicly, I was as busy as ever helping different people, charities, and organisations. I found that being an octogenarian was useful because I had a wealth of memories that I could draw upon. Things happen in cycles and by the age of ninety I had seen so much. If anybody young came to me with a revolutionary idea, I could tell them that I had lived through changes like that at least four times and it never did any good. This sometimes helped. If they listened to me, it often made it easier for them to formulate their thoughts and express them.

After the revolution when I had four students who were travelling to Brussels for a competition, for example, I explained how different their experience would have been under the old regime. They would have had to go to the minister, pass an interview, and only one of the four would have been selected to enter. If they didn't pass the first round of the competition, then they would have had to return straight home and not stay a day longer.

One of my students, who was vivacious and quite a character, said, 'I wouldn't care. I would stay until the end of the competition and then I'd go back.'

I smiled. 'That's fine, but what does your father do?'

'He is a surgeon.'

'Well, he wouldn't be a surgeon any longer if you didn't return immediately. Your whole family would have been held responsible for your behaviour, so your father and mother and everybody else would have had difficulties.' She was shocked.

Viktor's Concertino Praga competition was still going strong and I was happy to still be on the committee of that, as well as of the Philharmonic Chamber Music Society. I gave as much support as I could to Aleš Březina, the bright young man Viktor appointed to run the Martinů Institute, who had been diligently compiling, annotating and promoting the work of Martinů – as well as composing film scores and his first opera based on the trial of politician Milada Horáková during the show trials of the 1950s.

Fredy Hirsch had never been far from my mind and a group of survivors from Terezín decided to do something in his memory. I had reconnected with my friends Dana – who had become head of the Terezín Initiative – and Zuzana, so we talked about what we might do. I had a sculptor friend who had already completed portraits in bronze of Viktor and me, and he offered to sculpt Fredy's head from a photograph for free. A group of us held a small ceremony to install the small plaque in the ghetto memorial garden, and it remains the only statue that I know of to that remarkable young man.

In 1994, I was invited back to Hamburg by the city fathers, where I toured the memorial sites of the factories by the River Elbe where

Mummy and I had been enslaved with so many others all those years before. The buildings are still there, much the same and still used as warehouses for coffee and tea, only with small plaques now to commemorate those who were imprisoned and died there. As with any trip back to the scenes of my past, the visit only brought back unhappy memories. While there, I was awarded the Land Medal for Art and Science from the City of Hamburg, an award which conjures up memories of being in and around those warehouses on the Elbe in that terrible cold and wind, with daily raids and shrapnel in the river, and taking shelter in the water with the rats. Each award brings with it a different atmosphere, a different memory. When I received that one, I told them that I was accepting it not just for me but for everyone who was enslaved there.

I had virtually given up teaching, but I was proud to have three generations of harpsichord players among my former students, some of them already famous. Among my most notable students, I would list Christopher Hogwood, of course, but also Ketil Haugsand, Monika Knoblochová, Anikó Horváth, Borbála Dobozy, Giedrė Lukšaitė-Mrázková, János Sebestyén, Vojtěch Spurný, Václav Luks and Jaroslav Tůma. I was occasionally asked by piano professors to coach students in Bach, which I was happy to do if I had the time. I know how difficult it is to start being an artist so I tried to do as much work as possible with young people, who are the future of music, and – as Viktor always said – the future of this country. I taught them that once you fall in love with music, you never fall out of love with it.

There was one Iranian-American student named Mahan Esfahani who approached me several times after Viktor's death to ask to study with me, but I turned him down. I had cancer by then and the chemotherapy affected both my hands and my feet so that they did not function properly anymore. I could no longer play. I told Mahan I was too old and sick, and I didn't take on new students anymore. Then one day he came to Prague to play a song recital on the fortepiano. He asked if we could meet, but I was too busy. One hour before the recital, he telephoned and told me, 'Professor Růžičková, there'll be a taxi waiting downstairs at your building in ten minutes. In addition to the Haydn cantata and a few songs, I'm playing a solo Mozart fantasia and the big F minor variations of Haydn. There's a ticket for you at the front desk – see you afterwards!'

I admired his chutzpah and that was it. I came, I saw, and Mahan won, especially after I heard him play the Haydn variations.

Not long afterwards I told him, 'Okay then. Let's have a lesson to see how we get on together.' I remember one thing that entirely won me over. He was playing a fugue from the '48, and I told him that I usually liked it to be played on the whole instrument because it was like a Greek drama where the hero comes on stage as B flat minor. Mahan suddenly said, 'How about Oedipus?' and in that moment he became my student. It showed me he was thinking about things and was educated, as well as opposing me in a nice way. I like my students to oppose me with their own ideas. This made me think he would be a good person to work with.

Mahan is extraordinary. Whatever I suggest, he immediately does. It immediately resonates. A student is not really a student, they are a colleague, and Mahan understands how I feel, especially when it comes to Bach. You could say that everybody should listen as people listened in Bach's time, but that's not realistic. I am a synthesist who remains within the style of a certain period, yet does not eschew modern means. I took the Landowska way and Mahan takes it too. I want people to understand Bach. Mahan moved to Prague to be closer to me, and we have worked together for five years. Having thought that I would not teach again at my age, I came to look forward to his lessons enormously.

It was thanks in large part to Mahan that, to mark my ninetieth birthday in 2017, Erato and Warner Classics released a twenty-CD box set of my complete recordings of Bach for keyboard. I was a little bit frightened by that and wondered how the audience would be after fifty years. If I were to do it again, I would approach it completely differently, because you never play the same. You change as a person. And when you go on stage you have to be strictly truthful. You cannot be somebody you were two years ago.

You have to be yourself again. I listen to those recordings now and think I would be more frivolous. I think I was too heavy. It is funny because when you get older, you normally get heavier, but I would get lighter.

What strikes me most listening to those recordings is that they were the happiest days of my life. And even now when I hear the complete Bach, I am still surprised at the greatness of Bach's music, for the harpsichord especially. I still see places where I think, 'Oh goodness, this is so great.'

Thankfully, the box set created global excitement, which was helped by the release of *Zuzana: Music Is Life*, a documentary about my life and work created by American husband-and-wife team Harriet and Peter Getzels and screened worldwide, for which I am flattered and grateful. To mark my latest milestone, I received a beautiful letter from Prince Charles in England who had my Bach recording and had seen the documentary and expressed his admiration. And, perhaps, best of all, I was given a concert by some of my most eminent students at the Prague Academy, which gave me the greatest joy, especially as some of them are so busy performing. They even played 'Happy Birthday to You' in the style of Bach.

Despite my age and increasingly poor health, I continued to agree to almost every interview request from researchers, musicians and historians, some of which have been aired on television and radio. I had also never stopped taking the time to pen handwritten letters and postcards to anyone who contacted me about my music. I helped a young Czech harpsichord student with her thesis about me, and I took part in all sorts of programmes and documentaries, including a film about Fredy Hirsch, entitled *Heaven in Auschwitz*.

On several occasions, I was taken to the famous Pinkas synagogue in Prague, where the walls are inscribed with the names of the 78,000 Bohemian and Moravian Jews who perished. This is a place that moves me terribly. It is a place where you can see for yourself how Jews contributed in every sense to Czech culture. The memorial was created and opened in 1960, but closed for almost thirty years after the Soviet occupation in 1968. It was restored and reopened three years after the Velvet Revolution and the battle against flooding and damp is continual. On the first floor is a marvellous exhibition of pictures drawn by the children of Terezín, many of whom had once been in my care.

The mixture of Jewish, Czech and German culture that I grew up with produced so many remarkable people before the war, including Franz Kafka, as well as Gustav Mahler, Bedřich Smetana and the poet Rilke among so many others. I, of course, as a survivor of the Holocaust, deeply regret that this period was so violently stopped by the Nazis, and often think about how it would have been, or could have been, if many of the men, women and children who were slaughtered had survived and continued to contribute to Czech and world culture.

There is so much suffering in the Pinkas walls. The names look like some pretty decoration, but each little piece of the decoration is a life, a loss to humanity, which will never be made whole. Every year on the anniversary to commemorate the liberation of Auschwitz, the mourner's Kaddish is said for each and every name on the wall. People volunteer to do it, not even Jewish people. Famous actors come and recite all those names, including almost all of my family and so many of my friends from Plzeň and Dobříš – my father Jaroslav, my Uncle Karel and his wife Kamila, Milošek (just nine), my cousins Dagmar and Hanuš, my aunts Jiřina, Vlasta, Zdena, Hermine and Růžena, my grandparents Jindřich and Paula, and many, many more.

Very often I wonder about the miracle that my name isn't on the wall too.

These memorials are very important – first of all to warn against any dictators or terrorists who could do the same thing again – or who even do it now. And the second thing is of course to warn against things like the 'Auschwitz lie' – the denial that the Holocaust ever took place. The more we survivors die out, the more the Auschwitz lie will spread, because it is a terrible thing for humanity to remember. So, for me, these memorials carry great significance.

Czech TV once took me to a neo-Nazi demonstration outside the huge Plzeň synagogue where I'd had lessons as a little girl with the kind storytelling rabbi, and the scene that greeted me there was shocking. So many angry young men were on the streets, screaming and shouting and demonstrating against Jews, in a way that reminded me of the Nazis. I was furious. I didn't confront them because the anti-fascists did, but I came away very shaken and wondering when they would ever learn.

I had first come across this alarming rise in fascism as far back as 1993 when I was asked to take part in a series on Czech TV about leading intellectuals and artists. I had a crew follow me for seven days, filming how I lived and how I prepared for a concert of Viktor's music with the Suk Chamber Orchestra in the wonderful venue of the cloister of the thirteenth-century Convent of St Agnes in Prague. I arrived early that night to change in a little room they had set aside for me in the church, but when I reached the door I found a note pinned to it. The message said, 'You needn't play tonight because no one will be there. We bought all the tickets. Signed the Society against Jews in the Czech Culture.'

I was flabbergasted and upset and everyone in the orchestra was too. We didn't know what to do or what would happen. Should we go on, or would there be some sort of demonstration? In the end we went out and played anyway, although we were terribly tense, and there was a good audience in the end because quite a few people arrived spontaneously. Because of the note, I played badly and it was a horrible night for us all, as we didn't know if the protestors might try to interrupt us, or worse.

In the end the TV programme never even showed the concert, as they decided that to do so would only giving the protestors the publicity they wanted. As far as I know, this organisation did not target any other Jews, so it was just me who was unlucky.

I learned a lot about anti-Semitism when the Nazis first came to Czechoslovakia and I read everything I could about its origins. Even as a teenager, I came to understand that it stems from the need for an enemy from a different nation or race. To my mind anti-Semitism takes three forms in the Czech Republic. Religious – in which the Jews are blamed for killing Jesus Christ. Folklore – in which goblins and evil sprites are still portrayed as grasping figures with hook noses and beards, redolent of the Nazi propaganda posters of the 1930s. The worst form is the last – testosterone-filled young men from good families who want to be anarchists in order to gain importance within their peer group. They are the most dangerous because they are often charismatic and intellectual and they are good at presenting their ideology and infecting the group. It has always struck me as strange that those people who are paranoid, schizophrenic or megalomaniacal in some way often seem to have a kind of magnetism for the weaker ones. As soon as you get someone who speaks well and focuses on how the Jews are to blame for everything, then the trouble begins. The person may not have been anti-Semitic originally but Jews are an easy target.

If I have one dream it is to rid the world of hate and envy. Hate and envy fill me with despair and a depressing sense of always going round and round and ending at the same place, the aggression never ending. It is a very pessimistic view and was a theme of many a discussion I had with Viktor, who did not believe that human nature possessed innate aggression. He believed that it was up to the individual to oppose the evil in him or herself. I am not so sure. There is still so much animal in us, and because we have no natural enemies so we kill each other.

I still hope there is enough evolution left in our brains as they expand that we are able to share our experiences with the young so that they don't make the same mistakes. Sometimes being so old is a terrible thing, because I know from my own experiences that I could warn people not to behave in certain ways, if they would only listen. If we are able to develop that ability then, in a way, there is hope for us. Otherwise not.

I read a study about Holocaust survivors once and it said they fell into three categories: physically ruined, mentally injured or creative. I hope I fall into the last category, and especially when it comes to trying to do my bit against the rise of fascism in Europe and elsewhere, something that troubles me deeply. Educating the next generation is so important in this, and it is important to be as creative as possible. Whenever I go into schools to talk about the

Holocaust – something I feel it is my duty to do – I try to involve the pupils and bring the Holocaust to life for them. I ask them, 'How many of you have German names?'

The usual response is, 'Why? Do you want to punish us for the war?'

I'd shake my head. 'I want to know because there is a political party at the moment who call themselves "Czechs for Czech", so just imagine that they got into parliament and became influential and said that everyone with a German name had to wear a badge.'

I'd then take them through all the Nuremberg laws that banned Jews from so many everyday pleasures before the war, and then I'd ask them to imagine that they had a friend or relative in the Czechs for Czech Party who'd allow them to break just one of the rules. 'Which one would you break?'

The pupils would start to argue amongst themselves. Would they keep their dog, or prefer to be able to visit the cinema or travel on a tram? They had to choose just one. It made them really think.

My last question to them was, 'Okay, so now you have your invitation cards and you have to go to Terezín, but you have the possibility that someone could hide you, or you could go to the partisans and fight. Which would you choose?' Many chose to hide and a surprising number chose to go to Terezín. Only one wanted to join the partisans and she was Chinese.

When it was their turn to ask me questions, they had some interesting ones about my attitude to war, and my view on war crimes. I told them what I always tell people, 'I think the war criminals should be prosecuted, no matter how old they are. No one asked how old people like my grandfather were when they were persecuted and killed.'

Look at Dr Mengele, a man I knew personally, and who never expressed any regret after the war. Or Eichmann, Hitler's deputy, who was always so sure he did the right thing. 'It was the law,' he claimed. 'I followed my commands.' He never apologised and he never showed regret or guilt. If someone really would repent and tell me why they did what they did, then I might forgive – and only if they truly repented. I do admire Simon Wiesenthal for what he did in hunting down Nazis. He did not have a quiet life and he must have wrestled with so many things, but he chose that path.

I explain to the children that I still feel guilty for surviving, which is one of the reasons I talk to them. 'I often ask why me and not the others?' I say. 'I try to pay my debts to them all the time. I feel that I am responsible for living my life as well as I can, and never saying no if someone wants me to tell my memories, which I hope will in some way work out my guilt. This feeling will never leave me.'

They are surprised to learn of a service provided for all Holocaust survivors in Prague in which volunteers come once a week to help with shopping and chores. One year, a young German man volunteered to help me. I didn't know about his past and I didn't ask. Maybe he had his reasons or maybe he had relatives who were guilty, but he didn't say. I do know that many of the volunteers in the service are the grandchildren of Nazis. He just came and brought me my lunch and was very kind, for which I was grateful.

I think that the Germans have really tried to somehow digest their past, and I believe that is a good thing. I don't want revenge, or to feel hate, as these things hurt mostly those who hate. As my father told my mother in Terezín, revenge is up to God. I still feel that hating somebody is really poisoning yourself. Sometimes I felt a little bit characterless for not hating the Germans as much as I maybe should, but hating is such a negative emotion. I was often asked whether I could forgive a German, and I said that, first of all, he would have to ask forgiveness, and then I would consider whether I had the strength to forgive, but never forget.

My own faith is developing. It is a shy faith. I am a typical Jew, always asking my God questions like, 'Why this? Why do that? Why does this have to be like this?' Viktor had his own God and once wrote a piece of music he called his 'shy Hallelujah', but we always observed the Sabbath. Even if I forgot, he made me light the candles, which gave me comforting memories of my happy childhood and especially our family in Dobříš.

I rebelled against religion after the camps and then I found some solace and comfort in it, so when I was studying in Prague I used to go to the synagogue just to belong to a community again. Listening to the men singing in Hebrew made me think of my dear grandfather Leopold with his fine baritone, the smell of my grandmother's challah bread wafting from the kitchen.

For me, though, it is Bach that teaches me faith. He was a sort of mystic. He didn't adhere to any single church when he composed. He wrote his music in protest and passion. That spirit, the spirit of Bach, was always with me and it kept me alive. It has been my one constant since childhood. I have developed my spirituality through his music, which is transcendent. Bach is of the higher order. God is everywhere with him – making children, drinking wine, singing, being desperate, being sad.

With Bach, there is always solace. He gives us something eternal that surmounts being human.

He gives us grace.

Bach has sustained me through every trial of my life and remained with me as a comfort in old age. I owe him my life. When people ask me what he means to me, I tell them: Bach's music is order in chaos. It is beauty in ugliness.

I have seen enough of both in my life to know what I'm talking about.

My only hope is that when I die, people might say that I lived a good life and put some beauty back into the world with my music.

That would be enough of a reason to have survived. Besides, I like to think that this is what Bach would have wanted me to do…

Epilogue

Zuzana: Two Appreciations

A tribute by Aleš Březina, director of the Bohuslav Martinů Institute, Prague

Zuzana Růžičková was a phenomenon. Everything in her life was remarkable, starting with the privileged (as she would say) childhood as the only child of the owners of a toy store in Plzeň, through the fall to the deepest bottom of existence in the concentration camps Theresienstadt, Auschwitz II-Birkenau and Bergen-Belsen.

Then there was her miraculous survival and return to the beloved piano (despite her hands having been almost destroyed by hardships), the discovery of the harpsichord and the world career of the 'first lady' of this instrument, which she brought back to concert halls as a contemporary instrument, all the way to the legendary artistic partnerships; particularly with Václav Neumann, Josef Suk, János Starker, Pierre Fournier, Aurèle Nicolet and Jean-Pierre Rampal and almost a countless number of recordings among which stands out the first – and still the only – complete recording of the keyboard works of J. S. Bach.

That's all very well known about her, so I'll add only a couple of personal memories from the time of the fall of the former regime when – thanks to a collaboration and later a friendship with her husband Viktor Kalabis – I met her personally. At the age when others are slowly starting to end their professional career, she adapted absolutely perfectly to the new conditions and threw herself energetically into many new tasks. Apart from teaching at HAMU (the Faculty of Music and Dance at the Academy of Performing Arts in Prague), this included selfless work in many charitable organisations: including active work for the arts council of the Czech Chamber Music Society and in the chairmanship of the Circle of Friends of Music. All this during a period of a still-active artistic career. At that time, she was also affected by problems of faith and illness, particularly leukaemia against which she bravely fought for many years. Zuzanka faced all these troubles courageously and founded an endowment fund that supports many interesting projects in the long term.

However, she was struck most by the passing of her beloved husband in 2006. In the last year of his life, she stopped playing concerts and she devoted herself only to Viktor. Days after his death she told me, 'Now I've lost everything – both Viktorek and music.'

One doesn't even have to remember her war and post-war fortunes to see how uniquely brave and positive a person Zuzanka was. I remember how, in 2009, in the Prague hospital Na Františku, in spite of a broken leg, she was still full of energy and happiness and informed me that she had registered sixty-two performances of the works of her deceased husband. With her characteristic, fine humour she added, 'He's now sitting up there and laughing at how I'm holding forth from a hospital bed.'

She devoted herself so intensively to the promotion of her husband's music that she had entirely forgotten about herself and her role in the musical life of the second half of the twentieth century. She was surprised and happy when she was reminded of her ninetieth birthday by the press in many countries – particularly those where she used to play concerts regularly over the past half a century – and especially when (on the initiative of her student, Mahan Esfahani) Warner Classics issued a magnificently remastered and editorially perfectly new edition of her recording of Bach's complete legacy for keyboard instruments. Then I could see how much she had missed those more than ten years not only without Viktor, but also without an active concert career and how much she'd been troubled that her truly revolutionary and non-orthodox approach towards the interpretation of baroque music (which had been the cause of many disputes with the protagonists of the so-called 'authentic interpretation') had fallen into oblivion.

To put it simply and briefly: she considered the study of fundamental musicological literature of the times as a matter of course, but it wasn't a law to her or a manual of the only possible interpretation of the work. She did not recognise schools that professed dogmatism and produced performers unrecognisable from each other. The same applied to the choice of instrument: all her life Zuzanka promoted modern harpsichord and contemporary production for this instrument, which she successfully strived to emancipate from the ghetto of 'old' music and instrument-making stagnancy.

She also had an amplifier built which she used at orchestral concerts in large halls to compensate for the sound balance between the solo harpsichord and the orchestra. In this approach, often labelled as 'romanticising' (whereas it would have been more precise to call it 'individual' or 'distinctive'), she was a true rebel. A big part of this was her mastery of the piano, the instrument on which she began and which she played until the end of the 1950s. She would play piano concerts alongside her career as a harpsichord player and even switched between the instruments on a single stage.

She never wanted to be ranked under the label of 'early music', and she considered the esoteric approach to music interpretation to be limiting. She liked to compare her approach with the Shakespeare created by Laurence Olivier, who performed Shakespeare's plays according to original texts and in original costumes but didn't object to the use of modern means. The celebrations of her originality and inspirational approach on her ninetieth birthday filled her with pride and gave her a feeling of great satisfaction, not so much for herself alone – that wasn't important to her, I believe – rather she saw it as another opportunity to promote the harpsichord as an instrument of style and repertoire.

For me, Zuzanka's exceptionality lies in the unique combination of innate optimism and a long life of acquired scepticism. She was the embodiment of a 'survivor', but to survive was only a prerequisite for her to be able to provide continuous meaning to life. To her, much more important than mere surviving was the quality that a person gives to their life every day. In this aspect, she was and continues to be immensely inspiring for all of us who knew her.

In the sixties, her famous student Christopher Hogwood told her that if we could travel in space, we could also travel in time. It was a great honour for me to travel together with Zuzanka in this time and space for over twenty years – and a decade less with Viktor – to see how she enjoyed the love of her friends who didn't call her anything other than Zuzanka. Still today, they smile when they say her name and most of all remember her as a wonderful human being.

She showed us that even despite the war, the Holocaust and communist totalitarianism, it's possible to live a contented and fulfilled life.

A musical appreciation by Zuzana's final student, Mahan Esfahani

I would be giving the wrong impression were I to say that Zuzana Růžičková was universally acclaimed as the great harpsichordist of the close of the twentieth century. This is not a wholly accurate picture. Zuzana's reputation by the 1990s and 2000s had gone into an abeyance of sorts. She came to be seen as terribly passé, a relic of an earlier age. I think it's so important to emphasise this, since the hagiographies and tributes written of her elsewhere seem to forget that point. Really, when I went to study with her I received (and still do) a lot of derision from my colleagues for going to 'a dinosaur'.

This has mostly to do with the decline of the harpsichord as a serious modern concert instrument. And when she started to play in the early 1950s there were very few playable harpsichords at all. I'm not talking about the instruments in museums – those were in no acceptable concert or recording shape, since the art of restoration to bring these instruments to the glorious past state of their musical potential was still very much in its infancy. In the

Soviet bloc, the only harpsichord available was the Ammer (made by the Ammer family in East Germany since 1927) and that was pretty much it in the communist world, which probably explains why the idea of playing the harpsichord still elicits peals of laughter from most Russian musicians in particular. Russian pianists for the most part consider the harpsichord a 'toy instrument', as one rather famous Soviet pianist once said to me (in a tone that I will leave to your imagination).

Incidentally, Zuzana's Ammer – the one she used for touring and which was played on by a number of great harpsichordists on their visits to Prague in the communist period – recently came to live with me at my flat. It took three extremely strong professional Albanian movers (and an extra Czech from the local pub) to bring it up with straps. I sincerely thought it was going to kill at least one of them, it is that heavy. In contrast, two pipsqueaks like me can move a comparable historical copy (though with some effort).

This Ammer was what she had and her choices were limited. It's easy to blame that generation for not playing historical instruments, but it's what they coped with and it's what they made music with. I have tremendous respect for these people, because they were able to discover so much about the music with even, frankly, sub-par instruments that were bad hybrids of antiquity and modernity.

I was nine years old or so and insatiably curious about all things harpsichord-related when I first became familiar with Zuzana's name and reputation and I am quite certain that one of my first cassette tapes of harpsichord playing must have been of her playing sonatas by Domenico Scarlatti – but I can't verify that, as it came from the local library.

I think the initial impression I had from Zuzana's playing was how much authority it had. This was not authority in the intimidating or adversarial sense but more an authority based on someone who knows what they're doing and has something to say, an authority which derives its validity from a sincere intention to share the timeless qualities of a musical work. Her playing had verve and imagination and was almost confrontational; the sort of playing that seizes you by the collar and says, 'You really should get to hear this special piece of music.' This was very different from the sort of harpsichord playing that came into fashion by the 1990s, which instead says, 'This is correct and therefore you are wrong if you don't get it.'

To this day, when I put on a recording by Zuzana it grabs me like nothing else, save perhaps the recordings of Wanda Landowska, the other grand dame of the harpsichord who Zuzana sadly was never able to meet.

As a teacher Zuzana was an essentially no-nonsense person, and she was quite tough. She hated it if I brought anything to a lesson that wasn't completely prepared and at least quasi-memorised. Nothing could get past her in a lesson. If you hadn't thought through something completely you couldn't fake it with her for even a second, and I think the word she most often used in a lesson was 'sloppy'. She liked ideas to be stated clearly, but she also prized the ambiguity that even a strong literary narrative has, 'the fragile beauty … the pleasurable things that disappear with the morning light', as Kazuo Ishiguro described it. She expressed her dissatisfaction by tapping a pencil on the desk and shaking her head, muttering, 'Mahan, Mahan … no!' That was usually a signal to stop playing.

Her way of expressing pleasure was quite unique. She would stand up slowly and dance slightly to the music and breathe heavily – this was quite pronounced in the last year, as her lungs were pretty weak. And then she would say, 'Now we're getting somewhere.' I think that was the closest she came to a compliment in my presence. Actually, there was another time when I played Bach's *Capriccio on the departure of his beloved brother* (BWV 992) for her, an early piece with programmatic titles for each movement which can be read aloud before each part, and after the last movement, which is a difficult, virtuosic fugue, she let a few seconds pass and drily remarked, 'Well, you read the titles very well.'

Zuzana played quite a bit of modern music and was able to talk about a variety of music. Comparisons to other repertoire and composers inevitably came up in lessons. I'd like to stress that this is actually rare in the navel-gazing world of harpsichord enthusiasts. She often also shared all sorts of experiences, particularly about anything having to do with touring and travelling. As she was the last harpsichordist to have played the major orchestral concerto and recital circuit on the same scale as the great pianists, she had fifty years of experience to share. She'd say what to do before playing a recital on a relatively little sleep (play through anything *but* the music on the programme). She'd say what to eat, what not to eat (pasta and fruit fine, anything spicy not). She once said if you ran out of foundation (yes, male performers also use make-up!) that you could just do the right side of your face, since that's what the audience sees most of the time anyhow. She advised how to deal with fans, what to record, how to record, how not to record, who to avoid, how to deal with frustrations, and how to deal with badly played concerts.

Frankly, she didn't speak to me much about the war. At the beginning of our relationship I did ask her about it but, as we deepened our bond over music, it faded into the background. In hindsight I realise this was an unspoken decision on her part and on mine. In the last year of our studies, she would often sit with me in my kitchen after the day's lesson – which would end some time in the evening – and we would open a bottle of something (usually a nice whisky I had brought back from whichever duty-free shop I had been in the previous week. I expressly remember her helping me polish off half a bottle of very expensive Japanese whisky I brought back from Tokyo), and just talk about all sorts of things. Occasionally her parents, her life with Viktor and that sort of thing would come up, but nothing other than that. I sensed she valued the fact that I didn't come to her just to discuss the Holocaust.

By the time I came to study with her, Zuzana's hands were completely out of commission and she even had difficulty writing. The most she ever did with me was to once demonstrate the proper height of the knuckles in playing a certain trill. Another time she showed me, with considerable difficulty, how to phrase the opening of William Byrd's variations on 'Walsingham'. That's it. I saw films of her playing in the early 1990s and my impression is that by then the hands were already going. Obviously I never dared tell her this.

Two or three times I saw her lose herself to the music and she would wistfully say, 'I would do anything to be able to play!' Nonetheless, I have to say, it forced her to teach in a very different way. This had a tremendous impact on the way I have learned to speak about music.

In my view Zuzana played the harpsichord because she held on to it for dear life – I sometimes think of it as a co-dependent relationship between this neglected instrument and this damaged, traumatised person. I sincerely believe that the harpsichord gave her life and a chance of seeing and experiencing the world in a way that would have been unattainable to most people living in post-war Czechoslovakia. She met various and sundry of the greatest musicians and composers of her time, and, in a way, she made her father proud. He was the man she was closest to and about whom she spoke only after we had a drink or two.

As for her passion for Bach, each person sees something different in Bach. He is God-like in that sense. Everyone has a completely different view and will ultimately project onto him whatever they want to see. So the romantics will want to see 'Big Bach', the amateurs want to say that Bach's performances were never perfect, the feminists want to say he was a feminist, the atheists want to say he was anything but religious, the churchmen want to say he was the apex of devotion, ad nauseam.

For a thinking person like Zuzana, Bach gives every reason to live and work. I think she perceived J. S. Bach as a man very much 'above' such things as politics. Bach represents the apex of the musician's craft in every imaginable respect – the emotional aspect and the logical, mathematical aspect are each at a state of perfection and somehow neither seems to cancel the other out. Musicians who avoid Bach – and I believe Zuzana would have agreed with this – usually are avoiding confronting themselves.

Her comments about Bach becoming an ideology refer, I think, to the idea that Bach's own original practice should represent the ideal of what we aspire to as performers, which is a concern of some people in the historical performance movement. She basically thought that these people should go off somewhere and entertain themselves and leave the best work to the professionals – she was really quite unapologetic about this. In other words, I don't think she cared, in essence, what Bach originally did so much as what he left us. She didn't like a religion being made out of Bach-as-prophet.

Perhaps a good example of her views on Bach is the way she approached our lesson when I played her Bach's English Suite No. 5 in E Minor (BWV 810). This is about twenty-five minutes in total, no more. A dark, heavy piece, abounding in angular, thorny motifs and harsh dissonances, it has really sat in my consciousness for hours each time I've played it recently. The fourth movement of this suite is a sarabande – the most ancient and sophisticated of the baroque dances, a dance which originally came from the Americas in the sixteenth century as a wild song with lewd lyrics and fast movements which over time softened as it became adopted by the courts of Europe, particularly France.

In Bach's hands – and mind you, he was in his twenties when he wrote this piece – the sarabande becomes the central emotional point of the suite, the moment at which Bach the dance master is redeeming souls. His sarabandes are some of his most complex pieces from a lifetime of writing suites for the harpsichord (and other combinations besides) – not on a purely technical level, of course, but because of the ineffable emotional content within, which is particularly difficult to make sense of in an instrument which so many people deride as having no dynamic or expressive capabilities.

As some may know, the sarabande from this suite is what Zuzana copied out for herself before she and her mother went to Auschwitz. Now, here I should add a word about the English Suites as a whole. There are six of them, and in the second, third, and sixth suites, the sarabande is accompanied in Bach's score by what is called a 'double' or a variation of sorts, in which the composer essentially writes a new piece in the same basic harmony. It is a way of playing on the listener's memory of the sarabande and tugging at the nostalgic heartstrings a bit. Since the first, fourth, and fifth suites don't have these variations, one is, in theory, free to write or improvise one's own, as I do for the first and fourth suites (actually, it is already fairly ornate for the first anyhow, but that is beside the point).

When I first took the fifth suite to Zuzana, I went with a variation I had come up with for the sarabande. She didn't really explain why, but it didn't go over very well. (At this particular moment I hadn't really put two and two together to figure out that *this* was the sarabande copied out for Auschwitz.)

Rather than pulling an extra-musical excuse on me to tell me that I was doing the wrong thing, Zuzana tried to get me to reduce the piece to its fundamental aspects, to the core of its existence. This was something she did frequently, reminding me that, in essence, the only real evidence we have for how to play the piece is the score itself – so she'd get me to do the bare minimum to see what made the piece 'tick' first, and then see where certain notes or accents stuck out before we moved on to prise out an interpretation from the relationship between the notes. For the diehards, this would be enough because it would be 'objective' and thus 'correct'. But this was a stage of experimentation in Zuzana's lessons, and in any case she believed that all experimentation should be done in private before unlocking the real piece within, which by definition *had* to incorporate the subjective in a real, adult interpretation of the piece. She called the objective approach 'anti-interpretation', and I think the name sticks.

The first two bars of this piece, in E minor, are repeated in the next two bars in the relative major of G, with cadences, which are sort of like punctuation in a piece of writing, always occurring on the weak part of the measure. It is hard to overemphasise the remarkable colour the repetition of the theme in G major gives, as though the sun suddenly rises and envelopes the player further as the top voice then goes on to coax the other ones to join it in an extension of the nostalgic, rising melody in the successive bars. In the second half, that top voice really takes on a dominant character, stating a new theme alone while the bottom three voices – this is a choir of sorts, a cast of four characters in total – sing backup to the plaintive melody above. Bach takes us to some pretty harmonically distant places in this piece, to places in the human consciousness far beyond what a simple courtly dance usually concerns itself with. The return of the theme at the end is one of the most despondent, resigned statements I know from Bach, ending in the original minor version of the key of E.

Zuzana and I went over this piece for perhaps an hour and a half – certainly no less than that. She really insisted on keeping the rhythm quite strict in the beginning, as the voices were equals, sharing in the despondency of the theme until about the end of the fourth bar when she'd tell me to emphasise the top voice by slightly shortening the other voices in the cadence in the middle of the bar and then waiting a bit before the semiquaver leading into the third beat: 'Think that you can breathe no more, and then that's the perfect moment to say what you feel – except, you can't really say it, but you can sing to persuade your companions to move on.'

And at the end the most puzzling thing. Bach writes a G natural in the alto in the last bar. I played it and she said nothing about it one way or the other. But in Zuzana's recording of the piece she plays a G sharp – an enormous difference! One is sad and despondent, whilst the other gives some measure of hope. It's a bizarre effect, and I have never been happy with either one in performance since I heard this. It's not exactly what Bach wrote. But Zuzana may have had other priorities for herself than simply worrying about what he wrote. I've never quite figured this one out.

Bibliography

Berenbaum, Michael, *Witness to the Holocaust*, Harper Collins, 1997

Berney, Leonard, *Liberating Belsen Concentration Camp*, edited by John Wood, CreateSpace, 2015

Birenbaum, Halina, *Hope is the Last to Die*, Publishing House of the State Museum in Oświęcim, 1971

de Gaulle-Anthonioz, Geneviève, *God Remained Outside*, Souvenir Press, 1999

Frister, Roman, *The Cap: Or The Price of a Life*, Weidenfeld & Nicholson, 1999

Gaines, James, *Evening in the Palace of Reason*, Fourth Estate, 2005

Getzels, Peter and Harriet, *Zuzana: Music is* Life, documentary, www.zuzanathemovie.com, 2017

Gilbert, Martin, *The Holocaust: The Jewish Tragedy*, Collins, 1986

———, *Never Again: A History of the Holocaust*, Universe, 2000

———, *The Righteous: The Unsung Heroes of the Holocaust*, Black Swan, 2003

Haraszti, Miklós, *The Velvet Prison: Artists Under State Socialism*, Basic Books, 1987

Heimann, Mary, *Czechoslovakia: The State that Failed*, Yale University Press, 2009

Kluger, Ruth, *Landscapes of Memory: A Holocaust Girlhood Remembered*, Bloomsbury, 2003

Langbein, Hermann, *People in Auschwitz*, University of North Carolina Press and the USHMM, 1995

Lanzmann, Claude, *Shoah: The Complete Text of the Acclaimed Holocaust Film*, Da Capo Press, 1995
Lasker-Wallfisch, Anita, *Inherit the Truth, 1939–45*, Giles de la Mare, 1996
Lengyel, Olga, *Five Chimneys*, Academy Chicago Publishers, 1947
Levi, Primo, *Survival in Auschwitz*, Touchstone, 1958
Lieblová, Dagmar, *Someone Made a Mistake, So I Am Here Now*, McLeod, 2016
Longerich, Peter, *Holocaust: The Nazi Persecution and Murder of the Jews*, Oxford University Press, 2010
Lustig, Arnošt, *Night and Hope*, Northwestern University Press, 1976
Micheels, Louis J., MD, *Doctor 117641: A Holocaust Memoir*, Yale University Press, 1989
Muller, Melissa, *A Garden of Eden in Hell: The Life of Alice Herz-Sommer*, Macmillan, 2007
Pietraszewski, Igor, *Jazz in Poland: Improvised Freedom*, Jazz under State Socialism, Peter Lang, 2012
Posner, Gerald L., and Ware, John, *Mengele: The Complete Story*, Cooper Square Press, 2000
Redlich, Gonda (author) and Friedman, Saul F. (ed.), *The Terezín Diary of Gonda Redlich*, University Press of Kentucky, 1992
Smith, Lyn, *Forgotten Voices of the Holocaust*, Ebury Press, 2005
Solzhenitsyn, Aleksandr, *One Day in the Life of Ivan Denisovich*, Penguin Books, 1963
Sommer, Mark, *Living in the New Prague Freedom*, Mercury House, 1992
Vrba, Rudolf, *I Escaped from Auschwitz*, Robson Books, 2006
Weil, Jiří, *Mendelssohn is on the Roof*, Daunt Books, 2011
———, *Life with a Star*, Daunt Books, 2012
Whitworth, Wendy, *Survival: Holocaust Survivors Tell Their Story*, Quill Press, 2003
Wiesel, Elie, *The Town Beyond the Wall*, Schocken Books, 1982
Winstone, Martin, *The Holocaust Sites of Europe*, I. B. Tauris, 2010
Wolff, Christopher, *Johann Sebastian Bach: The Learned Musician*, Oxford University Press, 2000
Zygmuntowicz, Itka, and Goss, Jennifer, *Remember, My Child*, CreateSpace 2016

Acknowledgements

This book would never have been possible without dear Zuzana, who dedicated the final weeks of her life to telling me her story and making sure I had everything I needed to chronicle it for posterity. I shall never forget the precious time I spent with her and I shall always be inspired by her tremendous energy and passion.

I also owe much to a great number of people and organisations whose kindness and generosity of time, spirit, and enthusiasm allowed Zuzana's story to be told in full for the first time.

I am indebted to Aleš Březina and everyone at the Viktor Kalabis and Zuzana Růžičková Fund in Prague for supporting and facilitating my research, giving me the breathing space to continue with the project after Zuzana's death. Aleš further read, edited and helped corroborate much of the manuscript as well as correcting its many perplexing Czech accents and expressions. Throughout, he was unfailingly courteous and kind and even arranged for his own fascinating interviews with Zuzana over the years to be translated for my benefit.

Harriet and Peter Getzels, who made the award-winning documentary *Zuzana: Music is Life*, also deserve special mention – Harriet especially – for their infinite patience and for giving me the opportunity to see every transcript, rush and photograph related to their excellent film, which is currently touring the world.

Zuzana's cousin, Marie Winn, travelled to Prague to interview her in 1991, and then generously donated the transcripts and tapes to the United States Holocaust Memorial Museum for writers such as me to access, with her kind permission.

Frank and Emily Vogl, Zuzana's closest relatives, were a mainstay of her life and have devoted themselves to promoting and preserving her memory since her death. She always spoke of them so fondly and I was delighted to meet them in Washington, DC. I am extremely grateful for their assistance and support.

Mahan Esfahani, Zuzana's final student and musical prodigy, has been passionate and enthusiastic about this project from the start and kindly provided the insightful and touching musical appreciation of Zuzana in the Epilogue.

Dagmar 'Dana' Lieblová, head of the Terezín Initiative, first met Zuzana in the ghetto in 1942. They never lost touch. She kindly agreed to read the chapters relating to the war and corrected any mistakes. It was with great sadness that instead of thanking her in person as planned in March 2018, I attended her funeral instead. I am indebted to her daughter Rita McLeod for keeping me fully informed of the glowing tributes to both Zuzana and Dagmar before and since.

My translator and friend Anna Pocnarová did an excellent job translating various Czech historical documents from the archives for me, as well as reading aloud Zuzana's words. Holocaust survivor Hana Berger-Moran kindly also assisted me with some translations from Czech and German. The staff of the Jewish Museum in Prague have been as efficient and kind as ever in finding me relevant documents for my research. Special mention goes to Pavla Hermina Neuner, Curator of the Oral History Collection, Daniela Bartáková from the Shoah History Department, and Martina Šiknerová from the Collections Department.

Silvia Rathmann, archivist at Bergen-Belsen, shared her enthusiasm for this book from the start and was tireless in unearthing photographs, personal letters and documents relating to Zuzana's time in that camp. She also kindly arranged for senior archivist Bernd Horstmann to give me a guided tour of the camp, the museum exhibitions and the nearby Hohne barracks where Zuzana and her mother recovered after the war. Between them, Bernd and

Silvia helped bring that part of the story alive and both kindly fact-checked the Belsen section of the manuscript afterwards.

Nadia Ficara at the United States Holocaust Memorial Museum in Washington, DC, was as helpful as ever with contacts and other material. British harpsichordist Virginia Black kindly oversaw the chapters relating to this complex instrument and put me straight on a number of important points. Instrument-maker Keith Hill in Tennessee kindly explained the sixteen-foot stop and the finer points of pitches to me. I am also indebted to the many journalists and musicians who have interviewed Zuzana over the years and published their interviews online. There are too many to mention, but special thanks goes to Robert Tifft and his outstanding website jsebestyen.org, which features the most comprehensive list of tributes to Zuzana.

I would also like to thank the family of Clement Morgan, the young doctor Zuzana made such a connection with in Bergen-Belsen. Her sweet letters to him were saved and donated to the German authorities for posterity in an act of generosity and foresight.

My inimitable editor Michael Fishwick at Bloomsbury could not have been more supportive as I worked on developing this manuscript. His handwritten editorial notes proved invaluable (if occasionally illegible!) and his encouragement was pivotal to my continuing with it at my lowest moments.

Laura Williams, the book's literary agent at Greene & Heaton, helped deal with the highs and lows of this entire experience. I am indebted to her for bringing the project my way and for keeping it on track. I am also grateful to the rights department at Peters Fraser Dunlop, especially Laura Otal, for their able management of worldwide rights sales.

Thanks also to the Royal Literary Fund for the small research grant that allowed me to continue working on this when I might otherwise have been unable. Finally, my heartfelt appreciation to my husband Chris for his infinite patience, support and encouragement, as I put us both through the agonies of immersing myself in yet another all-consuming book. Sorry for the sleepless nights.

Wendy Holden

Index

A Note on the Type

The text of this book is set in Adobe Garamond. It is one of several versions of Garamond based on the designs of Claude Garamond. It is thought that Garamond based his font on Bembo, cut in 1495 by Francesco Griffo in collaboration with the Italian printer Aldus Manutius. Garamond types were first used in books printed in Paris around 1532. Many of the present-day versions of this type are based on the Typi Academiae of Jean Jannon cut in Sedan in 1615.

Claude Garamond was born in Paris in 1480. He learned how to cut type from his father and by the age of fifteen he was able to fashion steel punches the size of a pica with great precision. At the age of sixty he was commissioned by King Francis I to design a Greek alphabet, and for this he was given the honourable title of royal type founder. He died in 1561.

A Note on the Type

[illegible]

[illegible]